BUT
HE WAS GOOD TO HIS MOTHER

THE LIVES AND CRIMES OF JEWISH GANGSTERS

ROBERT A. ROCKAWAY

gefen publishing house בית‏הוצאה לאור

JERUSALEM ◆ NEW YORK

Typesetting: Marzel A.S. — Jerusalem
Cover Design: Studio Paz

Edition   9   8   7   6   5   4   3   2
Revised edition

Gefen Publishing House
POB 36004
Jerusalem 91360, Israel
972-2-538-0247
isragefe@netvision.net.il

Gefen Books
12 New Street
Hewlett, NY 11557, USA
516-295-2805
gefenbooks@compuserve.com

www.israelbooks.com

Printed in Israel   *Send for our free catalogue*

Library of Congress Cataloging-in-Publication Data
Rockaway, Robert, 1939-
But — He Was Good to His Mother: The Lives and Crimes of Jewish Gangsters
ISBN 965-229-249-4

1. Jewish Criminals—United States—History—20th century. 2. Jewish Criminals—United States—Biography. 3. Organized crime—United States—History—20th century. I. Title.
HV6194.J4 R63 2000
364.1' 06' 6089924073—dc21   99-059148
                                                                                    CIP

Contents

Introduction 5

Chapter One   Crime Barons of the East 7

Chapter Two   Rogues of the Midwest 44

Chapter Three   The Purple Gang 63

Chapter Four   In the Beginning 94

Chapter Five   The Perils and Pitfalls of the Gangster Life . . 113

Chapter Six   The Hit Parade 144

Chapter Seven   The Family Came First 182

Chapter Eight   Defenders of Their People 219

Epilogue 255

Author's Note and Acknowledgement 256

Source Notes 259

Bibliography 277

Index of Gangsters 284

Index of Photos 288

To my children, Eytan and Shiran

Introduction

*T*he concept for this book evolved out of a conversation I had with my mother. I had been doing research on American Jewish gangsters and was telling her about some of my findings. When I started to discuss the nefarious deeds of a Detroit gangster whose family we knew, she interrupted to say, "That may be true, but he was always good to his mother." Her reaction and that phrase stuck in my mind and I began to think about doing a different sort of book about Jewish gangsters.

As I collected material from FBI files, newspapers and books, I looked for anything that shed light on the personal and less publicized aspects of the gangster's life, such as his family and his relations with the Jewish community. I also focused my interviews with old-time Jewish mobsters, and people who knew them, in the same direction.

Wherever I lectured about Jewish gangsters, I found that what most interested audiences were the personal stories and anecdotes about these men.

I decided to write a book which combined the two impulses: tales and anecdotes about less well-known facets of the Jewish gangster in America. Above all, I wanted the book to be lively and entertaining, but factual.

Many of the stories in the book are humorous. However, the comic nature of the anecdotes is not meant to minimize the viciousness or ruthlessness of these men. They and their activities were not funny, yet, some of the things they said and did were farcical. I attempt to capture this in my narrative.

In no way do I seek to glorify the Jewish gangster. He was, however, part of the Jewish experience in America. What I have presented is an unconventional perspective on their lives.

Chapter One

Crime Barons
of the East

*T*hey had names like Louis "Lepke" Buchalter, Benjamin "Bugsy" Siegel, Arthur "Dutch Schultz" Flegenheimer, Meyer "The Little Man" Lansky, Charlie "King" Solomon, Max "Boo Boo" Hoff and Abner "Longy" Zwillman.

They had two things in common: they were all gangsters and they were all Jews.

They flourished in the period between the two World Wars and, together with the Italians, organized American crime and made it large, powerful and deadly.

"We're bigger than U.S. Steel," Meyer Lansky, one of the most important and longest-living actors in this drama, allegedly said.[1] And he may have been right.

In January 1919, three-fourths of the states ratified the Eighteenth Amendment to the Constitution, which forbid "the manufacture, sale, or transportation of intoxicating liquors... for beverage purposes." Congress then passed the Volstead Act to enforce the Amendment, making the Federal Government responsible for keeping the nation dry.[2]

When news of this event reached the Protestant evangelist and former baseball player, Billy Sunday, he exploded with joy. "Goodby, John Barleycorn," he exulted. "You were God's worst enemy. You were Hell's best friend. The reign of tears is over."[3]

The reign of tears may have been over, but the reign of the gangster had just begun.[4]

The ban on alcohol went into effect at midnight, January 16, 1920, and from that moment on it seemed that every American over the age of twelve had to have a drink. In response to this great American thirst, 200,000 unlicensed saloons selling illegal, or "bootleg," whiskey sprang up all across the United States. These bars and restaurants were euphemistically called "speakeasies" and "blind pigs."[5]

Large bootlegging organizations, led by tough, ruthless law-breaking sons of Irish, Italian and Jewish immigrants, arose to service them, making huge amounts of money. Income from the liquor industry ran into hundreds of millions of dollars annually, with smuggling alone bringing in over $50 million a year.[6]

Al Capone, who became a popular symbol of this era, spoke for his gangster colleagues, Jews and gentiles, and a lot of "respectable" Americans as well, when he declared, "You can't cure a thirst by law."

"They call Al Capone a bootlegger," he would say. "Yes, it's bootleg while it's on the trucks, but when your host at the club, in the locker room, or on the Gold Coast [Chicago's prime residential and nightclub district] hands it to you on a silver tray, it's hospitality."

Capone wanted to know what he did that was so awful. He supplied a legitimate demand. "Some call it bootlegging. Some call it racketeering. I call it a business. They say I violate the Prohibition law. Who doesn't?" To stress the point, Capone enjoyed telling his listeners that "The very guys that make my trade good are the ones that yell loudest at me. Some of the leading judges use the stuff."[7]

The morality of the age also contributed to the rise of the gangster. The post-World War I period was one of "anything goes," when an honest man was considered to be a "square" and a "sucker," and flaunting the rules was the norm, affecting every sector of society.

"People wanted booze, they wanted dope, they wanted to gamble and they wanted broads," reminisced former Detroit gangster Hershel Kessler. "For a price, we provided them with these amusements. We only gave them what they wanted."[8]

During Prohibition, fifty percent of the nation's leading bootleggers were Jews, and Jews and Jewish gangs bossed the rackets in some of America's largest cities.[9]

New York, with 1,700,000 Jews, more than 40 percent of the nation's Jewish population, contained the greatest number of Jewish gangsters. But the man who masterminded New York's underworld was not a gangster; he was a professional gambler and his name was Arnold Rothstein.

Best known, perhaps, as the man who allegedly "fixed" the 1919 World Series between the Chicago White Sox and Cincinnati Reds, Rothstein is recognized as the pioneer big businessman of organized crime in the United States. A man of prodigious energy, imagination and intellect, he transformed American crime from petty larceny into big business. One social historian described him as "the J.P. Morgan of the underworld; its banker and master of strategy."[10]

"Rothstein had the most remarkable brain," said Meyer Lansky admiringly. "He understood business instinctively, and I'm sure if he had been a legitimate financier he would have been just as rich as he became with his gambling and the other rackets he ran."[11]

During the 1920s, Rothstein put together the largest gambling and bookmaking empire in the nation, masterminded a million-dollar stolen bond business, and controlled most of New York's gangs, as well as that city's traffic in narcotics, bootlegging and gambling. These feats earned him the title of "Czar of the Underworld."

For Arnold Rothstein, a life in crime had been a matter of choice. He was born in New York City in 1882, the son of Abraham Rothstein, a wealthy and respected businessman. The elder Rothstein was one of the pillars of the Upper West Side's Orthodox Jewish community, was something of a philanthropist and was chairman of the board of New York's Beth Israel Hospital. New York's governor, Al Smith, called Abe "the Just," because of his high principles, selflessness and honesty in business transactions.[12]

Abe's younger son Arnold followed a different path. School and studying never interested him, but he did love to play cards and dice. "I didn't go to school much, but I used to gamble a lot and lose," he said. "Gradually, however, it dawned on me that if anyone was going to make money out of gambling he had better be on the right side of the fence. I was on the wrong end of the game."[13] In his late twenties, Rothstein opened his own gambling house on Forty-sixth Street.

Although Arnold never achieved the kind of respectability his family hoped he would, he did exceed their expectations in another area: he became both nationally famous and a millionaire by the time he was thirty.

With gambling as his base, Rothstein had access to the cash and political protection needed to make big deals in many other spheres

Arnold Rothstein

of activity. With the coming of Prohibition, Rothstein's business empire developed another dimension — bootlegging. Rothstein laid the foundation for the enormous profits of Prohibition by creating an organization to buy high quality liquor by the shipload in England and distribute it to buyers in the United States. This idea caught on and soon others were engaged in the same enterprise.

Always a loner, Arnold had no desire to be part of a venture he could not control. Prohibition was simply too big for him, or any one man, to dominate. After organizing eleven successful voyages, Rothstein retired from rum-running.

He next turned his talents to narcotics smuggling which, until he became involved, had been unorganized. Rothstein converted the racket into a businesslike machine by sending buyers overseas to Europe and the Far East, and by controlling the purchasing operation in the United States. The dope traffic attracted Rothstein because it offered the chance to make a huge sum of money with a very small initial investment: in 1923, a kilogram of heroin (2.2 pounds) could be purchased for $2,000 and sold for more than $300,000. By 1926, Rothstein was allegedly the financial overlord of the foreign narcotics traffic in America.[14]

It has been said that Jewish gangsters did not deal in dope. This is not true. Beginning with Rothstein, American Jewish underworld figures became heavily involved in smuggling and distributing opium and opiates in the United States. During the 1920s and 1930s Jews competed with Italians for dominance in the trade. After World War II, however, the Italian-American racketeers prevailed for one reason: the Nazis. When the Germans exterminated European Jewry, they also destroyed the Jewish criminals who supplied American distributors. And after Pearl Harbor, Asia was in chaos. This wrecked the American Jewish connections with European drug traders living in Chinese coastal cities.[15]

According to the testimony of persons engaged in the traffic, the quality of the product declined once the Jews left the scene. Jewish dope was purer and cheaper than that of the Italians, who cut their narcotics with chemicals.[16]

One long-time dealer offered another distinction between Jewish and Italian narcotics traffickers of the inter-war period. "The Jews," he said, "were businessmen. They wanted to make a buck on you today and a buck on you every day. The fucking wops, they wanted ten, and tomorrow maybe choke you for fifty." This dealer was himself an Italian-American![17]

Rothstein moved freely in all circles, from politicians and statesmen to bankers and bums. On his payroll at one time or another during the 1920s were gangsters who would become famous, such as Jack "Legs" Diamond, Charley "Lucky" Luciano, Dutch Schultz, Frank Costello and Waxey Gordon, as well as a goodly number of public officials.

Luciano always admired Rothstein not only for his business acumen, but because, as he explained, "He taught me how to dress, how not to wear loud things but to have good taste."

Apparently, when Rothstein first hired Luciano he was disturbed by Lucky's loud attire. Rothstein instructed the young hoodlum to appear less visible. "I want you to wear something conservative and elegant, made by a genteel tailor."

Luciano wasn't sure what Rothstein meant. "What the hell are you talkin' about?" he said. "My tailor's a Catholic."[18]

Luciano followed Rothstein's instructions and never regretted doing so. "He taught me how to use knives and forks, and things like that at the dinner table, about holdin' a door open for a girl, or helpin' her sit down by holdin' the chair. If Arnold had lived a little longer, he could've made me pretty elegant; he was the best etiquette teacher a guy could ever have — real smooth."[19]

However, Luciano and others learned something much more important from Rothstein: the good business sense of forming alliances, regardless of ethnic considerations, not only with underworld accomplices, but also with those who could handle the political fix.

Rothstein taught his charges that the dollar had one nationality and one religion — profit.

Arnold's persona and success in organizing criminal enterprises led the writer Damon Runyon to nickname him "the Brain," and to model Nathan Detroit, the main character in "Guys and Dolls," on him. And F. Scott Fitzgerald immortalized Rothstein in *The Great Gatsby*, as the gambler Meyer Wolfsheim. "He's the man," Gatsby told Nick Carroway, "who fixed the World Series back in 1919."[20]

Rothstein's life of crime, for which he never spent a day in jail, ended when he was shot to death over a gambling debt in New York's Park Central Hotel in 1928. True to his underworld creed, Rothstein refused to divulge the name of his assailant.

Detective Patrick Flood, who visited Rothstein as he lay dying in the hospital, asked him, "Who shot you?"

According to Flood, Rothstein replied, "I won't talk about it. I'll take care of it myself." He never did.[21]

Out of respect for the elder Rothstein, Arnold received an Orthodox Jewish funeral with the renowned Orthodox rabbi, Leo Jung delivering the eulogy. The Yiddish newspaper *Der Tog* matter-of-factly reported one conspicuous infraction of Orthodox tradition: Rothstein's body, wrapped in a *talith* (prayer shawl) was laid in a bronze casket — worth $5,000 the paper noted — rather than in the simple and inexpensive wooden coffin called for by religious law.[22] At the time of his death, Rothstein's assets totalled $3 million.

After Rothstein's death, no single individual was ever again able to dominate New York's underworld the way he had. Instead, the various criminal enterprises were divided up, a number of them going to his Jewish protégés. Bootlegging became the province of Waxey Gordon, Arthur "Dutch Schultz" Flegenheimer, and the Benjamin "Bugsy" Siegel and Meyer Lansky combine, better known as the Bugs-Meyer Mob.

Waxey Gordon's real name was Irving Wexler. He was nicknamed "Waxey" because, as a youthful pickpocket, he was able to slide a victim's wallet out of his pocket "as though it were coated with wax."

Waxey was born on the Lower East Side in 1888, "the son of poor tenement folk."[23] He never went beyond grade school, but loitered around street corners developing his talent for crime. In his teens, Waxey joined the Dopey Benny Fein Gang which terrorized much of the Lower East Side in 1910. By the time he was twenty, Gordon had worked as a labor goon, strikebreaker, bookmaker, burglar, dope peddler and extortionist, and had accumulated over $100,000 from gambling and other illicit activities. In the years before Prohibition, Gordon was a partner in five different cocaine mobs and was one of the major cocaine entrepreneurs in New York.[24]

So he was an experienced criminal when Prohibition went into effect. He quickly realized the enormous potential for profits and went about raising capital to import illegal liquor from Canada, England and the West Indies. One of the people he approached was

Arnold Rothstein, for whom he had worked as a slugger in the labor wars. Rothstein loaned Gordon the money and made him a junior partner in importing whiskey from Scotland.

When Rothstein abandoned bootlegging, Gordon expanded his operation. By the mid-1920s he was one of the East Coast's biggest bootleggers, with an estimated yearly income of well over $2 million. Gordon also owned speakeasies, nightclubs, gambling casinos, a fleet of ocean-going rum-running ships and blocks of real estate in Philadelphia and New York. He lived in a castle, complete with a moat, in New Jersey, and maintained a luxurious ten-room apartment on Manhattan's Upper West Side.[25]

Arthur "Dutch Schultz" Flegenheimer was born in 1902, the son of Herman Flegenheimer, a saloon and stable owner, and Emma Neu Flegenheimer. Arthur was not really Dutch. His parents were German Jews. His father deserted the family when Arthur was eight and his mother took in washing to support the family. Arthur contributed to the family's support as well, leaving school at age fourteen and selling papers, running errands, and working as an office boy and pressman in a printing plant. None of these occupations proved lucrative enough, so Arthur joined a gang and became a burglar.[26]

Arthur had little religious training, but his family were "traditional" Jews and his mother kept a kosher home. At various times when he was arrested, however, Arthur listed himself as Jew, Protestant and Catholic.[27]

His chums nicknamed him "Dutch Schultz" because his blue eyes, light brown hair and stocky build reminded them of a murderous member of a turn-of-the century Bronx gang, the Frog Hollows. Arthur liked the name Dutch Schultz and kept it "because it was short enough to fit in the headlines. If I'd kept the name of Flegenheimer, nobody would have heard of me," he said.[28]

Dutch was one of the flakiest, cheapest and cold-blooded gangsters of the Prohibition era. Few other gangsters, including his own men, liked or respected him.

The bank robber Willie "The Actor" Sutton recalled Schultz as "a vicious, pathologically suspicious killer who kept his people in line through sheer terror. Like anyone else who ever knew him I disliked him intensely."[29]

Schultz paid his men as little as he could get away with and would fly into a murderous rage whenever anyone asked him for a raise. One day he was arguing with one of his men, Jules Martin, about money. Schultz abruptly ended the argument by drawing his gun, shoving it into Martin's mouth and pulling the trigger. Schultz's lawyer, Dixie Davis, who witnessed the killing, was horrified. "It is wrong in the underworld to kill a fellow for no reason at all," he later said. "The Dutchman did that murder just as casually as if he were picking his teeth."[30]

Lucky Luciano called Schultz "one of the cheapest guys I ever knew, practically a miser. Here was a guy with a couple of million bucks and he dressed like a pig. He used to brag that he never spent more than thirty-five bucks for a suit, and it hadda have two pairs of pants. His big deal was buyin' a newspaper for two cents so he could read all about himself."[31]

Schultz viewed his parsimony differently. "I think only queers wear silk shirts," he said. "I never bought one in my life. A guy's a sucker to spend fifteen or twenty dollars on a shirt. Hell, a guy can get a good one for two bucks."[32]

In the mid-1920s Schultz formed a gang of over a hundred gunsels that dominated bootlegging in the Bronx and parts of

Manhattan, becoming the undisputed beer baron of the Bronx through sheer savagery and brutality. Two of his toughest competitors were a pair of Irish brothers, John and Joe Rock. After some initial resistance, John thought it wiser to step aside but Joe, apparently made of sterner stuff, refused to withdraw from the beer business. He paid a high price for his stubbornness: he was kidnapped one night, beaten, hung by his thumbs on a meat hook and then blindfolded with a strip of gauze which, so the story goes, had been dipped in a mixture containing the drippings from a gonorrhea infection. Whatever the potion was, Joe came out of the experience blind. Joe's family paid a $35,000 ransom to get back what was left of him.[33]

Schultz also moved into Harlem where he took over the numbers racket. His method was simple: he told those running the business to follow his orders or he would kill them. They agreed. Numbers proved to be a very lucrative part of Schultz's operation; his Harlem venture added approximately $20 million to his annual income.[34]

According to Dixie Davis, only one offense truly enraged Schultz. "You can insult Arthur's girl, spit in his face, push him around and he'll laugh. But don't steal a dollar from his accounts. If you do, you're dead."[35]

Once, while dining in Newark, Abner "Longy" Zwillman's territory, Schultz was accosted by an obviously drunk Zwillman cohort named Max "Puddy" Hinkes. Puddy walked over to Schultz's table and in a loud voice said, "Get the fuck out of Newark. You're nobody. Newark belongs to Abe. You're a fucking nobody."

The room got very quiet as all eyes were on Schultz. Dutch looked at Hinkes for a moment and burst out laughing. Before

Louis (Pretty) Amberg

Schultz's mood changed, Hinkes was hustled out of the club and driven home.

When he woke up the next day, Hinkes received a call that Abner Zwillman wanted to see him. When Hinkes entered his office, Zwillman asked him, "Puddy, were you drunk last night?"

"Yeah," said Hinkes.

"Do you remember what you did?" queried Zwillman.

"No," answered Hinkes.

"Did you go to the Blue Mirror?" asked Zwillman.

"I think so," said Hinkes.

"Did you tell someone to go fuck themselves?" asked Zwillman.

"I tell a lot of people to go fuck themselves," said Hinkes.

"Did you tell Dutch Schultz to go fuck himself and to get out of Newark?" asked Zwillman.

"How the fuck would I know, I was drunk," said Hinkes.

Zwillman told Hinkes that was exactly what he did. Zwillman smoothed things out with Schultz, and Hinkes lived to tell the tale fifty-five years later.[36]

Jack "Legs" Diamond was not as fortunate. For years he and Dutch engaged in a shooting war over bootlegging territory. For some time, Diamond led a charmed life, and every Schultz effort to eliminate him failed. In the early morning hours of December 18, 1931, Diamond's luck finally ran out. As he lay drunk and asleep in his boardinghouse room, someone entered and pumped three bullets into his head. The killer was never caught.

When he was informed of his rival's death Schultz remarked, "Just another punk caught with his hands in my pocket."[37]

The Bugs-Meyer mob was formed in 1921 by two of the most famous Jewish organized crime figures of the twentieth century, Benjamin "Bugsy" Siegel and Meyer Lansky.

At the time the gang was formed, Siegel was fifteen and Lansky nineteen years old. Lansky was born Meyer Suchowljansky in Grodno, Poland in 1902, and brought to the United States by his parents when he was ten. He completed the eighth grade and left school at age fifteen for a job in a tool and die shop. Despite his early departure from school, Lansky remained an avid reader all his life.

Siegel was born in New York in 1905 and evolved into the

Stacher

archetypal movie mobster: handsome, hot-headed, ambitious and ruthless. When Ben got angry he actually glowed with rage. He was so reckless and violent, people said that he was "bugs," slang for crazy. According to East Side folklore, that was how he got his nickname, Bugsy. Siegel hated the nickname and no one dared call him "Bugsy" to his face.[38]

Together, Lansky and Siegel made a fearsome combination, with Lansky providing the brains and Siegel the brawn. "He was young but very brave," Lansky recalled of Siegel. "He liked guns. His big problem was that he was always ready to rush in first and shoot — to act without thinking. That always got him into trouble."[39] The two fledgling gangsters recruited an expert group of gunmen and offered to transport illegal liquor for bootleggers, delivery guaranteed. The boys also supplied mobsters with stolen cars and trucks and expert drivers.

In the dangerous business of bootlegging, Siegel's fearlessness often proved an asset. Joseph "Doc" Stacher, an early member of the group remembered that Siegel never hesitated when danger threatened. "While we tried to figure out what the best move was, Ben was already shooting. When it came to action there was no one better. I've seen him charge ten men single-handed and they would all turn and run. I never knew a man who had more guts. And the Sicilians felt the same way."[40]

Later in life Lansky claimed that he always tried to avoid the use of guns. "It's always much better not to shoot if you can help it. It's better to use reason — or if that fails, threats." Violence, Meyer liked to say, was "a poor substitute for brains."[41]

In line with this philosophy, Lansky asserted that his gang killed no one, but operated as an efficient business. "We were in business like the Ford Motor Company," Meyer said. "Shooting and killing was an inefficient way of doing business. Ford salesmen didn't shoot Chevrolet salesmen. They tried to outbid them."[42]

That's not quite how others remembered the mob. Police recall the gang as particularly vicious, one that used violence, intimidation and murder if it had to. One veteran New York City detective, who dealt with them all, said Bugsy was the worst. "For two bucks that Bugsy-Meyer mob would break the arm of a man they'd never seen. They'd kill for less than fifty. Bugsy seemed to like to do the job himself. It gave him a sense of power. He got his kicks out of seeing his victims suffering, groaning and dying."[43]

By 1928, the Siegel-Lansky outfit sold protection to nightclubs, acted as troopers for the Italian mobsters Joe Adonis, Lucky Luciano and Frank Costello, muscled in on the labor unions and dabbled in armed robbery, burglary and narcotics.

Siegel and Lansky's friendship with the rising young Italian mobsters benefited both sides in the years to come, especially Meyer's relationship with Lucky Luciano. Lansky and Luciano had known each other since childhood and remained close all their lives. Bugsy Siegel once described the special affinity that existed between the two men to Joe Stacher. "They were more than brothers, they were like lovers, Charley Luciano and Meyer, although of course there was nothing sexual between them. They would just look at each other and you would know that a few minutes later one would say what the other was thinking. I never heard them argue. I never heard them quarrel. They were always in agreement with each other."[44]

In 1931, Luciano decided it was time to eliminate the old-time New York Mafia leaders and asked his Jewish associates, Lansky and Siegel, for help. The first man Luciano went against was his own boss, Giuseppe "Joe the Boss" Masseria.

On a beautiful spring day in April 1931, Luciano invited Masseria to dine with him at the Nuova Villa Tammaro Restaurant on Coney Island. They sat at a corner table. Never a big eater, Luciano ate slowly and sparingly. Masseria gorged himself on antipasto, spaghetti with red clam sauce, lobster Fra Diavolo and a bottle of Chianti. He was still eating when most of the other lunchtime diners had left. Soon Masseria and Luciano were the last patrons in the restaurant.

After the meal, Luciano excused himself to go to the men's room. Outside, a car drew up alongside the restaurant; in it were Albert Anastasia, Vito Genovese, Joe Adonis and Bugsy Siegel.

As soon as the bathroom door closed behind Luciano, the front door of the restaurant opened and the four men, led by Siegel, burst in. They pulled out revolvers and began firing at Masseria. More than twenty shots ricocheted around the room, six of them slamming into Masseria. He slumped, face down, on the table. The killing took less than a minute. Luciano left the restaurant before the police arrived and the police could find no witnesses to the shooting.[45]

In September 1931, less than six months after the killing of Masseria, four gunmen shot and killed the last remaining old-time boss, Salvatore Maranzano, as he sat in his office over Grand Central Station.

The assassins were never caught, but underworld lore has it that they were Jewish men organized on Luciano's behalf by Meyer Lansky and Bugsy Siegel. Dutch Schultz's bodyguard, Abe "Bo" Weinberg, later claimed that he was one of the killers. According to Joseph Valachi, a small-time hood who informed on the Mafia, Samuel "Red" Levine was another one of the gunmen.[46]

Luciano never forgot the invaluable help his Jewish associates gave him in his rise to the top of organized crime. With his blessings and assistance, Siegel and Lansky went on to bigger and better things: Meyer to creating a gambling empire in Cuba and the Bahamas and to notoriety as the alleged "chairman of the board" of the National Crime Syndicate, and Bugsy to renown as the dreamer who built the Flamingo Hotel and opened up Las Vegas to organized crime.

Labor racketeering became the province of Louis "Lepke" Buchalter, one of the most vicious gangsters in the annals of American crime. Lepke became boss of an extensive racket and smuggling empire, a man who "hired killers the way the average contractor hires day laborers."[47]

Buchalter was not at all typical of the gangster image usually held in the public mind. He was quiet and unprepossessing in appearance, "neat and almost apologetic in manner," and content to let his lieutenants get the spotlight as long as he got the money. Posing as a prosperous businessman, he became the symbol of the most deadly type of operator, skillful and successful in evading the law for many years.

Louis Buchalter was born on the Lower East Side of New York in 1897, the son of Barnett Buchalter, who had immigrated to the United States from Russia, and Rose Buchalter. As a result of previous marriages, there were eleven children in the Buchalter household. One of Lepke's brothers became a rabbi, another a dentist, and a sister became a teacher. Lepke was the only one to go bad.[48]

Louis's mother nicknamed him "Lepkele," an affectionate Yiddish diminutive meaning "little Louis."

Lucky Luciano remembered the first time he met Buchalter. "I took one look at him and all I could see was a guy with a fat face, a big head and so much muscle it was bulgin' out of his sleeves. Somethin' inside warned me that this guy was mostly strong-arm and very little brain. So I said to him, 'Listen, Lou…'

"He stopped me and said, kinda nice, 'You can call me Lepke.'

"I couldn't help it," recalled Luciano, "I started to laugh. I said, 'What the fuck kinda name is that?'

"He got all red and embarrassed and he explained that when he was a kid his mother used to call him by a pet Jewish name, Lepkele.

"So from then on we all called him Lepke. How can you not like a guy who always thinks about his mother?"[49]

J. Edgar Hoover didn't. In the 1930s, Hoover labeled little Louis as "one of the most dangerous criminals in the United States."[50]

Lepke got better-than-average marks in school and seems to have behaved himself. When he was fourteen his father died. One year later Buchalter quit school, despite the pleas of his mother and family, and went to work as a delivery boy. By the time Lepke was eighteen his entire family, except Louis himself, had moved out west.

Lepke turned down an elder brother's offer to put him through high school and college and, instead, moved into a furnished room on the East Side.

It was in this brawling neighborhood that Louis embarked on his criminal career. He joined a gang of local hoodlums who rolled drunks, picked pockets and robbed pushcarts. His close associate at this time, and for the next thirty years, was Jacob "Gurrah" Shapiro, a surly, loud-mouthed and hoarsely guttural 200-pound enforcer. One reporter called him "the Donald Duck of the New York underworld, constantly out of temper."[51]

Just after his nineteenth birthday, Lepke was sent to jail for stealing a salesman's sample case. Paroled in 1917, he was back in prison the next year on a larceny charge. He was arrested again in 1920 on a burglary charge and was sent up for two years. Upon his release, he turned his talent to labor racketeering and managed to avoid further prison sentences until his arrest in 1939.

In his private life, Lepke was a devoted family man who rarely drank or gambled, but outside his home he commanded an army of gangsters who extorted millions of dollars from his victims. It was estimated that payments to Lepke for "protection" amounted to over $10 million annually.[52]

The gang's weapons were destructive acids, bludgeons, blackjacks, knives, fire, ice picks and guns. For a fee, Lepke protected manufacturers from shop unionizers and strikers by intimidating workers and using strong-arm tactics. He also forced unions to do his bidding by installing his own business agents or by creating rival unions.[53]

Lepke explained that the trick was a captive union and a captive employer's association. "That way you got both management and labor in your pocket."[54]

His system worked and he became a legend. The few men who failed to heed the gang's orders or who dared to go to the police with their stories suffered destruction, acid burns, mayhem and murder. As a Buchalter associate once put it, "Lep loves to hurt people."[55]

In the same way that he gained control over the unions through terror, Buchalter moved into legitimate business. Those who tried to fight him found their plants wrecked or their stocks ruined by a special Lepke task force, expert in the art of acid throwing. When a manufacturer surrendered, Lepke would place his men in the factory as managers, foremen and bookkeepers.

By 1932 Buchalter dominated a wide assortment of industries and unions in New York, including the bakery and pastry drivers, the milliners, the garment workers, the shoe trade, the poultry market, the taxicab business, the motion picture operators and the fur truckers.[56]

Lepke also engaged in a sideline — drug trafficking. Before long he became one of the largest importers and distributors of heroin, cocaine and opium in the United States. Lepke used young women, chosen for their charm and personality, as his agents. Each lady received $2,000 plus her expenses to make the trip to Europe and bring back trunks loaded with narcotics. Lepke's syndicate operated in Mexico, Japan, China, France, Italy and Denmark, and such American ports as New York, San Francisco and Seattle.[57]

With all the money rolling in, Lepke became a multi-millionaire and lived accordingly. He resided in a plush mid-Manhattan apartment and maintained chauffeur driven cars for trips to racetracks and nightclubs. And he often spent his winters in Florida and California.[58]

Buchalter's reputation throughout the underworld was that he never lost his temper, but his own men feared him. They called him "The Judge," sometimes "Judge Louie." One associate, Shalom Bernstein, summed it up for all when he said, "I don't ask questions, I just obey. It would be more healthier."[59]

The history of organized crime in America is filled with myths. One of the more enduring, reinforced by Hollywood and crime writers, is that sometime in the 1930s Jewish and Italian mobsters in New York came together and set up a National Crime Syndicate to divvy up the rackets across the country in an orderly and businesslike fashion. Among the founders of this alleged syndicate were Lepke, Bugsy Siegel, Meyer Lansky, Dutch Schultz and Longy Zwillman, and Lucky Luciano, Frank Costello and Joe Adonis.[60]

At Lepke's suggestion, the syndicate supposedly created an enforcement arm of killers to maintain order. The primary members of this unit were a Brooklyn-based gang of Jewish thugs led by Abe "Kid Twist" Reles and his friends Harry "Pittsburgh Phil" Strauss, Abraham "Pretty" Levine and Martin "Buggsy" Goldstein, together with an Italian mob led by Harry "Happy" (because he wore a perpetual scowl) Maione and Frank "Dasher" Abbandando. A zealous crime reporter, Harry Feeney, dubbed this outfit of killers-for-hire Murder, Inc. And Murder, Inc. it has remained.[61]

Benny (Bugsy) Siegel

The Jewish members of this gang hung out in a tacky candy store located under the elevated subway tracks at the corner of Saratoga and Livonia Avenue in the Brownsville section of Brooklyn. Owned by a woman named Rose, who kept the place open 24 hours a day, the store became known as "Midnight Rose's."

Allegedly the two main topics of conversation in the store were how many runs the Brooklyn Dodgers would lose by that day, and murder. Wags claimed that more individual murders were planned in the store than at any other spot on earth.

Fact or fancy, what we do know for certain is that Italian and Jewish mobsters in New York did cooperate during the 1920s and 1930s (they also periodically fought each other), that various criminal syndicates across the United States maintained contacts with each other, that leading crime figures met intermittently, and that gangsters did put out contracts to kill rivals. We also know that while Lepke was hiding from New York's crime-fighting special prosecutor, Thomas E. Dewey, he used Abe Reles and company to execute persons he thought knew too much about him and might talk.

Somewhere between sixty and eighty men died on Lepke's orders. They were burned with gasoline, buried in quicklime, shot, stabbed with ice picks or garroted. It is said that Lepke even coined the word "hit" as a euphemism for contract murder.[62]

Although not a protege of Arnold Rothstein, Louis "Pretty" Amberg was a significant force in the New York underworld from the late 1920s until his violent death in 1935.[63] He was one of the city's best known killers, having "rubbed-out" between eighteen to 100 men, no one knows for sure. Arrested numerous times, luck and cunning kept him from being convicted of any of these murders.

His favorite technique was to stuff his live victims into a laundry bag, tied around the arms, legs and neck in such a way that they would strangle themselves as they struggled to get free. Damon Runyon commemorated this feat in a number of stories which portrayed Amberg in a thinly disguised form.

Amberg was nicknamed "Pretty" because of his ugliness. He was so ugly that the Ringling Brothers circus offered him a job, asking him to appear as the "Missing Link." Rather than being insulted, Amberg was flattered and often bragged about the offer.

Louis was born in Russia in 1898 and immigrated to the United States with his parents. The family settled in the Brownsville section of Brooklyn, where Louis's father peddled fruit. At the age of ten, Louis started peddling on his own, developing a unique method for selling fruit door-to-door. He would kick on a door until the resident opened up. Louis would then shove the fruits and vegetables forward and snarl, "Buy." One look at Pretty's face and they bought.

By the time he was twenty, Pretty was the terror of Brownsville. He and his older brother Joe ran a loansharking business that charged 20 percent interest a week. People who borrowed money from the Ambergs were told at the very outset that if they did not pay on time, they would be killed. No one was late.

During Prohibition, Pretty and his brothers Joe and "Hymie the Rat" (who later committed suicide in jail) controlled bootlegging in Brownsville. Any speakeasy that refused their product was bombed.

Prohibition made Amberg rich. He strutted around New York's nightspots spending lavishly. Waiters fought to serve his table because he never left less than a $100 tip.

Amberg later expanded his activities to include laundry services for Brooklyn businesses. He did very well by offering businessmen a

Zwillman

deal they couldn't refuse. If they used Pretty's service, they stayed in business. A morbid joke making the rounds claimed that Pretty got into the laundry business so he could have a ready supply of laundry bags for all his stiffs.

Pretty successfully defended his domain from inroads by other gangsters. Dutch Schultz once told Amberg that he was thinking of becoming his partner. "Arthur," Pretty said, "why don't you put a gun in your mouth and see how many times you can pull the trigger."[64]

Not to be put off, Schultz planted two of his men in a new loan office not far from Pretty's operation. Within 24 hours the two men were dead, their bodies riddled with bullets.

Pretty was good friends with Legs Diamond, but he even warned him about coming into Brownsville. "We're pals, Jack," said Amberg. "But if you ever set foot in Brownsville, I'll kill you and your girlfriend and your missus and your whole damn family."[65]

Not far from New York, in Newark, New Jersey, Abner "Longy" Zwillman reigned as king of the rackets. Over six feet two inches tall, Zwillman got the nickname "Longy" because he was the tallest kid in his school and neighbors called him, "der Langer," Yiddish for "the tall one." Next to Meyer Lansky, Zwillman was the most prominent Jewish mob boss in America. Together with his Italian allies, Richie Boiardo and Willie Moretti, Longy ran Newark from the Prohibition era until the 1950s. His influence was so great that he was referred to as the "Al Capone of New Jersey."

During his testimony before the Kefauver Committee investigating organized crime in 1950, Zwillman was asked by Senator Charles Tobey whether it was true "that you have been known in New Jersey for a long time as the Al Capone of New Jersey?"

The suave Zwillman laughingly replied, "That is a myth that has been developing, Mr. Senator, for a good many years, and during the time when I should have had sense enough to stop it, or get up and get out of the State, I did not have sense enough, and until the point where it blossomed and bloomed... I am not that, I don't intend to be, I never strived to be, and I am trying to make a living for my family and myself.

"But those rumors go around. They accuse me of owning places. I walk into a restaurant and I own the restaurant. I walk into a hotel and I own the hotel. I take a shine twice, and I own the bootblack, too."

"Well," replied Tobey, "those are the penalties of greatness."[66]

Zwillman was born in Newark in 1904 to immigrant parents who had come to the city from Russia before the turn of the century. Abner was the third of seven children. The father, Abraham Zwillman, peddled live chickens from a stall in the public market on Prince Street and barely made a living.

Longy was once asked why he was so strongly addicted to making money. He replied, "All I remember is that as kids my brothers, sisters, and I were always hungry."[67]

Longy's father died when he was fourteen. He quit school and went to work, renting a horse and wagon and peddling fruits and vegetables. But he saw that the men who made real money in his neighborhood, the kind of money he was after, were either politicians or gamblers. And he quickly realized that he would never get anywhere peddling. Prohibition provided him with the chance to get what he wanted — money, respect and power.

Using his brain and brawn, Longy began making his fortune by hijacking liquor shipments, muscling in on still operations, and rum-running. In these ventures he was assisted by his boyhood pal, Joseph "Doc" Stacher, and his gang, the Third Ward "Longy Mob."[68]

Longy expanded his operation by allying himself with Joseph Reinfeld, a saloon owner who perfected the system of shipping whiskey directly from the Canadian Bronfman brothers' distillery in Montreal to the shores of New Jersey.[69]

Reinfeld was born in Poland in 1899 and came to the United States and Newark in 1909. He was first arrested when he was nineteen, and fined $5 for a minor liquor offence. In 1925 he was charged with murder, shooting a prohibition agent in what police discreetly called "a dispute over money matters." Reinfeld was never indicted and the charge was dropped. His only federal conviction occurred in 1920, when he pleaded guilty to transporting ten barrels of liquor from Newark to New York. He paid a $200 fine.[70]

Zwillman started as a truck driver for Reinfeld, hauling liquor from unloading zones along the East Coast. Abe proved so ruthless and tough that no hijacker dared bother him. Smart as well as rugged, Zwillman quickly became a full partner in the combine.

Zwillman and Reinfeld ran one of the biggest and most profitable bootlegging operations in the United States, importing nearly 40 percent of all the illicit alcohol consumed in the United States during Prohibition. The syndicate maintained a sales office in Newark. A customer wanting to buy liquor came to the office, deposited his money and got a receipt entitling him to a specific amount of whiskey. He then took a boat out to the ship and collected his cargo.[71]

When the weather was rough, the gang found other ways to

distribute their liquor. For instance, one stormy winter night in 1928 off the coast of New Jersey, a Zwillman-Reinfeld ship, carrying a cargo of booze in copper-lined tanks, watched for a red light on the top floor of an oceanfront house. When the crew spotted the light, the ship anchored offshore. A small boat brought out a hose made of rubber on the outside and linen on the inside. The crew then connected the hose to the tanks and pumped twenty thousand gallons of Canadian whiskey into oaken vats located in three houses on shore. The customers then picked up their whiskey at the houses.[72]

Treasury agents estimate that from 1926 to 1933 Longy earned over $40 million from illegal booze alone.[73]

After Prohibition, Zwillman expanded into the numbers racket, bookmaking, slot machines, cigarette vending machines and gambling. He also muscled into labor organizations, installing his friends as heads of local unions such as the Wine and Liquor Salesmen of New Jersey, the International Union of Operating Engineers, the Retail Clerk's Union, the Teamsters Union and the Motion Picture Machine Operator's Union.

In 1942, a Newark businessman sent J. Edgar Hoover a confidential letter complaining bitterly about Zwillman's stranglehold on local businesses. "Longy Zwillman is interested in every industry, and openly admits being connected with over fifty firms who pay tribute to him and his henchmen," he wrote. The writer then went on to list a number of large concerns that paid Longy to keep the peace and allow them to operate.

"Do you know that Mr. Abner Zwillman sits in his office at the Public Service Tobacco Co., Hillside, N.J., while reputable business people come pleading and begging him to leave them alone so they can continue to conduct their business honorably."

As if to emphasize the un-American character of Zwillman and his cronies, the writer noted that "high officers at camps and draft boards are intimidated" to keep Longy's men out of the army, "and keep his friends in soft berths while others fight and die."

He closed his letter by assuring Hoover "that every word of this is true and correct. You will have no difficulty of checking on this because his employees are so bold, that they do not hesitate bragging of their accomplishments."[74]

Longy worked closely with New Jersey Italian mobsters Angelo "Gyp" De Carlo, Gerardo Catena and the Moretti brothers, Willie and Sal, as well as with New York organized crime figures Meyer Lansky, Bugsy Siegel, Lepke Buchalter, Frank Costello and Lucky Luciano.

Zwillman became especially close to Siegel. Whenever he traveled to Los Angeles, Bugsy was the first person he visited. The two men spent considerable time together and Zwillman often stayed at Siegel's home. Longy once remarked that he would not have hesitated to do any favor for Siegel, "no matter what the request might have been."[75]

As Zwillman's wealth increased, so did his political influence. He developed the payoff into an art, starting with the cop on the beat and including prosecutors and judges. The police did not merely look the other way when illegal whiskey was involved; they often convoyed trucks from the docks to the warehouses to prevent hijackings, and guarded the warehouses where the liquor was stored. Newark prosecutors became adept at "misplacing" evidence, or making unprofessional "mistakes" in drawing up indictments. Judges dismissed cases or levied small fines. Some of the bolder ones even bargained for bribes right in the courtroom.

Because of the corrupt policemen, prosecutors and courts, Newark became the bootleg capital of the country.

Zwillman's political clout continued long after Prohibition ended. The Democratic leader of Essex County New Jersey traditionally went to Longy to get his okay for the list of Democratic candidates. If Zwillman vetoed someone, he wasn't nominated. Well into the 1940s, the mayor of Newark and three of the city's five commissioners owed their jobs to Longy.

The mayor was a former dentist, Meyer Ellenstein. One Longy associate remembers that Ellenstein "was a wonderful dentist. Only he thought he could make more money being a mayor." But when he finished his term in office "he was broke. He didn't have one penny. He was the only mayor that left Newark that didn't have a quarter. He shoulda stayed a dentist."[76]

Longy's connections protected him the one time he was arrested and went to jail.

He was sent to prison for beating up a local pimp who was also a runner for his numbers racket. The pimp made the suicidal error of holding back money from his numbers route. Longy taught the man a lesson, beating him with a blackjack, breaking three bones in his face and leaving his body a mass of bruises and welts. The pimp was lucky. Longy said he felt sorry for the man because he was black, which was why he didn't kill him. Longy was found guilty of atrocious assault and received a six-month sentence.[77]

While in prison, Longy had a telephone in his cell, was permitted callers at all hours and ate meals prepared outside the prison.

A friend of Zwillman's, Itzik Goldstein, remembers standing on the corner of Princess and Springfield Avenue at 4 o'clock in the morning one spring day, when "a car stops and Longy and two other fellows get out. Now I knew he was supposed to be in prison, up at Caldwell. I says, 'My God, he's supposed to be in Caldwell.' So I asked him, 'Longy, what are you doing here?' He says, 'They let me out for a couple of hours.' Longy used to sleep at the jail all day and go out all night, go cabareting. That's how he spent his time in jail."[78]

Longy served three months. Upon leaving prison, he gave gifts of money to the guards and a new car to one of the jail officials.

Despite his reputation as a mobster, Longy always remained sensitive to his Jewish upbringing. When Hymie Kugel, a good friend of Longy's died, Zwillman would not go into the chapel where the casket lay. Hymie's son Jerry could not understand it. He felt hurt, because he knew his father loved Zwillman. After the service, he went over to Longy, who was standing outside, and asked why he had not gone into the funeral parlor to pay his respects.

"I can't, Jerry," Longy said. "I'm a Cohen."

Jerry looked confused, until someone standing nearby explained that as a Cohen, a descendant of the ancient Hebrew priestly class, Longy was not allowed to be in the same room with a dead body. As close as Zwillman had been to Jerry's father and family, he would not break this ritual prohibition.[79]

Perhaps the most incongruous Longy story involves the actress Jean Harlow, the sex symbol of the 1930s. Apparently, Longy met her in 1930 when she was an unsophisticated nineteen-year-old. At the time, Harlow was under contract to Howard Hughes and had just starred in his movie "Hell's Angels." Hughes recognized Harlow's potential and sent her on a personal appearance tour around the country promoting the film. One of her stops was Newark.

Longy's friend Doc Stacher had gone to Newark's Adams Theater to see the film. Harlow made an appearance before the movie began. Stacher was intrigued by Harlow's looks and raved about her to Longy. Zwillman had never heard Doc speak so enthusiastically about any woman, so he went to see for himself. One look and he was smitten.

Zwillman introduced himself to Harlow. The attraction was mutual and the two became lovers. He took Harlow under his wing and taught her how to walk, talk, dress and behave in public. He even coined the term "platinum blond" to describe her hair. And

Arthur (Dutch Schultz) Flegenheimer

from all accounts, Harlow loved Longy. Their affair lasted until Jean moved to Hollywood to become a star for MGM.[80]

Bootlegging in Prohibition era Philadelphia was directed by Max "Boo Boo" Hoff. Born in Philadelphia in 1893, the son of Russian-Jewish parents, Max was nicknamed "Boo Boo" when he was a kid, playing on the crowded streets of South Philadelphia. When the boy's mother called "bo," the Hebrew word for "come," his Irish and Italian playmates thought she was saying "boo boo."[81]

Hoff earned his first few dollars as a newsboy, then as a clerk in a cigar store, and later opened a high stakes gambling establishment which fronted as a political club in Philadelphia's Fifth political Ward.

Later, he managed boxers, promoted prizefights and became well-known in sporting circles. He made his real mark with the coming of Prohibition, heading a powerful gang of tough young Jewish hoodlums that supervised a considerable portion of Philadelphia's illegal liquor racket, gambling and other underworld operations. He was the city's major buyer of machine guns and bullet-proof vests, putting them to good use when dealing with competitors.[82]

Hoff maintained an ongoing relationship with the Jewish New York and Newark mobs and was reportedly on "close terms" with Al Capone. By 1927 he was acknowledged to be Philadelphia's "King of the Bootleggers."[83]

In keeping with his reputation, Max lived in a luxurious apartment in West Philadelphia and entertained lavishly. He became one of the city's most talked-about hosts, a man who thought nothing of hiring hotel ballrooms to honor local and visiting celebrities.

Hoff also achieved repute as someone who was generous to his friends. Every Christmas he distributed thousands of dollars in gifts to members of the police department; in 1926 alone he gave away a total of $250,000 in gifts. That was in addition to the bribes.

A 1928 grand jury investigation found over 80 policemen on Hoff's payroll. When questioned about the source of their wealth, some officers said they made extra money by being "lucky in crap games and poker games"; others said they "bet on the right horses." A few officers claimed that they had "loaned money to dead saloon keepers who left provisions in their will for the loan plus a large bonus." One police captain explained that he managed to accumulate $100,000 in bank accounts, from his salary of $2,000 per year by "building birdcages for the retail trade."[84]

When Prohibition ended, so too did Boo Boo's prominence in Philadelphia's underworld. He invested his bootlegging fortune in a series of nightclubs and jukebox dance joints, all of which failed. He died penniless in 1941 after swallowing dozens of sleeping pills.[85]

Hoff's successor as Philadelphia's dominant Jewish mobster was Harry Stromberg, alias Nig Rosen. He was called "Nig" because, as he said, "I was dark and they called me Nig." Stromberg was born in Russia in 1902 and immigrated with his parents to the East Side of New York in 1906. He was first arrested for juvenile delinquency when he was thirteen and went to jail on a burglary conviction when he was nineteen. Upon his release, he joined the Lepke mob that terrorized the New York garment industry. Police intelligence had him working with Meyer Lansky and Frank Costello as well.[86]

After moving to Philadelphia, Stromberg became a major power in the gambling business. He also led what was called the "69th Street Gang" that dealt in prostitution, extortion and labor racketeering. His influence extended as far as Washington, Baltimore and Atlantic City.[87]

Stromberg left Philadelphia sometime in the 1930s, but continued to run part of its numbers racket. In 1950, the Kefauver Committee still identified him as "Philadelphia's gambling czar." He later became involved in smuggling heroin into the United States from France, reportedly earning $20 million a year from the trade.[88]

He retired in the 1960s to Florida, where he died in 1984. When Stromberg left Philadelphia, he was succeeded by his driver and bodyguard, Willie Weisberg, a long-time member of the city's Jewish underworld.

Lester Schaffer, an attorney who represented Weisberg, remembers that as boss of the rackets, "he was under constant harassment by the police. He couldn't even walk down the street without being tailed and stopped.

"Weisberg knew he was being followed by the FBI. He got so used to it that when he saw agents in a restaurant, he would call them over to have a drink with him.

"Once he was sitting with Angelo Bruno (Philadelphia's Mafia boss) in a restaurant. It was snowing outside. So he went over to the FBI agents sitting in their car and told them his itinerary so they wouldn't waste time sitting out in the cold and could meet him where he was going."[89]

Weisberg was born in Russia and came to the United States with his parents when he was six. During the 1930s and 1940 he was arrested more than thirty times on charges of robbery, establishing lotteries, extortion and violations of the Firearms Act. From 1940 to 1950 the Philadelphia police barred him from setting foot in the city.

In 1950 he was investigated by the Kefauver Crime Committee, and again in 1957 by Senator John McClellan's Senate investigations committee. In 1961 he was listed by Attorney General Robert Kennedy on a "top echelon" roster of 40 leading American racketeers. Weisberg died in Philadelphia in 1978.[90]

Bootlegging in Boston was controlled by Charles "King" Solomon, alias "Boston Charley." He headed one of the largest liquor, vice and narcotics smuggling syndicates in New England.[91]

Born in Russia in 1884, Solomon was brought to Boston as a small boy and grew up in a middle class home on Boston's West End. Charley's father owned a theater and he had three brothers who all went straight.

Earning money legitimately never interested Charley. By the time he was twenty he was involved in prostitution, fencing and narcotics smuggling, mostly cocaine and morphine.

Solomon ran the Boston underworld during the 1920s. As a bootlegger he dealt with Seagrams in Canada and with associates in New York and Chicago. By bribing the local authorities, Solomon was never convicted of a single liquor charge in Boston.

Unfortunately for Charley, he did not outlive Prohibition. He was killed by gunmen in the washroom of the Cotton Club in Roxbury a day before he was to testify in court about his liquor smuggling operation.

According to witnesses, four men "escorted" Solomon into the men's room. An argument followed and a waitress heard Solomon say, "You've taken my money, what else do you want."

Another voice said, "You've got this coming to you, anyway."

Then three shots were fired and the men came running out.

Solomon staggered out of the washroom, bleeding. He cried, "The dirty rats got me," and fell to the floor. He died the next day.[92]

The killers were eventually caught and tried for robbery and murder. Three of the men were convicted of armed robbery and sentenced to seven years in jail, while the other was convicted of manslaughter and armed robbery and received a ten to twenty-year sentence.

Solomon's widow Bertha inherited a million dollar estate and remarried a year after Charley's death. Her second husband was legitimate.

During Prohibition, Charley Solomon, Longy Zwillman, Meyer Lansky, Dutch Schultz, Bugsy Siegel and Lepke Buchalter were known as the Jewish "Big Six" of the East Coast. But Jewish mobsters played important roles in other places as well.

Chapter Two

Rogues of the Midwest

*N*ot every Jewish gangster attained the stature of the East Coast bosses. Nevertheless, Jewish mobsters also played significant roles in organized crime in the Midwest.

Bootlegging and gambling in Cleveland were bossed by the "Cleveland Four" — Morris "Moe" Dalitz, Morris Kleinman, Sam Tucker and Louis Rothkopf. All were born at the turn of the century: Tucker in Lithuania, the other three in the United States of immigrant parents. The mob's recognized leader was Moe Dalitz. Moe was born in Boston in 1900, but grew up in Detroit where he attended elementary and high school. He began his career as a bootlegger while in Detroit, serving as one of the admirals in "the Little Jewish Navy." This gang of Jewish rumrunners ferried booze from Canada across the Detroit River to quench the thirst of many a Motor City resident.

For a time, Dalitz teamed up with members of Detroit's dominant Jewish mob, the Purple Gang, but he soon fell out with Joseph Zerilli, one of the local Mafia chieftains, and thought it prudent to shift his base of operation across Lake Erie to Cleveland. There he found his niche.

Abner (Longey) Zwillman

Through a skillful use of bribery and a judicious application of murder and mayhem, Dalitz and his syndicate dominated the bootleg liquor traffic to Ohio from Canada. They moved so much illegal booze across Lake Erie that it became known as "the Jewish Lake."[1]

Dalitz and his associates existed side by side with the Cleveland Mafia, led by Big Al Polizzi and his Mayfield Road gang. Together they eliminated competition posed by the Italian Porello brothers and Lonardo family. Relations between the Jewish and the Italian group remained cordial for many years.

When Prohibition ended, the Jewish syndicate operated gambling casinos in Cleveland, Kentucky, West Virginia and Indiana. Together with the Polizzis, they became involved in bookmaking, pinball machines, slot machines, and the lottery.[2]

Moe Dalitz and his syndicate were careful to form strong alliances with other mobsters around the country. And Dalitz was powerful enough to command the respect of America's top organized crime figures. One of the first things Lucky Luciano did when he became a national Mafia leader was to travel to Cleveland to meet with Moe.

Luciano was not the only top gangster to maintain ties with Dalitz. In 1952, Moe testified before the New York State Crime Commission hearings that he personally knew and was close to Abner Zwillman, Bugsy Siegel, Meyer Lansky, Joe Adonis, Frank Costello and other major mob figures. And when Lucky Luciano was deported from the United States in 1946, Dalitz attended his going-away party on the "Laura Keene," the ship that took him to Italy. Also present at that auspicious occasion were Lansky, Zwillman, Siegel, Costello, Albert Anastasia, Carlo Gambino and Joe Bonanno.

Eventually Dalitz, Kleinman, Rothkopf and Tucker pulled out of the Ohio area and transferred their interests out west, to Las Vegas, taking over the Desert Inn and becoming known as the Desert Inn Syndicate. In time, they gained control of a number of other Las Vegas casinos, including the Stardust Hotel, and remained a dominant force in the city's gambling industry for many years. The four partners shared everything equally and remained close friends all their lives.[3]

Dalitz invested his illegal gains wisely. In the early 1950s he became a partner in the Paradise Development Co., which built the Las Vegas convention center, Sunrise Hospital, a shopping center and several buildings at the University of Nevada-Las Vegas.[4]

Dalitz sold the Desert Inn in 1966 and helped develop Rancho La Costa, a $100 million resort near San Diego. Construction was financed in part by an $87 million loan from the pension fund of the Teamsters Union, at a time when the union was controlled by Jimmy Hoffa. Hoffa later disappeared and is presumed to have been killed by the Mafia.[5]

At the Senate crime hearings in 1951, Senator Estes Kefauver queried Dalitz about his substantial investments. "Now, to get your investments started off, you did get yourself a pretty good little nest egg out of rum-running, didn't you," asked Kefauver. "Well," replied Moe, "I didn't inherit any money, Senator."[6]

Although Dalitz was a small man, standing no more than five foot three inches, no one could frighten him. Once, in 1964, the 64-year-old Moe was sitting in the dining room of the Beverly Rodeo Hotel in Hollywood. Heavyweight champion Sonny Liston, in an ugly mood brought on by too much whiskey, approached him in a threatening manner. The two exchanged words and the angry Liston drew back his fist. Dalitz did not flinch. "If you hit me, nigger, you better kill me," he said. "Because if you don't, I'll make one telephone call and you'll be dead in twenty-four hours." Liston walked away.[7]

Altogether, Dalitz did quite well for himself. In 1982, *Forbes Magazine* listed him as one of America's four hundred richest men, worth $110 million.[8]

Across Lake Erie from Cleveland, Detroit's toughest, most ruthless mob was the all-Jewish Purple Gang. Led by a transplanted New York hoodlum, Ray Bernstein, the gang dominated the city's bootlegging and narcotics traffic throughout the Prohibition era.

In 1932, the Detroit police department compiled a confidential dossier on the gang members, a list of fifty names, which they forwarded to the FBI. At the time, ten members were serving prison sentences, seven were wanted for murder and kidnapping, four were dead and 28 members were at large and wanted by the police for questioning.[9] A few samples from this prospectus illustrates the composition and nature of a typical Jewish Prohibition-era mob.

"SAM DAVIS alias THE GORILLA (because he was only five feet one inch tall and weighed all of 100 pounds). Age 24. Eyes, Hazel. Hair, Light Brown. Complexion, Florid. Build, Medium Slim. This man has been arrested by the Detroit Police on charges of violating the U.S. Codes, Robbery, Armed, Extortion, and Carrying Concealed Weapons. He is now BADLY WANTED by the Detroit Police Department on a charge of murder. He is said to have killed one Harry Gold in Detroit, Mich. on the night of Feb. 17, 1932.

"HARRY FLAISH alias FLEISHER alias FLAISHER alias FLEISH alias FINK. Age 30. Height, 5-6. Weight, 190. Eyes, Hazel. Hair, Light Brown. Complexion, Medium. Build, Stout. This man has been arrested by the Detroit Police on charges of Kidnapping,

Receiving stolen property, Counterfeiting, Robbery, Armed, Extortion and Assault with intent to kill.

"PHILLIP KEYWELL. Age 31. Height 5-8⅛. Weight 148. Eyes, Hazel. Hair, Dark Brown. Complexion, Dark. Build, Slim. This man has a long record of arrests by the Detroit Police on charges of Grand Larceny, Robbery, Armed, Assault with Intent to Kill, Kidnapping and Murder.

"EDWARD SHAW alias LITTLE ABE alias JACK STEIN alias ROBERT GRAY alias ABRAHAM WAGNER. Age 25. Height, 5-3¼. Weight, 103. Eyes, Hazel. Hair, Black. Complexion, Medium Dark. Build, Slim. This man has been arrested in Eastview, N.Y., charge, Narcotics; New York City, Homicide; Los Angeles, Calif., charge, Suspicion Burglary; and in Detroit, on charge of Robbery, Armed. He is wanted on charge of Homicide in New York City.

"HARRY MILLMAN. Age 22. Height 5-7⅛. Weight, 135. Eyes, Blue. Hair, Dark Brown. Complexion, Dark. Build, Slim. This man has been arrested by the Detroit Police on charges of Robbery, Armed, Extortion, Kidnapping, Violating the Prohibition Laws, Carrying Concealed Weapons and also Hijacking.

"HYMIE ALTMAN alias HARRY ALTMAN alias NIGGER HYMIE alias JEW ALTMAN. Age 28. Height 5-7¼. Weight, 166. Eyes, Hazel. Hair, Dark Brown. Complexion, Dark. Build, Medium Stout. This man has been arrested by the Detroit Police on charges of violating Immigration Laws, Robbery, Armed, Loitering in a House of Prostitution, Violating the U.S. Prohibition Laws, Copyright Laws, Extortion and Murder."

This sterling cast of characters and their associates terrorized Detroit for thirteen years until a combination of the police and the Italian Mafia put them out of business.

A few hundred miles west of Detroit, Chicago had the second

Jack Guzik

largest Jewish population in the United States. Most East European Jews lived on the west side, in what was one of the poorest most congested areas of the city. The district spawned Jewish gangsters such as Louis "Diamond Louie" Cowan, Hymie "the Loudmouth" Levine, Sam "Sammy the Greener" Jacobson, and Maxie Eisen; however, they did not run things. Prohibition era Chicago was run by Irish and Italian mobsters, especially Al "Scarface" Capone.[10]

By a curious twist of fate, Capone's primary business strategist and financial advisor was a Jew, Jack "Greasy Thumb" Guzik, whom Capone called "the only friend I can really trust."

The two made an unlikely pair. Capone was an immaculately groomed man who wore custom-made suits. Guzik was a roly-poly slob. "Everything he ate for a week you could see on his vest," recalled Capone's driver George Meyer. "And the B.O.!"[11]

Legend has it that their friendship began when Guzik happened to overhear some men plotting to kill Capone. He immediately reported the plan to Al. Capone never forgot who saved his life and forever after protected Jack.

One May evening in 1924, Guzik, his face smeared with blood, staggered into Capone's office in the Four Deuces Nightclub on South Wabash street. "Who did this to you?" demanded Capone. Jack whimpered that Joe Howard, a small-time hijacker and roughneck, had slapped him around. The enraged Capone rushed out to look for Howard. He found him in Heinie Jacobs' saloon, not far from the Four Deuces. Al marched up to Howard, who was lounging at the bar bragging how he had "made the little Jew whine."

"Hello, Al," Howard said, never dreaming that anyone might object to his pummeling a slug like Guzik.

Capone grabbed Howard by the shoulders and shook him, demanding to know why he had hit his friend. Howard snarled something along the lines of of "G'wan back to your whores, you Dago pimp."

Without a word, Capone pulled out a revolver, shoved the muzzle against Howard's cheek and pulled the trigger. When Howard fell, Capone put five more slugs into his body.

At the inquest, no one in the bar remembered seeing or hearing anything. Just one more unsolved Chicago killing.[12]

Guzik was born in Russia in 1886, the son of Max and Fannie Guzik, who immigrated to the United States when Jack was one year old. In Chicago the elder Guzik supported his family of ten children by running a small cigar store. Jack found other means of employment, becoming a bartender and pimp in his older brother Harry's whorehouse.

When in a reminiscing mood, Jack would tell how policemen and judges would visit his home at all hours of the night. Each would want "a couple of dollars" or "a pass" so they could use the girls at the nearby whorehouse without paying. He never cared how many gentiles were within hearing when he declared, "Those cheap goys never wanted to spend a nickel. Always trying to get something for nothing. I never saw a goy judge after that I didn't want to vomit."[13]

When Prohibition began, Guzik joined Johnny Torrio's outfit. It was there he met Capone. After Capone killed Joe Howard, Jack became his trusted aid and spent the rest of his life enriching Capone and his heirs. Each of Capone's successors, Frank Nitti, Paul "The Waiter" Ricca, Sam Giancana and Tony Accardo, trusted Jack implicitly, allowing him to exercise his own judgment in what was best for the mob.

There are two versions of how he got the nickname "Greasy Thumb." According to the first, "Greasy Thumb" alluded to Jack's beginnings as a clumsy waiter whose thumb constantly slipped into the soup. The second has it that his thumb was always greasy from counting Capone's money.[14]

From 1927 to 1929 Guzik earned $1 million but only paid $60,240 in income tax. According to the Internal Revenue Service, he should have paid $250,000, and in 1932, Jack went to prison for five years for tax evasion.

While in prison, Jack underwent a series of physical and psychiatric tests. He was found to have a history of gonorrhea and syphilis, and was judged to have "a mental age of 13 years 2 months, with an intelligence quotient of 82 indicating subnormal intelligence."[15]

In his later years, Jack became outspoken on nearly every subject and made good copy for the Chicago press. He especially loved to pontificate about judges, for whom he had little regard. "You buy a judge by weight, like iron in a junkyard," he said. "A justice of the peace or a magistrate can be had for a five-dollar bill. In the municipal courts he will cost you ten. In the circuit or superior courts he wants fifteen. The state appellate court or state supreme court is on par with the federal courts. By the time a judge reaches such courts he is middle-aged, thick around the middle, fat between the ears. He's heavy. You can't buy a federal judge for less than a twenty-dollar bill."[16]

Guzik also became thin-skinned regarding his image and sued the press whenever he felt slighted by them. In 1955, he sued the *Chicago American*, one of William Randolph Hearst's newspapers, for a story that appeared on February 20, 1955. The article was written in a humorous vein by Elgar Brown, one of the paper's reporters. Brown's article referred to Guzik variously as "Old Baggy Eyes," "Mr. Fix," "Dean Jake, of Old Scarface U," "Chief Pander," "a potbellied toughy," and "Gangland's Fearless Fosdick."[17]

A fellow journalist remarked that most people who knew Jack, from his frequent court appearances, felt that Brown had pretty much caught the flavor of the man.

Jack charged that the Hearst Publishing Company had libeled him, but Judge Quilici of the municipal court dismissed the suit.

His friends told him to forget about it, but Jack was adamant. "I'm paying those judges," he said, "so why shouldn't I use them?" But he never won any of the lawsuits.

Undeterred, Jack kept suing. He knew exactly what he was doing, however. "Never be afraid to sue," he told his gangster confederates. "Go into court at the drop of a hat, anytime you don't like what some newspaper guy writes. You pay your lawyers a retainer. The judges are on our payrolls.

"You can sue in Cook County for fifteen dollars. Just the fact that a suit has been filed will cause most people to shut up. They can never be sure that some nutty jury won't award you a million dollars in damages." Excellent logic for a man with an IQ of 82.[18]

Although Minneapolis, Minnesota could not match any of the other cities in the size of its Jewish population, much of that city's illicit business was managed by Isidore "Kid Cann" ("If anyone can, the Kid can") Blumenfeld and his all-Jewish syndicate. Born in Rumania in 1901, Blumenfeld came to the United States as a child. Two of his brothers, Harry and Yiddy, who changed their last name to Bloom, served as his lieutenants. In 1942, the FBI identified Kid Cann as "The overlord of the Minneapolis, Minnesota underworld"; local journalists called him "the Godfather of Minneapolis."[19]

This Jewish syndicate oversaw a goodly portion of Minneapolis's bootlegging, gambling and vice. They also controlled a number of police and politicians. Anyone who got in their way was eliminated.

A crusading newspaperman named Walter Ligget, publisher of the *Midwest American*, ran a series of editorials exposing the syndicate's involvement with local officials in a variety of illegal activities. In December 1935, he was shot and killed by two assassins as he came home from Christmas shopping with his family.

Blumenfeld was arrested after Ligget's wife, Edith, identified him in a police line-up as one of the killers. "Oh that face," she sobbed to the police. "It passed inches from me and it was grinning, grinning. I'll remember that face to my dying day."[20]

Morris Dalitz

During the trial, Blumenfeld claimed that at the time of the killing he had been at a barbershop nineteen blocks away. And he had the witnesses to prove it. The jury deliberated less than four hours and acquited Blumenfeld of the murder.

Edith Ligget blamed the acquittal on the city's mayor, who had been accused of corruption by her husband. Kid Cann celebrated by taking a vacation in Florida. He liked what he saw, and he and his brothers invested in real estate and hotels in Miami, taking up residence in that city when they "retired."[21]

Minneapolis's sister city, St. Paul, was the home of two large Jewish bootleg gangs; the Bennie Gleeman-Harry Gellman syndicate, and the Leon Gleckman syndicate. Of the two, Gleckman rose to become "the most powerful syndicate leader in St. Paul."[22]

Gleckman was born in 1894 in Minsk, Russia, the third of eight children, and came to the United States in 1903 with his family. As a teenager, Gleckman married clerical worker Rose Goldstein, by whom he had three daughters. Described as "a salesman by inclination, a bootlegger by vocation, and a sports buff by avocation." Gleckman was bright, self-confident and glib. With his money and power, Gleckman played an active role in the politics of St. Paul and became a strong factor in that city's government.[23]

Gleckman's prominence — he was called "the Al Capone of the Northwest" — exposed him to a hazard common to bootleggers of the 1930s: being kidnapped by other gangsters. In September 1931, he was kidnapped from his home and held captive in a cottage located in Wisconsin. The initial ransom was thought to be $200,000, but after negotiations with Gleckman's partner, Morris Roisner, the amount dropped to $75,000. The final sum was reduced to $5,000, plus the $1,450 in cash that Gleckman had in his pockets. He was released in October 1931, after eight days in captivity.

Rumor had it that some of Gleckman's "friends" had engineered the kidnapping.

Gleckman later told the FBI that he intended to investigate the rumors and "would take care of them in his own way." Shortly thereafter, one of Gleckman's kidnappers, hotel owner Frank LaPre, was found dead with multiple gunshots to the face. Immediately after LaPre's death, the other conspirators were apprehended and convicted of the kidnapping.

After the trauma of being kidnapped, Gleckman had police guard his house, ostensibly to guard against another kidnapping. Many underworld bosses controlled members of their police departments, but not many could command police officers to stand guard outside their home.[24]

What did Jewish community leaders think of all this? They evinced shame and horror at the activities and notoriety of these men because the gangster epitomized the "bad Jew," the evildoer who would bring onus and hatred upon the entire community. Chicago Jewish leader S. M. Melamed warned his coreligionists in 1924 "that there is arising now among American Jewry an element which in the course of time may become a danger to us and which already is causing much shame. I refer to the great number of Jews in the underworld." He deplored the fact that in Chicago "not a single day passes by during which some Jewish criminal is not arrested. Something must be rotten within American Jewry, if such a phenomenon is possible."[25]

Reacting to a 1928 grand jury investigation exposing the role of Boo Boo Hoff and other Jews in Philadelphia's underworld, Rabbi

Mortimore J. Cohen of Congregation Beth Shalom bemoaned the shame "that has come to all Israel in the crimes of a lawless few. What disgrace is ours through these men, less than human, who have, without let or hindrance, dragged the Jewish name in the mud and filth of murder and bribery and corruption! As ever, all Israel is responsible one for the other, and the deeds of these men will be held against a whole people for all time to come. Let any cry break out against foreigners, and the Jews will be hounded for the dark sins of these reprobates."[26]

Cohen's fears were born out in Minneapolis. In November 1927, the Minneapolis *Saturday Press*, ran an article claiming that "ninety percent of the crimes committed against society in this city are committed by Jew gangsters." The author went on to state, "I am launching no attack against the Jewish people as a race. I am merely calling attention to a fact."[27]

These fears increased during the 1930s, when the Great Depression and the rise of Hitler and Nazism in Europe fueled a precipitous rise in anti-Semitism in the United States. Jewish leaders worried that Jewish gangsterism would provide ammunition for Jew-haters. Consequently, they steadfastly refused to acknowledge the problem in public. "We knew about the Jewish gangsters," confesses Detroit community leader Leonard Simons, "but we were afraid to admit it."[28]

Long-time Detroit Jewish journalist Philip Slomovitz concedes that the community knew about the Jewish criminals, yet the English-Jewish press printed nothing about them. "We panicked," he admits. "We worried about what the gentiles would say and submitted to our fears." In retrospect, Slomovitz believes this was a mistake. "It wouldn't have hurt if we were unafraid and said, 'Yes, we have them, but our morality is above that'."[29]

If Jewish morality was above this, what motivated these men to engage in criminal activities. Poverty? Perhaps. Meyer Lansky and Longy Zwillman said they did what they did because they grew up poor and never wanted to endure it again. Yet some criminals, such as Arnold Rothstein, were raised in comfortable circumstances. Their environment? Maybe. But these gangsters were no more deprived or suffering than their peers who grew up in the same slum or overcrowded immigrant quarters, but went legitimate.

Anti-Semitism? Possibly, because the United States of the 1920s was not always a pleasant place for Jews to live. From 1920 to 1927 Henry Ford vilified Jews in the pages of his *Dearborn Independent* newspaper and in pamphlets entitled "The International Jew." Ford required his automobile dealers to give a pamphlet to everyone who purchased one of his cars, and millions of Americans bought Fords.

The Ku Klux Klan instigated boycotts of Jewish merchants, vandalized Jewish-owned stores, burned crosses outside synagogues and terrorized prominent Jews in southern Jewish communities. Colleges and professional schools, including Harvard, Dartmouth, Rutgers, Columbia and New York University, imposed quotas on Jewish enrollment. And Jews encountered economic discrimination in commercial banks, industrial corporations, public utilities and insurance companies, as well as widespread social discrimination.[30]

Blocked from respectable avenues to success and status, many Jews selected alternate routes to fame and fortune, such as sports (especially boxing), and the entertainment industry. And some tough young Jews may have been angry enough at American society to choose crime.

More likely, however, these men selected careers in crime

Louis (Lepke)
Buchalter

because they wanted money, power, recognition and status, and they wanted it fast. Crime offered them a quick way to realize their dreams. And crime was exciting, certainly more glamorous than the tedium of studying or the drudgery of working long hours in a shop or factory.

By the age of twenty-three Harry Fleisch owned a Cadillac, wore fancy clothes, cavorted with blond girlfriends and lived in a fine house. "I had been to Europe before I was twenty-five," he recalled. "My brother, the schlemiel, studied day and night as a kid and later worked like a dog in his store. He went to Europe for the first time when he was forty-five years old. And you know who paid for the trip? I did."[31]

Meyer Lansky always considered his father to be a failure and something of a fool for having worked so hard all his life, in the sweatshops of the garment industry, for so little reward. While still a youngster, Lansky determined not to repeat his father's mistakes, swearing that "When I grew up I'd be very rich." He chose crime as the way to reach his goal.[32]

Lester Schaffer, the Philadelphia attorney who defended Willie Weisberg, believes his clients became criminals because their options were limited. "They were uneducated men, but they wanted the good life," he says. "There was little else they could do to get it."[33]

Herb Brin, a crime reporter in Chicago during the 1930s and a feature writer for the *Los Angeles Times* in the 1940s, personally knew many Chicago and Los Angeles Jewish mobsters. He agrees with Schaffer's assessment. "They were uneducated. Crime was the easy way to make a buck," he says. "That's all it was."[34]

West Coast mobster Mickey Cohen echoes this analysis. Reflecting on what a life in crime did for him, Cohen explained that he was uneducated. "So where could I have had the opportunity to meet the people that I've met in my life? Being an uneducated person, what walk of life could I have gotten into that I could have become involved with such people? I'm talking about celebrities, politicians, people in higher walks of life and education. Where could I have ever come to meet these kind of people if I had gone into some other line of work than I did?"[35]

Contrary to the image promoted by movies and crime exposes, not every Jewish gangster was a boss, like Mickey Cohen. Most of the hundreds of Jewish mobsters who toiled during Prohibition and the Great Depression were members of gangs, and took orders rather than gave them.

Chapter Three

The Purple Gang

*O*n the afternoon of September 16, 1931, three transplanted Chicago Jewish hoodlums, Herman "Hymie" Paul, Joseph "Nigger Joe" Lebovitz and Joseph "Izzy" Sutker, members of Detroit's "Little Jewish Navy" gang of rumrunners, and a local bookmaker, Solomon "Solly" Levine, pushed the buzzer for Apartment 211 at 1740 Collingwood Avenue on Detroit's west side.

Levine had brought the others to the apartment house ostensibly to discuss a "peace treaty" with rival gangsters. They came unarmed.[1]

Waiting for them inside the apartment were Irving Milberg, Harry Keywell, Ray Bernstein and Harry Fleisher, all members of Detroit's notorious Purple Gang.

The men all knew each other. The Purple Gang had imported Hymie, Nigger Joe, and Izzy to Detroit in 1926, to help them in their wars against other local bootlegging organizations.

For a while, the trio did their job well. But then they decided to go into business for themselves. They hired their own gunmen and tried to get a piece of the Detroit action, something even Al Capone himself declined to do.

The boys moved into the rackets and affiliated themselves with the Third Avenue Navy, a gang so named because it landed its river cargoes of Canadian whiskey in the railroad yards between Third and Fourth Avenue. Because all its members were Jews, the outfit was also referred to as the "Little Jewish Navy."[2]

The Chicagoans quickly acquired an unsavory reputation in the Detroit underworld. They hijacked from friend and foe alike and double-crossed almost everyone who worked with them. Local mobsters found them so untrustworthy that no one dared collaborate with them. Worse, they refused to stay within their own boundaries in the alcohol and whiskey trade, encroaching on the domain of other gangs. They especially angered the Purple Gang by brazenly selling bootleg whiskey in the Purple's territory.[3]

In 1930, the trio began extorting protection money from blind pigs* and bookmakers. Their targets included friends of the Purples as well as establishments that were already paying the Purples for protection. Moreover, they behaved deceitfully in their bootlegging deals with the gang by failing to pay what they owed.

The stage was set. Sutker, Paul and Lebovitz had pushed their luck once too often. Their activities spelled death. It was only a matter of time.

Ray Bernstein, the accepted leader of the Purple Gang, was 28 years old, short and slightly built, with a dark complexion and prominent blue eyes that gave his face a perpetually devious expression. He was the one who had organized the meeting between the two groups, and he was the one who answered the buzzer and ushered the visitors into the apartment.

The men shook hands and the visitors sat together on a long couch facing the Purples. After chatting for some minutes, Bernstein asked, "Where's Scotty with the books?"

---

* A place that sells intoxicants illegally.

He then got up and left on the pretext of calling their bookmaker. The others continued talking about details of their mutual financial transactions.

Crowded together on the sofa, the visitors failed to see any significance in the fact that the Purples stood or sat some distance apart, directly across from them.

Meanwhile, Bernstein had walked down to the alley behind the apartment house and started the engine of the getaway car. After making sure the escape route was clear, he tooted the horn and waited.

Suddenly the Purples drew guns and began shooting.

Levine sat frozen to his seat as bullets whizzed around him. One bullet zipped past his nose and struck Sutker in the head. His three companions made desperate but futile efforts to flee as slugs from blazing guns slammed into them. It was over in seconds.

When the smoke cleared, Lebovitz, Sutker and Paul, their bodies riddled with bullets, lay dead.

Keywell, Milberg and Fleisher huddled for a moment, then one of them turned to Levine and said, "Come on!"

As they retreated through the kitchen, the killers dropped their guns into a can of green paint they had left on the floor near the stove. The registration markings on the weapons had been filed off and the green paint would eliminate any fingerprints.

They rushed down the back stairs to the waiting car. With Bernstein at the wheel, the car sped away, nearly hitting a truck and barely missing a woman and child. After driving a short distance, they stopped the car and let Levine, a pal from their school days, get out.

Letting Levine go proved to be a mistake. Within hours, he was seized by detectives who were rounding up known underworld figures. He fingered the Purples as the killers.

The authorities apprehended Keywell and Bernstein two days after the murders. Heavily armed lawmen surrounded their house, but both surrendered without a fight. Milberg was captured in an apartment on September 19. Police confiscated five pistols and a rifle. He, too, yielded without a fight.

Fleisher, also named in the murder warrant, vanished and was not heard from until months later.

Solly Levine testified at the preliminary hearing against the three men, who were bound over for trial on first degree murder charges. Levine remained the key witness in the trial, which took place on October 28, 1931, although the caretaker of the Collingwood apartment building and the boy who was almost run over also testified and identified the Purples.

The police's greatest tasks were keeping Solly alive so he could testify in court, guarding the jurors against intimidation and protecting the accused from retaliation by the slain men's friends.

The defendants were transported to and from court in a patrol wagon with machine and riot guns protruding from the rear door. The jurors rode to the trial in a special bus escorted by five police cruisers in front and back, a detail of motorcycle police on either side, and a squad of armed police within.

Detroit had never seen anything like it.

Throughout the trial, Solly Levine had a personal bodyguard of twelve fast-shooting policemen. He voluntarily chose to live inside the police headquarters building.

Sitting slumped down in the witness chair, a pale, nervous and frightened Solly told his story. As he spoke, eight of his bodyguards flanked the witness chair, hands close to their revolver holsters.

Solly admitted that he was a partner of Hymie Paul, Joe Lebovitz and Izzy Sutker. "We owed Bernstein several hundred dollars for alky and I guess, too, they thought that we had been responsible for trying to cut in on their business and that we had hijacked some of the dope they were transporting," he said. "But we didn't have any idea that they were trying to get us.

"Anyway, we were over in the bookie (illegal betting parlor) at 700 Selden Avenue that is — Hymie and Joe and Izzy and me — when a call came from Ray Bernstein that he wanted to see us, because he had some suggestions he wanted us to get together on. He gave me the address of where he said his new office was at 1740 Collingwood Avenue, and I wrote it down on one of the pink slips we used for making bets.

"I wanted to know if I couldn't leave Izzy to watch the book for me, but he said no, we were all to come. We wanted to go and get cleaned up and shave, but he said come now. We all got into Sutker's car and drove over to Collingwood Avenue."

Solly then recounted what happened inside the apartment and immediately afterward. He said that just before the killers released him, "Bernstein shook hands with me again and said, 'I am your pal, Solly.' He gave me three or four hundred dollars and said to go back to the book and he'd pick me up later.

"I found out later that they were going to make me tell where some dope was and then bump me off. Bernstein, my 'pal,' had kept one of the murder guns. I'd be found in the ditch with that gun, and a dead man would be blamed for the murder."

Solly said that detectives arrested him a half hour after he arrived at the book.

That ended Solly's testimony.

The jury deliberated just one hour and thirty-seven minutes

before finding Bernstein, Keywell and Milberg guilty of first degree murder.

The verdict created bedlam in the courtroom. Friends and relatives of the defendants began to scream hysterically and court officers climbed onto tables and chairs to restore order.

One week later, on November 17, 1931, Judge Donald E. Van Zile sentenced each man "for murder in the first degree to imprisonment in the branch of Michigan State Prison at Marquette for life."

The prisoners, clean-shaven and dressed in new suits and shiny shoes, remained silent. Guards led them away after the judge spoke.

The next day the three killers were placed aboard a special Pullman car attached to a northern Michigan-bound train. They were shackled to their seats with a heavy chain. Seven Detroit policemen rode with them.

The three Purples remained cool. They joked and gossiped with their guards, read newspapers, munched corned beef sandwiches and played cards.

Bernstein, still the leader, flashed a roll of bills and tipped a Pullman waiter five dollars after breakfast.

As the train neared the end of its fifteen-hour trip, Keywell asked Bernstein. "I suppose it will be tough at first?"

"Yeah," replied Bernstein. "Like everything else, you have to get settled and organized. It'll be new and strange at first, but we'll get organized. We always did."

"Sure we will," said Keywell.

Once inside Marquette prison, however, the men lost their identities. Bernstein became No. 5449. Keywell, not yet 21 years old, became No. 5450. And Milberg, 28 years old, became No. 5451.[4]

Harry Milberg died in prison in 1938. Bernstein suffered a crippling stroke and was left partially paralyzed. He was released on mercy parole in 1964, after serving 33 years, and died two years later. Harry Keywell had a spotless prison record for 34 years before his life sentence was commuted. He was freed in 1965.[5]

Levine, the key witness, disappeared. Some said the police paid his way to France, other rumors placed him in St. Louis, Mobile, Oklahoma City or elsewhere.

Fleisher escaped and never was tried in connection with the killings. Although his name was linked with various crimes, he remained free for many years.

Thus ended what Detroit newspapers called the "Collingwood Massacre." Despite its notoriety, this slaying was merely the latest in a long series of crimes perpetrated by the all-Jewish Purple Gang, Detroit's most famous Prohibition era mob.

The Purple Gang had its origins in the Jewish section of Detroit's east side. During the first two decades of the twentieth century, the east side contained a turbulent and colorful mix of ethnic groups, including Italians, Poles, Germans, Russians, Hungarians, African-Americans and others. In 1920, Detroit's Jewish community numbered 34,727 persons, about 3.5 percent of the city's total population of 993,678. While Jews predominated in their quarter, other ethnic groups lived there as well.[6]

One former resident of the old neighborhood joked that it was easy to distinguish the Jewish dwellings from those occupied by non-Jews. "The non-Jews grew flowers in front of their houses," he said. "The Jews grew dirt."[7]

Variously dubbed "New Jerusalem," "Little Jerusalem," and "the Ghetto" by the city's press, the Jewish district abounded with

Police Department picture shows "Purple Gang" of the late '20's: From left, Harry Fleisher, Abie Zussman, Jack Stein, Willie Laks, Harry Levine, Philip Keywell, Sam Goldfarb, Sam Axler and Edward Fletcher.

"Hebrew stores of every description: butchers, bakers, clothiers, shoemakers, printing shops and restaurants," as one observer wrote. "A Hebrew might live his lifetime in the quarter and never leave its confines."[8]

Detroit's east side differed significantly from the classic tenement districts of New York's Lower East Side in that it remained a city of single and two-family dwellings throughout the pre-World War I period and for many decades afterwards. Although congestion existed, it never came anywhere near the pushcart-laden streets of New York.[9]

Nevertheless, the east side was one of the least desirable areas of Detroit in which to live. It continually lagged behind the other districts in the number of water pipes laid, sewers installed, streets paved and streetcar lines extended. The district was also more crowded, had higher rents, and higher disease and death rates than other parts of the city.[10]

The *Jewish American*, Detroit's Anglo-Jewish weekly, ruefully admitted that the Jewish quarter contained "tenement houses that are actually unfit to live in: old, decrepit, polluted and infected hovels, where human beings endeavor to exist and where a young generation is reared."[11] The members of the Purple Gang were bred in this environment.

The gang members were second-generation Americans whose parents had immigrated from Eastern Europe. Most of the boys had been born in the United States during the first decade of the twentieth century. Their parents were working class and, strictly speaking, non-Orthodox Jews. However, the parents did observe a number of Jewish holidays and traditions, such as the Jewish New Year and Day of Atonement, the Passover festival, and lighting the Sabbath candles in the home. Some of the fathers were active members of their synagogues, and one of Harry Keywell's uncles was president of the Orthodox congregation B'nai David.[12]

On one particular Day of Atonement the FBI sent two agents to monitor the service at B'nai David in hopes that some of the wanted Purple gangsters would show up. The agents dressed as Hasidic Jews, believing this would allow them to blend in, unnoticed, with the other worshippers. They sat at the rear of the synagogue.

Everything went along smoothly until the recess between the morning and afternoon service. It was a mild autumn day, and the two agents stepped outside along with the other congregants. To the consternation of those around them, the agents lit cigarettes and began to smoke. Because striking a match, or lighting a fire is strictly forbidden on this holiest day in the Jewish calendar, their cover was completely blown.[13]

As children, the future Purple gangsters lived near each other and attended the same grade school. Few of them ever finished high school. They started off in crime as petty thieves stealing fruit and candy from peddlers and stores; they also stole money when they had the chance. Later they graduated to rolling drunks and waylaying pedestrians late at night. Occasionally they teamed up to shake down Jewish merchants or to take revenge on an enemy.[14]

Gradually the boys, who were too young to serve in World War I, grew up. They stopped preying on storekeepers and hucksters and turned their attention to bigger things — the blind pigs of the Prohibition era, the gambling joints, and the bawdy houses.

Detroit boomed during Prohibition. By 1929, smuggling, manufacturing and distributing liquor had become Detroit's second largest industry, exceeded in size only by the production of automobiles. Detroit's illegal liquor industry was three times larger than her chemical industry, eight times the size of her stove and heating appliance industry, ten times the size of her cigar and tobacco industry, and about one-eighth the size of her automobile industry. Illegal booze employed fifty thousand people and grossed over $300 million a year.[15]

In 1923 there were 7,000 blind pigs in the city. By 1925 the number had risen to 15,000; three years later the figure stood at 25,000. The *Detroit News* reported that in some areas of the city "every house is either a bootleg stand or a blind pig." One newspaper investigator found 150 blind pigs on one single block, and more than 500 blind pigs in one twenty-block neighborhood.[16]

A.B. Stroup, deputy administrator in charge of Prohibition enforcement in Detroit complained that "Detroit is the wettest city I have been assigned to. I have worked in several parts of the country and observed conditions carefully, and I can say without hesitation that nowhere else is the law so openly violated as it is here."[17]

In 1923, the local police asked the federal government to help them crack down on the booze business. Washington responded by sending their number one Federal Prohibition Agent, Izzy Einstein, to Detroit.[18]

Izzy was one half of the team of Izzy and Moe, the most famous and wackiest Prohibition agents of all. Izzy Einstein and Moe Smith fit right into the Roaring Twenties. Both men were short and fat, weighing over 200 pounds, and looked nothing like government agents. This was the secret of their success. They became so successful that some speakeasies posted pictures of them as a warning to customers. Hundreds of hilarious newspaper stories were written about the pair, most of them probably true.[19]

The variety of disguises they used when making their raids seemed endless. They wore false whiskers and noses. They put on blackface. Once they donned football uniforms to bust a blind pig serving thirsty athletes playing in a Brooklyn park.

In order to bust one particular Coney Island speakeasy in midwinter, Izzy went swimming with a polar bear club, and almost froze. A concerned Moe rushed the shivering Izzy into the establishment. "Quick," he cried, "some liquor before he freezes to death." When the solicitous bartender complied, he was arrested.

From 1920 to 1925, the pair confiscated five million bottles of liquor and arrested 4,392 persons. Ninety-five percent of those arrested were convicted.

Izzy was a product of New York's Lower East Side. He spoke fluent Yiddish, Italian, Hungarian, German and Polish. He had been a dry goods salesman and post office clerk before becoming a Prohibition agent.

Once, Izzy met his namesake Albert Einstein. He asked Einstein what he did for a living. "I discover stars in the sky," replied the scientist.

"I'm a discoverer too," said Izzy, "only I discover in the basements."

The team worked primarily in the New York area, but their reputation led local bureaus in other cities to ask for their help in busting problems in their own towns. Thus it was that Izzy came to Detroit.

Izzy's methods proved successful. Sporting a mustache and dressed as an auto worker, Izzy walked into a Woodward Avenue blind pig and asked for a drink. Now most illegal drinking saloons refused service to a prospective drinker if he was not known to the bartender or other customers, thus keeping plainclothes law officers from purchasing alcoholic beverages. As added protection, many blind pigs kept photographs of local and federal law enforcement officers in an album behind the bar.

The bartender refused to serve Izzy because, he said, pointing to a black-framed photograph of Einstein, "Izzy Epstein's in town."

"You mean Einstein, don't you?" asked Izzy.

"Epstein," insisted the bartender.

"I bet you a drink it's Einstein," said Izzy.

"You're on," said the bartender.

The bartender poured him a shot of whiskey which Izzy emptied into a secret funnel sewed to his breast pocket and connected by a long rubber tube to a concealed flask he used to gather evidence.

"There's sad news here," Izzy announced in a mournful voice. "You're under arrest."[20]

Izzy and Moe retired in 1925. They went into the insurance business and soon numbered among their clients many of the people they had arrested for liquor violations.

Supplying the blind pigs with alcoholic beverages became an extremely profitable enterprise. Booze smuggled across the Detroit River from Canada was the main source, supplemented by locally produced products. By 1928, five thousand Detroit stills bubbled forth alcohol to slake the city's thirst. Many of these enterprises were large-scale operations, but most were small setups in family basements, living rooms, closets and attics.[21]

In Detroit, most branches of the illegal liquor business, from brewing and distilling to rumrunning and blind pig management, were controlled by well-organized underworld gangs. To Detroiters, the best-known gang operating in the city by the mid-1920s was the Purple Gang.

The Purples originated in the 1920s with the merger of two

Jewish gangs. The first was called the Oakland Sugar House Gang because their base of operation was a sugar warehouse located on Oakland Street.[22]

The original members of the Oakland Sugar House Gang were Harry Fleisher, a hefty youngster who started out as a driver for the gang and later became a vicious thug and killer; Henry Shorr, a former potato sacker at a produce market who was the gang's financial genius and business head; Irving Milberg, only 17 years old in 1920, but already known to be good with his fists, a club or a gun; Harry Altman, whose arrest sheet included armed robbery, extortion and murder before he was 21; Harry Keywell, a handsome, wavy-haired slugger and strong-arm man; and Morris and Phil Raider, two brothers who excelled at larceny and extortion.[23]

The Sugar House Gang sold corn to moonshiners, provided protection for local gambling establishments and manufactured alcohol for bootleg liquor.

The second group of east side Jewish criminals was originally formed by Sammy Cohen, a stout gunman and enforcer who was also known as "Sammy Purple." In the early 1920s the leadership of the gang was assumed by the three Bernstein brothers — Abe, Isidore and Ray — who immigrated to Detroit from New York. At one time or another, each of the brothers had been arrested for robbery, extortion and murder.[24]

During Prohibition this group, like the Sugar House Gang, turned from shoplifting and extortion to distilling and brewing. To earn extra cash, the gang shook down blind pigs and gambling houses.

Eventually, instead of competing, the two groups joined forces under the leadership of the Bernsteins and branched out into the business of importing liquor across the Detroit River from Canada.

Detroit's Canadian border and the existence of Jewish-owned Canadian distilleries, such as those owned by Sam and Harry Bronfman, offered opportunities to Detroit's Jewish gangsters that rivaled bootlegging operations in Chicago and New York.

Instead of transporting the liquor themselves, the Purples arranged for the Jewish-dominated "Little Jewish Navy" gang to bring it across for them. The Purple Gang then managed the operation on the Michigan side of the border.[25]

The Purple Gang's dealings also extended to the sale of stolen diamonds, narcotics and prostitution in Canada.[26]

The origin of the gang's name is in dispute. One story has it that the name stemmed from the remark of a Hastings Street shopkeeper who had been victimized more than once by the gang. "They're tainted, those boys," he told a policeman. "Their characters are off-color. They're purple. They'll come to a bad end."[27]

Another account says the nucleus of the gang, while cutting classes at the old Bishop School on Winder Street, spent hours at a cottage near Lake St. Clair. There the boys traipsed about in purple swimming trunks, calling themselves the "Purple Gang." When an older and rougher group took command, they adopted the name the younger boys had chosen. And some say the gang simply took the name of Sammy Purple.[28]

David Levitt, a neighborhood associate and friend of the boys, has yet another version. "I was at the warehouse on Oakland Avenue where the boys hung out. It was a sugar warehouse. The boys called themselves the Sugar House Boys.

"We were sitting around and the boys discussed changing their name. One of the members, whose name was Silverstein, had a purple sweater on. Someone suggested Purple Gang. It stuck."[29]

The name meant little in the early years. But as the gang's deeds became more brazen, and their activities in shaking down blind pigs and gambling houses more widespread, the name came to mean terror, violence, slugging and clubbing. Sometimes it meant murder.

Police sources claim that the gang first achieved prominence in 1926 when local gamblers employed them to defend their establishments against pilfering by a gang of invaders from St. Louis known as "Egan's Rats."[30]

The Rats were a powerful St. Louis mob that had been founded at the turn of the century by Jellyroll Egan. He specialized in hiring out his army of thugs to anti-union businessmen as strikebreakers. Prohibition gave the gang a boost and they expanded their activities. Under the leadership of a hood named Dinty Colbeck, the Rats went into safecracking and jewelry heists, and supplied men to other criminal gangs that needed out-of-town talent.[31]

The Purples had imported several Rats to help them in their war against Detroit's Italian mobs. A number of Rats then double-crossed the Purples and began operating on their own.

These men were blamed for the March 1926 kidnapping of Meyer "Fish" Bloomfield, a croupier at the Grand River Athletic Club, Charles T. "Doc" Brady's gambling place. A $50,000 ransom was paid for Bloomfield's release.[32]

The "snatching" of Bloomfield was the first in a series of kidnappings of rich gamblers for ransom. A debate raged as to whether the Purples played a defensive or an offensive role in the crimes.

A few defectors from the St. Louis gang then merged with the

Detroiters. This combination was further strengthened by the addition of a dozen or so certified tough guys from New York.

Two of the most ruthless of the New York hoods were Abe Axler and Eddie Fletcher. Both men grew up in New York and came to Detroit in 1923, while in their early twenties. In Detroit, they became inseparable pals and partners, and hitmen for the gang.

One observer described them as "sawed-off Napoleons," with "dark, furtive, beady eyes and abnormal ears, Axler's protruding and overgrown by nature, and Fletcher's flattened and hammered close to his head by the punches of too many pugilists during his early ring career."[33]

Axler was never a pug. His nose had not been knocked askew as Fletcher's was, and his large ears had never been "cauliflowerized." But his face was the more sinister of the two. He had an aquiline nose, high cheek bones, deep shadows under his small eyes, sunken cheeks and a thin, tight mouth. By repute, he was a more vicious killer and rougher fighter than Fletcher.

Axler was dour, moody and quick on the trigger of a machine gun. Fletcher was a second-rate pug who became a fifth-rate fight manager and, ultimately, a first-rate gunman. Both men were "larceny-minded schemers and killers, with an abundance of what police and newspapermen call 'crazy nerve'," wrote one journalist.[34]

By 1927 the Purple Gang had grown to between forty and fifty members and felt strong enough to move against their competitors and those who had betrayed them.

In March 1927, Fletcher and Axler rented a suite in the Milaflores Apartments at 106 East Alexandrine Avenue and invited three St. Louis gangsters — Frank Wright, Reuben Cohen and Joseph Bloom — to a parley. When the trio entered the flat, Fletcher and Axler opened up with machine guns. The three callers were dead before they hit the floor.[35]

Underworld gossip had it that the Purples had imported the three men from St. Louis as "rod men" (hired killers) to help protect the gang's lucrative alcohol trade while it was waging a war with rival bootlegging gangs. The trio became greedy and double-crossed the Purples with the Bloomfield kidnapping. They had to be taught a lesson.

Crime historians refer to this incident as Detroit's first machine gun execution and the event which introduced machine guns into Detroit gangster warfare.[36]

Axler and Fletcher, along with a colleague and former Egan Rat, Fred "Killer" Burke, were arrested as suspects in the killing. Police grilled them for hours without results, and, in the end, were forced to let them go.

Despite their release, Axler and Fletcher's activities earned them the odious distinction of being named Detroit's Public Enemies No. 1 and 2, respectively.[37]

By 1928, the Purple Gang was at its peak. It dominated the Motor City's rackets and acquired a reputation for ruthlessness and violence that matched Chicago's Capone outfit. The consensus was that the Purples were the toughest Jewish mob in the nation.

Jazz musician Milton "Mezz" Mezzrow, who played in Detroit and Chicago, knew many of the Purples. He claimed that they were "a hard lot of guys, so tough they made Capone's playmates look like a kindergarten class."[38]

Mezzrow had first-hand experience of just how violent the Purples could be. On the evening of August 13, 1927, Mezz was working in a black cabaret at 1708 St. Antoine Street when Abe Axler and Irving Milberg came in with two women. The Purples and their dates sat at a table and ordered drinks. At another table across from them sat two local black hoodlums, Godfrey Quales and Hobart Harris. The men exchanged words and an argument ensued. In a flash, Axler and Milberg pulled out guns and began shooting. Quales and Harris were killed.

Axler and Milberg were arrested. They admitted to the killings but maintained it was in self-defense. Witnesses supported their claim and they were released.[39]

The major source of the gang's income was bootlegging. The Purples controlled the liquor traffic from Canada, as well as a number of blind pigs and gambling houses. They operated them outright or forced them to pay "protection" money to stay in business.

The gang also organized a phoney Detroit business, the Art Novelty Company, to facilitate the interstate shipment of their Canadian Whiskey. Liquor conveyed to Detroit from Canada was brought to the company's building where it was packaged under false labels and then shipped by train or truck to other cities.[40]

For several years, the Purples ran the lucrative business of supplying Canadian whiskey to the Capone organization in Chicago. The hijacking of a shipment of Purple Gang whiskey (Old Log Cabin) by the Bugs Moran Gang of Chicago led to the St. Valentine's Day Massacre of seven Moran gangsters in 1929.[41]

The massacre was part of a prolonged war between the Capone mob and Chicago's North Side gang headed by George "Bugs" Moran. Although he got his nickname because of his often outlandish behavior, Moran was known, especially to Capone, as a brutal and efficient killer.

A regular churchgoer, Bugs considered Capone to be a lowlife because he dealt in prostitution. "We don't deal in flesh," Moran

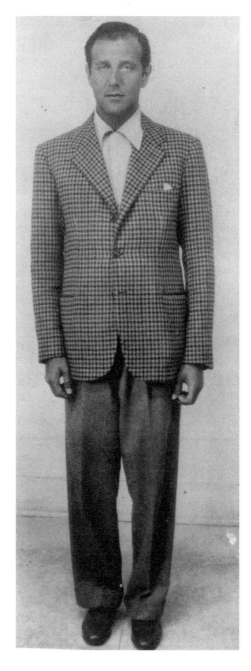

Bugsy Siegel

said. "Anyone who does is lower than a snake's belly. Can't Capone get that through his thick skull?"[42]

In public Moran referred to Capone as "the Beast," and "the Behemoth." Just to aggravate Capone, Bugs would make peace with him and then break the agreement within a matter of hours.[43]

Because Capone refused to sell him Old Log Cabin at what he felt was a fair price, Moran made the foolish decision to supply his customers with the whiskey by hijacking Purple Gang shipments to Capone. Soon nothing coming from Detroit was safe.

Capone was enraged. He decided to set Moran up for a hit and eliminate his gang once and for all. Through freelance hijackers never identified, but rumored to be Purples, Capone's people arranged for a load of Old Log Cabin to be sold to Moran, with a promise of more to come.

Moran's men went to the gang's headquarters, a garage at 2122 North Clarke Street, to await delivery. Suddenly, several unknown men, dressed in police uniforms, rushed into the garage at the appointed time. They lined the Moran henchmen up against the wall. Thinking this was just a routine police bust, the gangsters offered no resistance. All at once, two of the "policemen" cut loose with Thompson submachine guns, mowing the seven victims down.[44]

Purple gangsters Harry and Phil Keywell and Eddie Fletcher were identified from photographs as men who, a week earlier, had arrived with baggage and rented front rooms in the boardinghouses overlooking the garage. This was never proven and the culprits in the killings were never identified.[45]

In order to earn additional money, the Purples branched out into other fields during the late 1920s. They hijacked prizefight films and forced movie theaters to show them for higher fees. Detroit theater owners, distrustful of the local authorities and fearing for their lives, sent a confidential letter to J. Edgar Hoover of the FBI pleading for help. "We think that this is an outrage and you should investigate this matter right now and not let these gangsters make thousands every year at this racket and pay no income tax and get away with it," they wrote. "Can't we have some protection please?"

The owners requested anonymity "because we don't want no stink bombs put in our theaters or else the back blown up, or worse."[46]

The Purples also dealt in gambling and narcotics and defrauded insurance companies by staging fake accidents. They kidnapped people and accepted contracts for killing the enemies of various hoodlums who did not want to do the job themselves. Abe Axler was singularly proficient at this.[47]

In the summer of 1927, Axler undertook a contract to eliminate a visiting St. Louis gunman named Milford Jones. On the evening of June 15, 1927, Axler followed Jones into the Stork Club at 47 Rowena Street. Jones made the mistake of sitting at the bar with his back to the door. Axler walked up quietly behind him and without saying a word pulled out a revolver and shot Jones in the head. He then walked out the door.

Acting on a tip, the police arrested Axler on June 25. He was questioned and released. No one who was in the club could recall what the killer looked like and the Jones killing remained unsolved.[48]

The Purples' wide-ranging activities caused them to become overextended, forcing them to bring in "specialists" from the outside. One of these was Morris "Red" Rudensky, a premier safecracker who later wrote an autobiography entitled *The Gonif* (thief). Rudensky operated strictly on a contract basis and his "fees" ranged from $5,000 to $15,000, depending on the value of the goods to be stolen. Red pulled a series of jobs for the Purples and enjoyed working for them so much that he remembered them in his book.[49]

Detroit police credit the Purple Gang with over 500 killings, more than the Capone mob. This caused Herbert Ausbury, a historian of American crime, to call the gang "the most efficiently organized gang of killers in the United States."[50]

During 1927, members of the gang extorted thousands of dollars in protection money from Detroit cleaners and dyers. The laundry business attracted many Detroit Jews because it seemed a logical adjunct to tailoring and because of the ease with which a family could maintain the business. By the 1920s Jews owned most of Detroit's dry-cleaning establishments. They became the prime targets of the Jewish gang.[51]

Most of the laundries paid their monthly or weekly "dues" without protest. "It was not worth getting beaten up or losing your life or your business," one owner recalled. "So we paid the collector when he came."[52]

Recalcitrant owners were subjected to fires, dynamitings, stench bombings, thefts, beatings and kidnappings. This so-called "Cleaners and Dyers War" lasted for two years, and at least two cleaners, Sam Sigman and Sam Polakoff, were murdered in cold blood.[53]

The police finally stopped the war and arrested twelve Purples, among them the Bernstein brothers, Abe Axler and Eddie Fletcher, Harry Keywell and Irving Milberg. They were charged with conspiring to extort money from wholesale cleaners and dyers. The trial lasted for weeks, but ended with all of them being acquitted.[54]

The gang extorted money from other legitimate businesses as

well. One terrified businessman wrote to J. Edgar Hoover describing his fear and predicament.

"Several years ago this mob came to my office and announced that they would take charge and if I didn't like it my body would be found floating in the Detroit River." As a result, "I was compelled to let these parasites run my business and take the biggest cut of the profits or face death."

He explained that he "dare not give you my name," and asked Hoover to "do everything in your power to rid Detroit of this menace and put these rats where they really belong."[55]

After the Cleaners and Dyers War, the Purple's interest in extortion declined. They continued to operate, however, as bootleggers, rumrunners, hijackers, smugglers, betting parlor operators and dope peddlers.

The Purple's reign ended because the police moved against them when gang members got careless and left behind too much evidence of their crimes, and because the rival Sicilian mob, tired of competing with the Purples, decided to eliminate them. One by one, the Purples were murdered until most of them were either dead or afraid to remain in Detroit. The Sicilians moved so secretly that neither the Purples nor the public knew what was happening.[56]

In July 1929, Prohibition agents brought liquor violation charges against four members of the gang and made the charges stick. Eddie Fletcher, Abe Axler, Harry Sutton and Irving Milberg were sentenced to twenty-two months in Leavenworth penitentiary and fined $5,000 each.[57]

Two months later, Phil Keywell shot and killed a young boy he thought was spying on the gang. David Levitt was there at the time and remembers what happened.

"My brother Nate Levitt owned a warehouse and liquor cutting headquarters in the rear of Jaslove's butcher shop on Henry and Hastings. One of our employees, a man by the name of Eddie Keller, went up to the office to tell them he saw a black boy looking under the stable door. The boy lost his ball; it rolled under the door.

"Phil Keywell and my brother Nate found the boy in front of a candy store between Henry and Medbury on Hastings Street. The kid was confused and couldn't answer their questions. Phil shot the boy.

"However, the police did not want Nate, as he would have been charged because he was with Phil. The police wanted to get Morris Raider, who was the sidekick of Philly Keywell.

"Morris Raider had an alibi which he did not use. And both men were sentenced to life at Jackson.

"The boy should not have died. The police let him bleed to death instead of calling for an ambulance. They were taking reports."[58]

In November 1929, Morris Raider was sentenced to twelve-to-fifteen years in Jackson State Prison for the shooting. In October 1930, Philip Keywell was sentenced to Jackson Prison for life for this same killing. He served 32 years and was paroled in 1962.[59]

In 1931, Ray Bernstein, Irving Milberg and Harry Keywell were sentenced to life imprisonment in the Collingwood case.

And in 1936, Harry Fleisher was tried in federal court for violation of the internal revenue law. He was charged with part ownership of a $100,000 six thousand gallon still. Fleisher and his brother Sam were sentenced to serve eight years in the Federal Penitentiary at Leavenworth.[60]

Harry was released in 1944. In December 1945, he was convicted for the armed robbery of an Oakland County gambling spot and received a sentence of 25 to 50 years. He was released again from prison in 1965 at the age of 62. He never went back to prison again.[61]

Louis Fleisher, Harry's other brother, was arrested in 1938. A longtime member of the Purples, Louis's record of arrests included bootlegging, assault, carrying concealed weapons, arson, robbery and murder. Louis specialized in "muscle tactics" and intimidation in Detroit's meat-cutting and packing industries, and during the Cleaners and Dyers War.[62]

Some Detroiters remember Louis as an open-handed, big-hearted, boisterous, fun-loving, friendly guy. Others remember him as a nut.

Detroiters recall how Louis enjoyed aiming his moving car at people he knew walking across Twelfth Street, where the Purples' favorite restaurants were located. He thought it was great fun to chase them to the curb and then down the sidewalk.

One acquaintance claimed he would "always get out of a joint when Lou walked in. You never knew what would happen."

Another friend felt differently. "I was always glad to see Lou walk in a place," he said. "Things livened up every place he went."[63]

After searching for him for over a year in connection with robbery and arson, Federal agents located Louis in his car outside an apartment at Highland and Second Avenue. Louis's wife Nellie fled, throwing away a pistol as she ran. Agents seized her before she got too far.

Inside Fleisher's apartment, agents found an arsenal consisting of submachine guns, revolvers with silencers, brass knuckles, a dozen teargas shells and a thousand rounds of ammunition. Fleisher was sentenced to 30 years at Alcatraz. His wife got ten years.

Louis was paroled in 1957, after serving nineteen years, but was jailed again in 1958 for violating parole after Detroit police arrested him for attempted arson. Louis had been caught on the roof of the Dorsey Cleaners, at 1348 East Seven Mile Road. A hole had been bored in the roof and a can of gasoline was next to him.

Fleisher pleaded guilty to arson and was sentenced to five years in prison. By playing with matches on the cleaning plant roof, Louis had violated his federal parole. He served the rest of his federal term, eleven years, in Leavenworth and the Milan, Michigan prison, with his Detroit sentence running concurrently. He died of a heart attack in the Michigan State Prison at Jackson in 1964.[64]

Remaining leaders of the gang were systematically and mysteriously executed. In July 1929, Irving Shapiro, who had been a gorilla for the gang, was taken for a ride and slain, his head shattered by four bullets fired at close range from behind.

In October 1929, Ziggy Selbin, a Purple Gang enforcer, was cornered in a doorway on Twelfth Street and shot to death. Few persons mourned his death because Selbin was wild, unpredictable and totally unprincipled. Born in Detroit in 1910, his father was a deli owner who also dabbled in petty crime. By the time Ziggy was a teenager he had committed several murders and was doing considerable freelance work. Once Selbin got into an argument with a drinking companion who refused to surrender a ring Selbin admired. Ziggy solved the stalemate by cutting off the man's finger.[65]

Despite his good work for the gang, the hard-to-control Selbin had become an embarrassment. The Purples felt they had no choice but to eliminate him.[66]

In November 1933, the bodies of Abe Axler and Eddie Fletcher were found, side-by-side and holding hands, in the back seat of

Axler's car on an isolated road in Oakland County. Each man had been shot in the face a dozen times.[67]

Henry Shorr, for many years the gang's brains, disappeared in December 1935 after meeting Harry Fleisher in a Twelfth Street delicatessen. Fleisher's automobile was later found with bloodstains on the cushions and Shorr was never seen again. The police concluded that Shorr had been taken for a ride. His body was never found and Fleisher had an airtight alibi.[68]

In November 1937, Harry Millman, the gang's last surviving torpedo, was gunned down in the cocktail bar of Boesky's delicatessen on Hazelwood and Twelfth Street where he had gone for dinner.[69]

More hooligan than hoodlum, Millman had swaggered through the Detroit underworld with a chip on his shoulder, rye whiskey on his breath, and an eagerness to be a tough guy. Although considered the clown of the gang, Millman was serious enough to try and carry on the Purples' extortion rackets. But his post-Prohibition career consisted mostly of shaking down whorehouses.

An earlier attempt had been made on Millman's life that summer when someone placed a bomb under the hood of his car, set to go off as soon as he stepped on the starter. Only Millman had sent Willie Holmes, the doorman at a local nighclub, to pick up his car for him. The hapless Willie started the engine and was blown to pieces.[70]

From then on, Millman was living on borrowed time. Detective-Sergeant Harold Branton predicted his death. "His number is up and it's only a question of time. He has kept himself on the streets with his gun and his fists. He is going to die one of these days and die violently."[71]

Those out to get Millman tried again, but this time they brought in outside help. It was long rumored that Harry Strauss and Happy Maione, two of Murder Inc.'s best gunmen, had been hired to do the hit. According to witnesses, two armed men strode into the crowded restaurant as Millman ate. They pumped nine slugs into Millman and wounded four innocent diners in the process. The killers then calmly sauntered out and disappeared down a dark street. No one ever saw them again.[72]

Millman had liked to think of himself as Detroit's No. 1 Tough Guy and gang leader. This status lasted only a few months, when the unknown assassins cut him down to size. His death signalled the end of the Purple Gang as a force in organized crime in Detroit.

No one has ever been convicted for killing the Purples. But law enforcement officials agree on who benefited the most from their elimination: the Mafia family headed by Joseph Zerilli.

During the 1920s, the local Italian combination was run by Samuel Catalonotte, who acted as an arbiter, resolving differences between Detroit's various Sicilian factions. Catalonotte kept the peace between them until his death in 1930. When he died, the Italian coalition disintegrated into several competing and hostile groups. Chester LaMarre, who liked to think of himself as the "Al Capone of Detroit," headed one large contingent, Joseph Zerilli another.[73]

In late 1930, LaMarre made a bid to become Detroit's crime czar, but failed. He was murdered in the kitchen of his own home by two "close friends" in February 1931.

Joseph Zerilli replaced him and instituted a new peace pact between the warring Sicilians.[74]

Zerilli had come to the United States from Sicily at the age of seventeen. Starting out as a common laborer, he eventually built a criminal operation that made a profit of $150 million a year from loansharking, extortion, narcotics, bookmaking and labor racketeering.

Posing as a respectable baker-businessman, Zerilli lived in a $500,000 home located on a twenty-acre estate in the exclusive suburb of Grosse Point Park. During his lifetime he was convicted only twice: for speeding and for carrying concealed weapons.[75]

Throughout the 1920s the Purples coexisted, albeit uneasily, with the Italians. The Purples even imported two Italian brothers from St. Louis, Yonnie and Peter Licavoli, to gun for them, and joined Zerilli in a number of criminal ventures. The Licavolis later left the Purples and became their rivals in bootlegging and other rackets.[76]

As long as the Purples remained powerful, Detroit Mafia families made do with the territories ceded to them by the Jewish mob. After the murder convictions of the Keywells, Bernstein, Milberg and Raider in 1930 and 1931, the Italians moved against them.

Detroit turned into a battle zone. Elsie Prosky was a schoolgirl in Detroit at the time. "I lived in the middle of the city just off Woodward Avenue, where much of the fighting went on," she says. "I recall many times dodging into a store on my way home from school to avoid gunshots."[77]

As long as the gangsters killed only each other, the authorities displayed a singular lack of interest in the goings-on. The police commissioner explained that "so long as they confine their shootings to their own kind there will be no police drive or any increase in the squad assigned to such cases."[78]

After an especially wild eleven-day shooting spree in July of 1930, during which twelve hoodlums were gunned down on city streets, Mayor Charles Bowles remarked that "it is just as well to let these gangsters kill each other off, if they are so minded. You know the scientists employ one set of parasites to destroy another. May not that be the plan of Providence in these killings among the bandits?"[79]

Bowles's nonchalant attitude toward the violence outraged Detroit's respectable citizens. On July 22, 1930, they deposed the mayor in a recall election.[80]

By the end of Prohibition in 1933, the Purples had been elbowed aside by the Sicilians, spearheaded by Joseph Zerilli. The war ended and the city quieted down. Zerilli remained the crime boss of Detroit until his death in 1977.[81]

Despite their apparent power and reputation for ruthlessness, the Purples were, in truth, a local gang that never made it big; a neighborhood mob that, for all its swagger and braggadocio, remained small-time.

When asked how he rated the Purples, Meyer Lansky, a major figure in American organized crime, replied, "They were nothing."[82]

Because the Purples were flamboyant and well-known in the city's night spots, and because many of them liked to dress well, be seen in public and live in elegant homes, a romantic aura surrounded the gang which distinguished it from other Detroit mobs.

Hollywood believed in this image and hoped to capitalize on it. In 1960, Allied Artists produced "The Purple Gang," starring Barry Sullivan as the heroic, honest detective, and Robert Blake as the Purple's brutal, neurotic leader.[83]

The film was a "B" movie that flopped at the box office.

In the final analysis, Meyer Lansky may have been right.

Chapter Four

In the Beginning

*J*ewish involvement in American crime did not start during Prohibition. By the end of the nineteenth century, Jews were appearing more and more frequently on police blotters.

From their earliest residence in the United States, dating back to the mid-seventeenth century, Jews had enjoyed a reputation for being among the country's most law-abiding and least violent citizens. Journalists visiting jails in search of a story frequently noted how they rarely saw "the face of an Israelite" among the prisoners.[1]

This spotless reputation began to tarnish in the nineteenth century.

Due to an influx of Jews from Germany, the nation's Jewish population rose from 50,000 in 1860 to 250,000 by 1880. An increase in Jewish crime accompanied this growth.

In 1886, Thomas Byrnes, a former New York City police inspector and chief of detectives, published a compendium of "America's leading professional criminals," most of whom actually lived in New York City. Over four percent of the men on his list were Jews. At the time, Jews made up less than one percent of the American population, but 10 percent of New York's population.

Scanning Byrnes' lists, we find that Jews were primarily thieves and confidence men and rarely engaged in crimes of physical violence. For example, Abe "the General" Greenthal, was one of America's premier pickpockets. Although born in Poland in 1826, Abe called himself a German. This was a common tactic among nineteenth century Polish-Jewish immigrants, many of whom spoke German and wished to identify with the more westernized German Jews.

Lawmen knew the General as the leader of the "Sheeny Mob" ("sheeny" being a derogatory term for an untrustworthy Jew) of Jewish pickpockets. Abe's home and base of operation was in New York City, but his gang traveled all over the United States picking pockets. The mob's technique was to enter a crowded place and while "jostling" through the throng, relieve someone of their purse or wallet.

In March 1877, Abe, together with his brother Harris and his son-in-law Samuel Casper, was arrested in Syracuse, New York, and charged with robbing a farmer of $1,190. The farmer had sold his farm in Massachusetts and was moving west with the proceeds. He made the mistake of flashing his newfound wealth in Albany.

Working the train station, the Sheeny Gang saw him and followed him to Rochester. They befriended the man at the Central Railroad Depot in Rochester and told him he would have to change cars. One of the trio kindly helped the farmer with his valise and the entire party entered another car. While pushing through the crowd of passengers, Abe divested the farmer of his pocketbook containing the money. The gang escaped, but were arrested a few hours later in Syracuse.

They were all indicted, tried and convicted. The court sentenced Abe to twenty years at hard labor in the Auburn New York State Prison. Harris Greenthal received a sentence of eighteen years and

Casper fifteen years. Governor Grover Cleveland pardoned all of the men in 1884.

One year later, Abe was arrested in the company of one Bendick Gaetz, alias "the Cockroach," for robbing a resident of Williamsburg, New York. Abe pleaded guilty to grand larceny in the second degree and received a five-year sentence. He was released in 1889 and died in his own bed in 1895.[2]

A rarity among the nineteenth century thieving set was Frank Lowenthal, alias "Sheeny Irving," alias August Erwin. He was a college graduate. Small and slightly built, Lowenthal was born in Cincinnati in 1844 to wealthy German-Jewish parents. At age sixteen, Frank's parents sent him to Germany to be educated. After two years at the high school in Magdeburg, he entered the University of Heidelberg as a student in the natural sciences. He graduated with a B.A. degree in 1866, returned to the United States and got married. Frank and his wife moved to St. Louis, where he wrote for a newspaper. In 1870, the family moved to New York. Frank failed to make much money legitimately and embarked on a career as a shoplifter and receiver of stolen goods.

When his wife's father learned of his son-in-law's criminal occupation, he pleaded with his daughter to leave Frank. She agreed and made plans to travel with her father to Europe. Frank discovered her intentions.

In July 1885, a distraught and drunk Frank confronted his wife in the Allman House Hotel on East Tenth Street in New York City. He begged her not to leave but she refused to change her mind. Frank pulled out a pistol, shot his wife and tried to kill himself. He botched the job and both of them recovered.

Frank Lowenthal pleaded guilty to assault in September 1885

and was sentenced to five years in prison and fined $1,000. He left jail in 1890 and was not heard of again.[3]

At the time he shot his wife, Lowenthal was awaiting trial for filching opera glasses from a jewelry store in Maiden Lane, New York. His accomplice in this robbery was twenty year-old Julius Klein, alias "Sheeny Julius," alias "Young Julius," a German-born Jew who worked as a sneak thief, shoplifter and pickpocket.

Julius was markedly unsuccessful as a thief and kept getting caught. For example, he was arrested four times in 1882. He was arrested in June in New York City for filching a gold watch from a passenger on a ferry boat and was released on $1,000 bail. In September, he was arrested for robbing a jewelry store in Brooklyn, but was not held. Then he was arrested in October for snatching $100 from a young woman as she was window-shopping on Sixth Avenue in New York. The lady must have been taken by Klein's boyish looks, because she refused to press charges.

Klein left New York, hoping a change of locale would improve his luck. He was mistaken. Still in October, Julius and two accomplices were arrested for stealing $3,500 worth of goods from the W. A. Thomas tailor's trimming store in Boston. Julius received two years in the Boston House of Correction.

In 1885, just six months after he was released from prison, Klein was arrested again in New York for shoplifting $60 worth of velvet and braid from a woman's clothing store. He received one year in the penitentiary on Blackwell's Island, New York. After his release, he disappeared from view.[4]

A somewhat more successful thief was Michael Kurtz, alias Michael Sheehan, alias "Sheeny Mike," one of America's most celebrated burglars. Born in New York in 1850, Mike joined a gang of burglars when he was fourteen years old. He became a highly valuable asset because of his ability to quickly analyze the construction of a building the gang wanted to rob, and to locate its weak spots. Kurtz also became adept at cutting through floors and partitions, and at blowing up safes.

Sheeny Mike was arrested numerous times, but usually got off. The one time he was convicted, he originated a scheme to gain his release that became a classic among criminals.

In March 1877, Mike was arrested and convicted of robbing a silk emporium in Boston and received a twelve-year sentence. While in jail he contrived to secure a pardon as a man on the verge of death.

First, he made himself sick and thin by drinking soapy water. He then made an incision in his side and with the aid of a chemical preparation caused pus to flow out. The physicians who examined him concluded that he would not live a month. On the basis of their report, the governor of Massachusetts pardoned Kurtz in 1880.

After his release, Kurtz recovered his health so quickly that he was arrested just three months later on a charge of robbing a dry goods store in Washington, D.C. He was released for lack of evidence.

One February evening in 1882, thieves entered a diamond and jewelry store in Troy, New York, by boring a hole through its twelve-inch thick basement wall from an adjoining building. Using heavy sledge hammers, they broke open the safe and took $50,000 in watches, jewelry, diamonds and cash. Immediately after the heist, Sheeny Mike and his accomplice and pal, Billy Porter, another gifted burglar, sailed for Europe on a White Star liner. The ship's crew and passengers knew Mike as Henry Appleton, a retired California mine owner; Billy masqueraded as Leslie Langdon, the proprietor of a large cattle ranch.

The two fashionable gentlemen traveled to Paris and London together, stopping at the best hotels and leaving lavish tips wherever they went.

During their stay abroad, a number of daring robberies were committed in the heart of London by persons who obviously knew their craft. Safes were blown open so noiselessly that people in adjoining buildings were not alarmed. In every instance, the burglars escaped with their booty.

Oddly enough, suspicion fell, at length, upon the two wealthy American tourists, Messrs. Appleton and Langdon. The men deemed it wise to cut short their stay abroad and return home. A few days after landing in New York Billy Porter was arrested for the Troy robbery. Upon learning this, Sheeny Mike hurriedly moved to Jacksonville, Florida with his wife and brother. Once there, they opened a large wholesale tobacco warehouse under the name of "Kurtz Brothers."

Not too long afterwards, Mike was arrested for the Troy robbery while surveying a plot of land he had purchased to build his house. After a long legal battle, Florida extradited him to New York.

In 1886, Mike was tried, convicted and sentenced to eighteen years and six months' imprisonment in the state prison at Dannemora, New York. His case, however, went to the court of appeals on a technicality and Mike was discharged after a few months in jail.[5]

A contemporary account claimed that while under arrest, Mike made "reckless confessions" which implicated some of his associates in crimes. Because of this, he was "blacklisted by his old associates, in all parts of the country, as a professional 'squealer'."[6]

Samuel Brotzki was listed as a "star" confidence man of "the first magnitude" by the denizens of the Boston police department.

Jack Zelig

According to the police, the 50-year-old Brotzki was an "expert in every confidence game from years of practice in every state of the union." Brotzki's wanted poster describes him as a Russian Jew who also went under the names Schwartzman, Tzigainer ["gypsy"], Schetman, Leitchman and Greenberg. Among his habits, Brotzki was a "constant smoker of cigarettes that he makes himself," he could always "be found amongst Jews," and he was "very fond of women."[7]

Just as the earlier German Jewish immigrants were the vanguard of a much larger wave, these criminals were the forerunners of more menacing Jewish gangsters and Jewish gangs in the decades to come.

Beginning in 1881 and continuing until the outbreak of World War I in 1914, almost two million East European Jews entered the United States; over 75 percent of them came from Russia. They increased the country's Jewish population from 250,000 in 1880 to 3.3 million by 1917. Jews comprised 9 percent of the nearly twenty million immigrants who came to America during this period.[8]

The causes of this Jewish immigration lay in overpopulation, pogroms and devastating economic restrictions in Russia, government-sponsored discrimination in Rumania and grinding poverty in Austria-Hungary. Jews were also lured to America by tales of wondrous opportunity in the "Golden Land," and by the advent of cheap trans-Atlantic ship fares.

The East Europeans, commonly called "Russian Jews," crowded into the great cities of the East Coast and the Midwest. Like other urban immigrants of that era, Russian Jews congregated in ethnic enclaves, often called "Jewtown," "Little Jerusalem," or the "Jewish Ghetto" by the local press. Boston's North End, Chicago's West

Side, Philadelphia's South Side and New York's Lower East Side were among the better-known of these.

The Jewish gangster sprang from these densely populated districts.

The most notorious breeding ground for Jewish gangs and gangsters before World War I was the Lower East Side of New York. By 1910, 540,000 Jews lived within its 1.5 square miles, a population density greater than that of Bombay, India. In 1913, a report on crime conditions on the lower East Side listed 914 hangouts, mostly saloons where various forms of gambling took place, 423 houses of prostitution, over three hundred gang hideaways and 374 pool parlors, which were fronts for horse betting. Dance halls, a rendezvous for pimps and procurers, and gambling establishments could be found on almost every block.[9]

Immigrant poverty, the trauma of transition from the Old World to the New, and loss of family and religious structure generated these conditions, and the district spawned men like Joseph "Yoski Nigger" Toblinsky, Dopey Benny Fein and hundreds of gangsters like them.

Yoski (or "Yoshke") Nigger led a gang that specialized in stealing and poisoning horses. The gang modeled themselves after the Italian Black Hand, an organization which terrorized newly arrived Italian immigrants by threatening to harm their families unless they paid for "protection." Calling themselves the "Yiddish Black Hand," Yoski's outfit wrote letters to stablemen or businessmen whose companies used horses. They demanded a certain sum of money to insure the horses from unforeseen "accidents." Should the victim refuse to comply, his horse would disappear or be poisoned. If he complained to the authorities, he risked bodily harm.

Yoski concentrated on the produce market, truckmen and livery stables, leaving the ice cream trade, seltzer and soda water dealers to others. He planned the gang's strategy and routinely boasted of personally poisoning over two hundred horses. This feat earned him the title "King of the Horse Poisoners."[10]

Benjamin Fein was born of poor immigrant parents on the Lower East Side in 1889. He started off in crime at an early age, stealing packages from express wagons and delivery carts, rolling drunks and picking pockets. He acquired the nickname "Dopey," because adenoidal and nasal troubles from infancy gave him a sullen, sleepy appearance. By the time he was sixteen, Fein commanded one of the toughest gangs of *shtarkes*, or strongarm men, on the Lower East Side.

Benny was the first Jewish gangster to make labor racketeering a full-time and profitable business. He institutionalized the practice of supplying gangs of hoodlums to unions in their wars against employers. Jewish labor unions in New York, including the butchers, bakers, garment workers, neckwear makers, ragpickers, sign painters and others, turned to Benny at one time or another to help them during strikes. Using bats, clubs and blackjacks, but not guns, Dopey's gang protected striking workers from being attacked by management's hired thugs. At other times, Dopey's gang wrecked non-union shops and beat up some of the employees.

Dopey also employed a gang of female thugs, who attacked non-union female workers with sharp hairpins and umbrellas weighted with lead slugs, to persuade them to join the union. For these services, Benny charged between $25 and $50 a week and an additional $10 a day for each of his men. He also had a schedule of prices for different tasks. Shooting a scab in the leg cost the union $60. Breaking an arm cost $200. Demolishing a non-union shop ran from $150 to $500, depending on its size. Murder cost $500 per victim.

Bosses also hired gangsters, but never Dopey Benny. He remained loyal to the unions and refused to work for management. "My heart," he once explained, "lay with the workers." In 1912, one manufacturer offered Dopey $15,000 to take his side, but Dopey refused. "He put fifteen $1,000 bills in front of me," said Dopey. "And I said to him, 'No, sir, I won't take it,' I said... I won't double-cross my friends." Dopey Benny had his principles.[11]

As tough as Yoski and Dopey were, the most dominant Jewish gangsters of the pre-1914 era were Monk Eastman and Big Jack Zelig.

Herbert Ausbury, the contemporary chronicler of New York's early criminal gangs, called Monk the prince of gangsters and "as brave a thug as ever shot an enemy in the back or blackjacked a voter at the polls."[12]

Monk's real name was Edward Osterman. He was born in Williamsburg, New York in 1873, the son of a respectable restaurant owner. Monk began life with a bullet-shaped head and a short, bull neck. During his turbulent career, he acquired a broken nose, a pair of cauliflower ears and heavily veined, sagging jowls. His face was pocked with battle scars and he seemed always to need a haircut. He accentuated his ferocious and unusual appearance by wearing a derby hat several sizes too small, which perched precariously atop his shock of bristly hair.

Monk would have made an excellent movie caricature of a gangster, but he was the real thing. His appearance belied the fact that he stood only five feet and five inches tall and never weighed more than 150 pounds.

Eastman was one of New York's first Jewish major underworld

figures. He bossed a Jewish street gang and could field as many as 1,200 gangsters on short notice.

He and his mob derived most of their income from delivering votes to the local Democratic Party political machine, Tammany Hall, and from a variety of protection rackets. And Monk was one of the first underworld figures to furnish strongarm men to warring unions and employers.

Monk also had an interest in houses of prostitution and stuss (card) games, and shared in the earnings of prostitutes who walked the streets under his protection. He directed the operation of pickpockets, loft burglars and footpads (holdup men who traveled on foot), and provided thugs for men who wanted to rid themselves of enemies. Eastman set his fees according to the degree of "disability" desired, from broken limbs to total elimination.

Eastman patrolled his domain armed with a huge club, a blackjack and brass knuckles. In an emergency, he could expertly wield a beer bottle and a piece of lead pipe. Monk was also a skillful boxer and street fighter.

When he was a youngster, his father opened a pet store for him, but Monk abandoned it for the crime-ridden streets of the Lower East Side. Nevertheless, he retained his love for animals, especially cats and pigeons, all his life. He was said to have owned more than a hundred cats and five hundred pigeons at one time.

"I like de kits and boids," Eastman would say, "and I'll beat up any guy dat gets gay wit' a kit or a boid in my neck of de woods."

His love for animals didn't extend to people.

Monk enjoyed violence. He would personally lead members of his gang on raids against stuss games, which flourished throughout the East Side, and he occasionally accepted blackjacking jobs himself.

"I like to beat up a guy once in a while," he said. "It keeps me hand in."

In all fairness, it should be mentioned that Monk never struck a woman with his club, no matter how much she annoyed him. When it became necessary to discipline a lady, he simply belted her with his fist.

"I only gave her a little poke," he would exclaim. "Just enough to put a shanty on her glimmer. But I always takes off me knucks first."[13]

Eastman was the instrument of his own downfall. In February 1904, he held up a well-dressed young man who was drunk. It was a robbery Monk did not have to commit, but could not resist. The kid seemed like such an easy mark.

Unfortunately for Monk, the young drunk turned out to be the son of a wealthy and well-connected family which had hired a Pinkerton detective to follow the boy and keep him out of trouble. When the detective saw Eastman accost the young man, he opened fire. Eastman returned the fire and fled — right into the arms of a policeman who knocked him out with his nightstick.

Eastman was tried for highway robbery and felonious assault. He was convicted and sentenced to ten years in Sing Sing Prison in 1904.

Six years later he was paroled after serving a little more than half his sentence, and returned to the East Side hoping to pick up where he had left off. Things had changed, however. New leaders had arisen and Eastman's power was gone. So he became a sneak thief, a burglar, a pickpocket and a dope peddler.

When the United States entered World War I in 1917, Eastman enlisted. He served throughout the war with bravery and distinction. Bullets held no terror for him and Monk led the charge

Harry Horowitz

whenever his unit went over the top. In recognition of his actions, Monk was awarded a full pardon for his misdeeds by Governor Al Smith of New York after the war.

Monk promised to go straight. The police found a job for him and he did not come to their attention again until the morning of December 26, 1920, when his body was found lying on the sidewalk in front of the Blue Bird Cafe on East Fourteenth Street. He had been shot five times.

Eastman had been killed by a corrupt Prohibition enforcement agent with whom he was running a small bootlegging and dope-peddling operation. The agent had quarreled with Eastman over tipping a waiter. Eastman was buried with full military honors.[14]

Monk was succeeded as leader of the gang by his right-hand man, Max "Kid Twist" Zweibach, when he was sent to prison in 1904. Zweibach was aptly named "Kid Twist" because of his treacherous nature. Detective captain Cornelius Willemse, who knew Zweibach, remembered him as "a brutal, double-crossing criminal whose own men hated him. He couldn't be trusted even by his friends."[15]

Zweibach was no Eastman and the gang he inherited lost its supremacy over the various Irish and Italian gangs. Had he paid more attention to the gang's business, Zweibach might have been able to maintain its dominant position in the New York underworld. But an affair of the heart distracted him and caused his downfall.

The Kid was in love with Carroll Terry, a Coney Island dance hall girl of exceptional beauty. It so happened that Carroll was also being courted by one Louis Pioggi, better known as "Louie the Lump." Since Louie the Lump was rather undersized, Kid Twist took to battering him around every chance he got. The Kid was no fool and usually picked on Louie when the Lump was alone and could not draw his gun.

The Lump was a member of the Five Pointers, a gang that controlled the Five Points section of Manhattan which encompassed the area between Broadway and the Bowery, and Fourteenth street and City Hall Park. The Five Pointers were an Italian mob led by an ex-prizefighter named Paolo Antonini Vaccarelli, alias Paul Kelly. The gang, whose alumni included such luminaries as Johnny Torrio, Al Capone and Lucky Luciano, was continually at war with the Eastman gang.

The rivalry between Kid Twist and the Lump reached a climax on May 14, 1908, when the Kid and his companion, Cyclone Louie, a local strongman and hired killer, forced the Lump to jump out of the second-floor window of a Coney Island bar. Unluckily for Zweibach, the Lump landed on all fours.

Determined to exact vengeance, Louie called the Five Pointer's headquarters to report that Kid Twist was nearby with only one other gunman for protection. Within an hour, 20 Five Pointer gunmen appeared on the scene.

Louie the Lump was given the honor of gunning down his hated foe. When Kid Twist came outside, Louie shot him through the brain, and then shot him in the heart as he toppled to the sidewalk. Cyclone Louie tried to run, but was cut down by a hail of bullets.

The police were so delighted to have Zweibach out of the way that Louie received only eleven months in jail for assault.[16]

Kid Twist's successor was William Alberts, better known as Big Jack Zelig. Zelig was born in 1882 to middle class Jewish parents. He began his criminal career at the age of fourteen when he ran away from home to join a gang of juvenile pickpockets led by a youngster called "Crazy Butch."

Zelig was an apt pupil with a real gift for theft, and he soon developed a reputation as someone whose services were always available to anyone for a price. It was said that Jack never turned down any job of violence. By the age of twenty he was one of Monk Eastman's prize gunmen.

Jack seems to have been a youthful-looking lad with large brown eyes who took advantage of his boyish appearance whenever he had a run-in with the law. Each time he was arrested, Jack would hire a frail and sickly-looking girl to come timidly into court to plead for him. "Oh judge, for God's sake, don't send my boy-husband, the father of my baby to jail," she would wail.

Few magistrates were hard enough to resist these tearful pleas, and Jack was invariably released with a warning to be a good boy and go home to his wife and baby. This ploy worked frequently during Zelig's early career.

Once Zelig became the Eastman gang's leader, he expanded its operations and offered clients a fixed rate for services performed. A Zelig associate once gave the police Big Jack's price list:[17]

Slash on cheek with knife	$1 to $10
Shot in leg	$1 to $25
Shot in arm	$5 to $25
Throwing a bomb	$5 to $50
Murder	$10 to $100

As his fame increased, Zelig's following was augmented by a number of young and ambitious sluggers and gunmen. One newcomer to Zelig's mob was Harry Horowitz, who went under the nom de guerre of "Gyp the Blood." Gyp was a vicious brute of extraordinary strength, which he relished demonstrating.

He used to boast that he could break a man's back by bending him over his knee. He performed this feat several times before witnesses. Once to win a two dollar bet, he grabbed a total stranger and cracked his spine in three places.

Gyp became an expert shot with a revolver and was extremely accurate at throwing a bomb. He enjoyed bomb-throwing because, as he explained, "I likes to hear the noise."[18]

With gifted thugs such as Gyp under his command, Big Jack carried on his various activities with great success. For several years he did a booming business in slugging, stabbing, shooting and bomb-throwing. And he knew how to protect his enterprises by making friends with politicians and business people on the East Side and uptown as well.

Jack's demise came in 1912 when he agreed to do a killing for police Lt. Charles E. Becker, head of New York's gambling squad. Becker was a silent partner with a gambler named Herman "Beansie" Rosenthal. They had a falling out and Rosenthal threatened to go to the district attorney and expose Becker.

Becker asked Zelig to take care of Rosenthal. Jack was given $2,000 and he delegated the job to Gyp the Blood and three other gang members.

Late in the evening of July 15, 1912, Rosenthal was dining in the Hotel Metropole on West Forty-third Street, just east of Broadway. A man came in and told him he was wanted outside the hotel. Rosenthal stepped to the sidewalk and was gunned down by the four killers who waited for him in an automobile. The murderers then sped away.

After the deed was done, it appeared that the killers would get away clean, since Becker was in charge of the investigation. However, a reform-minded district attorney named Charles

Whitman launched his own investigation and found witnesses who identified the four gunmen.

Gyp soon confessed and implicated Zelig and Becker. Zelig also broke the underworld's code of silence by testifying before the grand jury about Becker's links to the crime.

But on October 5, 1912, the day before he was to appear in court, Zelig was shot and killed by Red Phil Davidson as he stepped aboard a Second Avenue trolley car at Thirteenth Street.

Even without Zelig's testimony, the four gunmen were convicted and sentenced to die in the electric chair at Sing Sing Prison. They were electrocuted on April 13, 1914. Becker was also found guilty and was electrocuted on July 30, 1915.[19]

With Zelig's death, the Eastman gang's reign as the dominant Jewish gang in New York came to an end. It was not until after World War I that Jewish gangsters once again achieved a dominant position in that city's criminal underworld.

Chapter Five

The Perils and Pitfalls of the Gangster Life

*B*eing a gangster was never easy. Hunted, wiretapped, harassed and jailed by the authorities, shot at by rivals, and haunted by the specter of an early and violent death, the gangster led a life of tension and risk. Many Jewish gangsters probably felt as Lucky Luciano did when he mused that "there must be an easier way to make a living."

Cops and Robbers

Sometimes being chased by the police could deteriorate into comedy, resembling in a scene from an old Keystone Cops movie. Jake "Mohawk" Skuratofsky was one of Newark's more colorful bookmakers. Trusted by everyone because he was thoroughly honest in the way he ran his business, Jake claimed that a bookmaker was the most honest person alive, because he had only one asset, his reputation. No matter what happened to Jake, whether arrested or his money confiscated by the law, he always paid off, immediately.[1]

Jake's love, next to his wife Faye, was shooting craps. Long before Jake had his own club, he could be found playing on street corners at night. When the law put the "heat" on, he would take the crap game to the cellars of apartment houses or to his own home.

One cold October night in 1938, with a beautiful harvest moon in the sky, Jake decided to start a crap game. The "fix" was in with the law, with the okay scheduled for Tuesday. However, the participants began arriving one day earlier and Jake felt it no great risk to start the game on Monday.

Unknown to Jake, there was an enthusiastic rookie cop on the beat who was unaware of the okay for Jake to run his game.

That night Jake's home was filled with Damon Runyanesque characters with names like Big Ann, Sid Red, Tanks, Tootsie Roll and twenty or so other mobsters and gamblers. Somehow this group caught the attention of the rookie policeman, who called the station house for backup.

Police in the precinct were faced with a dilemma because they could not admit to knowing that a dice game had been okayed for the following day. So they were forced to act.

Suddenly, Jake's crap game was raided by the police, and the dice shooters and bettors scattered all over the house looking for places to hide. Harry Levine bolted down the basement steps and jumped into the coal bin. Abie Markowitz darted into Jake's bedroom and slid under the bed. Sam Gold flung himself into a clothes closet and huddled behind the coats. Jules Stein clambered into a cedar chest filled with linen, but couldn't close the top. Morrie Marks sprinted into a bathroom, stripped off his clothes, climbed into the tub and turned on the water. The police found them all.

Sidney "Big Red" Klein, who weighed close to 300 pounds and looked like he was nine months pregnant, managed to run up to the second floor, open a bedroom window and crawl out onto the roof.

A policeman appeared and seeing the bedroom window open, stuck his head out. He saw Klein lying on the roof, still and quiet, as though he were asleep.

"What the hell are you doing out there," he hollered.

Quick as a flash, Sid looked up at the moon and bellowed, "What the hell does it look like I'm doing? I'm taking a damn moon bath!"

The cop seemed convinced, since Big Red was the only one who wasn't booked that night.

Most of the time, however, the law's pursuit of the gangsters was serious business and no laughing matter.

Stop Bugging Me

The FBI kept Meyer Lansky under surveillance for years. In the spring of 1962, Lansky, 60 years old, was recovering from heart trouble. He had been released from the Trafalgar Hospital in New York City and was staying at the Volney, a quiet, unobtrusive hotel, spending most of his time in his room chatting with his wife, Teddy, and with friends who came to visit. With the hotel management's permission, the FBI wiretapped the room and listened to every word Lansky said.

In one of his recorded conversations Meyer discussed how the FBI harassed him, his family and friends.[2]

"So they started to come to my house when I wasn't there. 'Is Lansky in, FBI.' The bastards wouldn't come at six, six-thirty or at nine in the morning. They always came at two in the afternoon and hours like that. Teddy was having trouble with the help. Every maid I got, got contacted by the FBI, and they were quitting.

"So I decided I better call these bastards, and I called. So they said we'd like to come and see you at your house."

Agents arrived at Lansky's home and the men sat together on the terrace. They engaged in a discussion of morality and Lansky recounts asking the agents just how moral they were.

"They said, there's a moral complication. I said, would you like to discuss morals with me? I know I'm not equipped to discuss it. I don't know if you are. Are you Socrates or some kind of philosopher or something? So I turned to the other guy. I said, what's moral? So he said, we're not here to talk about that. So I straightened him out as to what was moral. I said are you a lawyer and he said he was not. I said, you understand the law and he said yes. I said, you're going around questioning people about my income. You're going to people that are so devoted to me, it's not even funny. Then if you don't like what they say, you say 'Don't you know he's a big gambler? You only know the good side.'

"I said, what the fucking side do you know of me? Was I a thief? Sure I was a gambler. My doors were as wide open as the Fountainbleau Hotel (a Miami Beach hotel). But it didn't take in a poor unfortunate worker. It took in a class of people that could afford it. Nobody was forced to gamble or to come there. Your fucking reformers that came there and ate my food and your newspapermen and many big officials... they didn't pay their fucking check. If it was so terrible, why the fuck didn't they pay their fucking check?

"I said, I know you know everything, but will you tell me what you're trying to accomplish? Will you tell me what do you want to make out of this? You don't want to see me make a living? I don't intend to starve. Before I do, I assure you I'm going to do something to feed myself. Only a moron would refuse. I said, I don't intend to do anything immoral. I have sympathy for a thief if conditions force him to steal. But I have no sympathy for an immoral thief.

"He said, we don't want to hear all this. We just want to ask you four questions.

"I said, if the Commies were getting on the beach here, you'd be worried about a broken-down Meyer Lansky."

At the end of the transcription, the FBI warned their agents that Lansky "should be considered armed and dangerous."[3]

Death and Taxes

The most persistent, successful and certainly the most publicized pursuer of Prohibition-era mobsters was Thomas E. Dewey, special district attorney for New York in the 1930s. Dewey came from Owosso, Michigan, where he had been born in 1902. His forebears had immigrated to America from England in 1634. Tom's grandfather, a crusading abolitionist and prohibitionist, moved to Michigan just before the Civil War. He bought the *Owosso Times* and used it to campaign against the evils of the world. Dewey's father carried on the tradition when he became the paper's editor.[4]

Dewey was a model child and adolescent, never late or absent during twelve years of school. He remained diligent, reliable and conscientious all his life. After graduating from the University of Michigan, Tom went to Columbia University Law School, then stayed in New York City to work for a Wall Street law firm.

Of average height and build, and with a round, boyish face, Dewey always looked younger than he really was. To give himself a more mature and serious look, he grew a mustache which became his trademark. According to people who later worked for him,

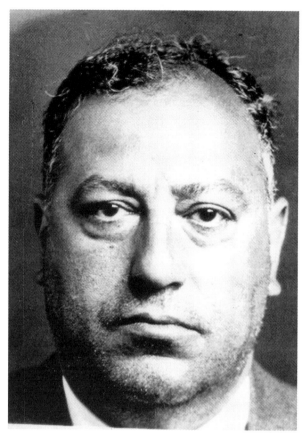

Waxey Gordon

Dewey was "never a great relaxer," but was always serious, sober and humorless. He was a man on a mission.

True to his heritage, Dewey was a Republican and participated in local reform politics. With other members of a Young Republican Club, he served as a poll watcher on election day in 1928. The experience would influence his future career.

He saw "gangsters with guns that you could see sticking through their clothes" bring unregistered voters to the polling places, while the police looked the other way. Some of his friends who protested were beaten up. From then on Dewey was determined to fight against organized crime. Through a contact, he was appointed chief assistant district attorney for the Southern District of New York in 1931. Dewey commanded a staff of sixty lawyers, most of them older than himself.

Dewey had another motive as well. He had his eyes on higher political office and saw crime-fighting in corrupt, Democratic New York City as his ticket to the top. He would later capitalize on his gang-busting reputation to become governor of New York and the Republican candidate for president in 1944 and 1948.

Dewey's first target was Irving Wexler, alias Waxey Gordon. Tom decided to get Gordon the way the government got Al Capone: for evasion of income tax.

Gordon had many enemies, not the least of whom was Meyer Lansky. Gordon's feud with Lansky started in 1927 when Meyer and Bugsy Siegel hijacked four truckloads of whiskey destined for Mafia boss Joe Masseria. Unknown to them, Masseria had promised the shipment to Waxey Gordon.

Lansky, Siegel and their gang ambushed the convoy, killing three men and wounding four others. One of the wounded truck drivers recognized Lansky and later told Gordon. Waxey was furious. From then on, he and Lansky quarreled openly, accusing each other of being double-crossers and liars. Once they came to blows and Lucky Luciano had to physically separate them.

The bad blood between the two men persisted and among New York's mobsters became known as the "War of the Jews." Lucky Luciano decided to do something because the feud disrupted business. Favoring Lansky, his boyhood partner, Luciano and Lansky hatched a plot to dispose of Gordon the best way possible: they would let the federal government do it for them.

Luciano and Lansky knew that Thomas Dewey was investigating Gordon's income taxes, and decided to help him out. Beginning in 1931, they had Meyer's brother Jake, a member of Lansky's outfit, secretly deliver information about Gordon's bootlegging operation to Internal Revenue officials in Philadelphia. Dewey used this material to convict Gordon.[5]

Waxey maintained a ten-room apartment with four baths at 590 West End Avenue, paying $6,000 a year in rent. The apartment contained a bar costing $3,600 and a library with $3,800 worth of books, none of which had ever been opened. Five servants looked after the apartment and waited on Gordon, his wife and three children. Gordon also kept a summer residence at Bradley Beach, New Jersey and sent his son to a private military school in the South.[6]

Gordon drove around in three expensive cars and indulged his taste in flashy and expensive clothes. Socks, which he bought by the dozen, cost him $10 a pair. He paid $45 for silk briefs. His suits cost $225 each and were bought from the tailor who made clothes for Al Capone. He also liked luxurious furniture and bought it in quantities. He paid $2,300 for a bookcase made to order by an interior decorator.

Waxey reported a net annual income of $8,125.

In April 1933, Waxey was indicted on four counts of income tax evasion. He tried to avoid arrest by hiding out in a small cottage on White Lake in the Catskill Mountains, but treasury agents found the cottage and paid Waxey an early morning visit. They found Gordon and two bodyguards still asleep.

"This is nonsense," said Waxey after they had awakened him. "I ain't Waxey Gordon," he insisted. "I'm William Palinski. I'm in the tobacco business."

"Look, Waxey," said one of the agents, tired of Gordon's protests. "You oughtn't to keep saying you're William Palinski and walk around in silk drawers that have I.W. embroidered on them. I.W. means Irving Wexler, Waxey."

At Waxey's trial, Dewey showed that in 1930 alone Gordon earned $1,427,531 and paid the United States government $10.76 in income tax.

Gordon's attorney defended his client by saying that his only ambition had been to provide for his family and that Gordon had only two vices, "his love of a beautiful home for his family and his love of good clothing."

The jury took 45 minutes to find Gordon guilty of income tax evasion. In December 1933, he was sentenced to ten years in prison and fined $80,000.

When Waxey got out for good behavior in 1940 he was flat broke. All his property and wealth had been seized or was gone. At the time of his release, Waxey owed the government $1,603,427 in income taxes plus a $40,000 fine. He agreed to pay it off at a rate of $6 per week. At that rate, it would take him 273,903 weeks, or 5,267 years, to clear his debt.

He smilingly told reporters waiting for him at the gate that his life in crime was over and that he was a new man. "Waxey Gordon is dead," he said. "From now on it's Irving Wexler, salesman."[7]

He did become a salesman of sorts, only it was in the black market during World War II. In 1942, he was caught diverting 10,000 pounds of sugar to a distillery and went back to jail.

Released after a few years, he returned to sales, this time dope. In 1951, he was caught trying to pass a $3,600 package of heroin to a federal narcotics informer.

As the officers arrested him, Waxey began to weep. "Shoot me," he pleaded. "Don't take me in for junk. Let me run, then shoot me."

One of the old gangster's confederates took $2,500 from his pocket and slipped two diamond rings off his fingers. "Take this," he said. "Take me. Take the whole business. Just let Pop go."

Ignoring his plea, the officers handcuffed Gordon and took him away.

At the age of 63, Gordon was sentenced to 25 years to life in Alcatraz. This was a cruel punishment. Alcatraz was a place for dangerous prisoners; Gordon was a threat to no one.

In the end, it made no difference as he only lived six months. Waxey Gordon, once a millionaire bootlegger, died in prison of a heart attack in 1954.[8]

Failure to pay income taxes also tripped up Joseph "Doc" Stacher, Longy Zwillman's buddy and right-hand man. Stacher was born in Poland in 1902 and came to Newark at the age of ten. His police record included arrests for atrocious assault and battery, robbery, burglary, larceny, bootlegging, hijacking and murder.[9]

During Prohibition, Stacher aided Zwillman in his bootlegging and gambling enterprises and worked with Meyer Lansky, Bugsy Siegel and other New York Jewish mobsters. Later, Lansky chose Stacher to head the group that built the Sands Hotel in Las Vegas and to represent the mob's interests there. Stacher also operated as the official paymaster to Cuban dictator Fulgencio Batista, who permitted Lansky and his friends to build and operate casinos on the island.

Although they pursued Stacher for years, it wasn't until 1963 that the government was able to convict him. Stacher reached a settlement with the Internal Revenue Service and instead of jail, was deported.

Stacher had never become a citizen, but flatly refused to go to Poland or Russia. Moreover, the law prohibited the government from sending anyone to a communist country. As a Jew, Stacher was entitled, under the Law of Return, to immigrate to Israel and become a citizen. He accepted and moved to Israel in 1965.

If the government thought Doc would suffer in exile, they were sadly mistaken.

Doc set up residence in the Sheraton Hotel on Tel Aviv's seacoast and enjoyed an idyllic retirement. He had a car and driver every day and, at the grand old age of seventy, acquired a twenty-three year old girlfriend who was a law student at Tel Aviv University.

Doc enjoyed Israel and Israelis found him entertaining and generous. His largess attracted the attention of Agudat Israel, an ultra-Orthodox political party. One of its rabbis, Menachem Porush, convinced Stacher to invest $100,000 in a plan to build homes for young, strictly Orthodox Jewish couples. But instead of applying the money to this end, Porush used it to build a kosher hotel in Jerusalem.

Stacher and Porush quarreled and the matter went to court. Stacher claimed he had loaned Porush the money to build a charitable institution. Not only was he unable to get back the loan, but he had not received any interest on the money.

Israelis found the episode hilarious: the famous American gangster being ripped off by a rabbi.

Wild scenes punctuated the trial, with Stacher's lawyer calling the rabbi a swindler and Porush's attorney accusing Stacher of being a criminal.

Stacher won the case and Porush had to return the loan. As Stacher left the courtroom, a reporter asked him what he thought about the affair. "I can't believe it," Doc replied. "A rabbi stole my money, a rabbi stole my money."

Standing nearby, another reporter was heard to say, "This rabbi may be a bigger crook than you were."[10]

For a time, Israel became something of a refuge for old-time Jewish mobsters on the lam. Stacher's friend Meyer Lansky also moved to Israel to avoid standing trial in the United States. In 1970, he applied for citizenship under Israel's Law of Return. After a protracted trial and public debate, Lansky's request was denied and he was expelled from the country in 1972.

The proceedings against Lansky spurred a national debate in Israel. Prime Minister Golda Meir was told that Lansky was the alleged boss of the American underworld and if he were allowed to stay, Israel would become a center for Mafia activities. Golda knew nothing of Meyer Lansky and little about American organized crime, but she had heard of the Mafia. That word was enough to seal Lansky's fate in Israel.

According to Yosef Burg, who was then Minister of the Interior, Golda was horrified when that word was mentioned in connection with Lansky's application to remain in Israel.

"Dr. Burg, Mafia?" she asked. "No Mafia in Israel."[11]

Golda had grown up in the United States and was extremely sensitive to American, especially Jewish American public opinion. She knew that if Israel gave shelter to an alleged crime boss, it might encounter difficulties in raising money among American Jews. Therefore, the word "Mafia" held dangerous connotations for her.

Golda may also have worried that if she allowed Lansky to stay in Israel, the Nixon administration, which wanted to extradite Lansky, might have deferred sending Israel the Phantom jet fighter-bombers Israel needed to counter the new Soviet weapons going to Egyptian positions on the Suez Canal.

In September 1971, Yosef Burg rendered his decision based on FBI files, Justice Department documents, the Kefauver Committee hearings and books on organized crime. None of these had ever been enough to convict Lansky. Although Lansky had been involved in organized crime for over fifty years, he had only served three months in jail: in 1952, after pleading guilty to gambling charges in Saratoga Springs, New York. After carefully studying the evidence, Burg concluded that Lansky was a person with a criminal history and likely to endanger the public welfare. He therefore denied Lansky's application for Israeli citizenship and ordered his extradition.[12]

After undergoing open heart surgery in 1973, Lansky stood trial in Miami for income tax evasion. He was acquitted. The government also failed to convict Lansky in two other cases against him. In November 1976, the Justice Department gave up trying to put him behind bars.

While in Israel, Lansky became friends with a journalist, Uri Dan. Their friendship continued for a number of years and Lansky told Dan a great deal about his past. Unbeknownst to Lansky, Dan would use this material in a book about Lansky. After the book's publication, Lansky felt betrayed, which only reinforced his deep distrust of writers and journalists. When asked how he felt about Dan's actions, Lansky looked his questioner in the eye, and without the trace of a smile said, "Some people will do anything for money."[13]

During his stay in Israel, a small-time Israeli criminal named Ilan plotted to kidnap Lansky and hold him for ransom. The plot failed to materialize when Ilan disappeared mysteriously. His body was later discovered in the northern part of Israel, chopped into pieces and stuffed in bags. His killer was never caught.[14]

Doing Time: Hard and Soft

Being sent to prison could be a terrible experience for men accustomed to freedom, power and the action of the streets. If you were "well connected," however, you might pass the time in relative comfort and security, as in the case of Max "Puddy" Hinkes, a stalwart enforcer in Longy Zwillman's Newark mob.

"In my stay at these various prisons I had nothing but money," recalls Puddy. "Always everything that was done for me was through Longy's connections, for which I was always entirely grateful to him. And to the day he died, I loved him."[15]

In 1939, Puddy was sentenced to the minimum security prison at Leesburg, New Jersey. "At Leesburg we gambled very freely," he says. "Once when I was called in by the superintendent, I told him we would only gamble for cigarettes. And here I am standing there, without exaggeration, with thousands of dollars in my pocket.

"I had a private room above the barracks, and I ate nothing but the best. I also had a person by the name of Playboy Figer, who used to come down and visit me, bring down a girl that I used to associate with when I was off the premises. This was a sneak job.

"I also went to town. I would get whiskey, which I would bring back and let certain inmates, friends of mine, drink as much as they could. And the next day they would say, 'That lousy Jew done it again.'

"The guards were pretty hip to what went on, but apparently being they knew that I was connected pretty good, they didn't bother me too much.

Jack Guzik

"I was arrested, I would say, roughly around fifty times. It wasn't too bad. I only done two sentences."

Sometimes, the more famous the gangster, the harsher the treatment. Jack Guzik, who was sent to jail for income tax evasion in 1932, had a difficult time of it. Jack felt that he was not being treated fairly because of his notoriety, and that he was being singled out for sterner treatment by the guards. True or not, he continually petitioned the authorities to alleviate his situation by transferring him from the Federal Penitentiary at Lewisburg to Alcatraz in California. He asked for Alcatraz because Al Capone, his pal and boss, was there.

In June 1934, two years after he was incarcerated, Jack wrote to Sanford Bates, director of the federal prisons, portraying himself as a misunderstood and wronged man, and pleading for relief.[16]

"As you may or may not know," wrote Guzik, "I have met with quite a few disappointing experiences as a prisoner in your custody. I entered the penitentiary at Leavenworth, Kansas, with an artificial evil reputation as the result of newspaper 'ballyhoo' ascribing to me so-called 'gang' or 'mobster' activities and connections that found their origin in the fertile imaginations of professional publicity hounds in the employ of the press. Why it was permitted to follow me once the prison doors clanged shut is an unanswerable riddle.

"But follow me it did. For some reason, despite the declared policy of your department that all inmates are treated alike, with no favoritism or oppression shown to any particular individual behind the walls of federal penitentiaries, I have been given to understand by various acts and the attitude of your subordinates — even including the parole board that has denied me a well-earned parole despite the provisions of a wise law — that the odium of unjust and unfair evil must still be mine and I must be treated accordingly."

Guzik went on to complain that at Leavenworth and at Lewisburg Prison, Pennsylvania, "I have been the subject of what I honestly believe to be a repressive and studied espionage over and above what is the lot of the average prisoner: my goings and comings within the inmate body being the subject of unusually severe scrutiny over and above what is accorded others; all of my visits being held under the sharp supervision of a high official of the institution; my mail extraordinarily scrutinized and censored; and the general tone being one of distrust and suspicion."

Because of his treatment, Guzik concluded that Bates must "consider me a real bad character, an evil man, despite my good birth and parentage, my magnificent family and the all-important item to a prison administrator, that I have no criminal record of any kind."

Should this litany of injustices fail to sway Bates, Jack included health and medical reasons for being transferred. "I am in poor health all-around, with but one kidney. I am suffering acutely with sinus trouble and am existing solely on such low-protein diet as they can afford here. The climate of the west coast has, in the past, been most beneficial to me, and I honestly believe it will help me again were I there."[17]

Guzik's request was denied. But this did not prevent dozens of friends and acquaintances from bombarding the parole board with letters requesting his parole. They usually based their pleas on family considerations.

Jack's parents, Max and Fannie, had moved to Los Angeles in the late 1920s to be with their other children. Jack's mother died there of heart trouble in 1931. When Jack was sent to prison, the elder Guzik wrote to the parole board on Jack's behalf and asked his Los Angeles acquaintances to do the same.

"I'm asking you to have pity on an old sick man," wrote Max. "I am 84. My health failing me, my eyes failing me. I am on the way and I want to see my dear son before anything happens. He was good to everybody, especially to his sick father and mother. His mother passed away from trouble on account of him. She found out that her son must go to prison. She passed away suddenly from a heart attack."[18]

Guzik's father explained that his "dear son supported us for a long time with all the goods, with doctors and medicine. Now I am holding a vacant flat for him to live together in my building." He guaranteed the board that Jack would "be a very good boy," if released.

"Your honor," writes Max, "I ask you a second time and a million times more, have feeling and pity on me, an old and very sick nearly blind father. Please don't throw away this letter in the waste basket and help me to get my dear son and supporter home."

Max concluded his letter by promising the board that if they would release Jack, he would "pray for you and your dear family all the rest of my life. Even in my grave I will remember what you did for me and my good son."[19]

Max's Los Angeles friends also tried to help Jack out by writing the parole board. Dr. Herman Lando, the elderly Guzik's Los Angeles physician and family friend, sent a letter asking for Jack's release. "I have known Jack Guzik for many years; also his family," he wrote. Jack "has been a good friend, good husband, and an extremely good son. He has always been a good provider and has helped his family just for the asking."

The doctor asked for Jack's release "for the sake of his father, who is in his 84th year, is rapidly failing in health and losing the sight of his eyes." He ended by saying that he would "gladly vouch for Jack Guzik anytime and all the time."[20]

Rabbi M. Kohn of Congregation B'nai Jacob in Los Angeles, the synagogue Max attended, also pleaded for Jack to be released for his father's sake. The good rabbi wrote that Guzik's "father has absolutely guaranteed me that if Jack is paroled he will not return to his old haunts, but will come to live with his father."[21]

Another Los Angeles resident, Mike Lyman, wrote that he and Jack had grown up together and were "real close pals." He assured the parole board that, at heart, Jack "was as fine a boy as you could possibly find in any walk of life." Lyman was positive that, should Jack be released, "he could easily rehabilitate himself." Furthermore, if a parole were granted, Lyman "would be more than happy to take him in the business with me, and personally guarantee that he would not break any of the laws of the land."[22]

One of Jack's friends in Youngstown, Ohio, tried another approach. "Whenever I think of the New Deal our president, Franklin D. Roosevelt has inaugurated," wrote Fred Kohler in October 1933, "my mind goes out to an old friend that I have known for a good many years. Mr. Jack Guzik is the man I refer to." He then went on to praise Jack as a man "very much attached to his family and home," and "interested in his children to a degree that made him outstanding as a father."

Kohler believed that if Jack was given "a new deal," he would "prove himself worthy of parole in every respect."[23]

The appeals were of little avail. Jack's first petition for parole was denied "upon the premise that this subject is a menace to society and a dangerous criminal; that in all probability his intentions... are to resume his criminal activities as soon as he is released."[24]

The parole board's analysis proved correct. Jack was released from prison in December 1935, after serving three years of his four year sentence and resumed his criminal career immediately upon his return to Chicago. He never went to prison again.

Guzik died of a heart attack at age 69 in 1956, while dining on a couple of lamb chops and a glass of wine. His friends gave him a lavish funeral. The bronze coffin alone cost $5,000. One attending gangster remarked that "For that money, we could have buried him in a Cadillac."[25]

Like Waxey Gordon, Jacob "Gurrah" Shapiro, Lepke Buchalter's sidekick of many years, died in prison. Shapiro was born in Russia in 1895 and came to the United States with his parents when he was twelve. One of nine children, Jacob left school at an early age and never learned to read or write properly. This proved to be no handicap in his chosen profession of slugging and strong-arming.[26]

Jake's nickname "Gurrah" allegedly evolved from his difficulty with the English language. When annoyed at someone, he would shout "Gurrarah here." Translated, this meant "Get out of here." Jake usually tendered this command with a blow or kick. To his peers and the police he became "Gurrah Jake."

Jacob grew up ugly. He was five feet, five inches in height, weighed 200 pounds, had a flattened nose, thick lips, fat fingers, brown, tightly curled hair, and large ears.

He also grew up bad. Before he was eighteen, he was a pushcart thief, bully and East Side hoodlum. While still a teenager, Jake met Lepke on the Lower East Side while they were both attempting to rob the same pushcart. Rather than compete, they decided to form a partnership. Lepke realized he could use Jake's muscle, and Jake likely realized he would need Lepke's brain. The duo became known as "L and G," or simply "the boys."[27]

Both men started off working for New York's criminal mastermind, Arnold Rothstein. At first, their only jobs were those they received from Rothstein, but this changed during the New York garment center strike of 1926. Both sides used gangsters in the conflict. Rothstein supplied mobsters, among them Lepke and Gurrah, to the unions. When the strike ended, Lepke and Gurrah stayed on, taking over the unions. After 1926, Lepke and Gurrah worked with Rothstein, instead of for him.

Once the boys gained control of a union local, they would take kickbacks and skim off the dues from union members. At the same time, they extorted huge payoffs from garment manufacturers who wished to avoid strikes.

Between 1915 and 1933, Gurrah was arrested fifteen times on charges including burglary, assault, kidnapping, carrying concealed weapons, larceny and violation of the federal antitrust laws. He served five prison sentences, all short. Though underworld gossip and police information linked him with murder, especially the killing of Jacob "Little Augie" Orgen, the evidence was always too obscure to make the charges stick.[28]

Gurrah was happiest when he could use force. He believed a punch in the mouth was better than a harsh word, and that a bullet or a bottle of acid was more fun than a bust in the chops.

In 1936, Gurrah and Lepke were convicted by the federal government for violation of the antitrust laws. Both men received sentences of two years in jail, but were released on bond pending appeal. U.S. Circuit Court Judge Martin T. Mantin overturned

Buchalter's conviction, but not Shapiro's. It was rumored, although never proven, that Judge Mantin had been bribed.

Gurrah jumped bail and completely disappeared. The New York State and federal government searched for him everywhere, including Poland and Palestine, but he surrendered to the FBI after hiding out for less than a year.

In 1938, Shapiro was tried and convicted of labor racketeering and sentenced to life in prison. He died in prison at age 50 in 1947. A few months before his death, Gurrah bitterly told other convicts that he had been a fool to follow Luciano, Lansky and Lepke. If only he had done things his way, using more violence, "I wudda been free," he said.[29]

Lepke Buchalter's real troubles started after Judge Mantin released him. Special District Attorney Dewey, who had already convicted Waxey Gordon for tax evasion and Lucky Luciano for prostitution, went after Lepke with a vengeance. Dewey believed that catching Lepke would deal a death blow to organized crime in New York, and ensure his own election to the governorship. He conducted midnight raids on union and company offices and seized their books. He tapped telephones and subpoenaed hundreds of witnesses. Anyone connected to Lepke in any way was brought in, questioned, threatened with indictments and put under enormous pressure to talk.

Lepke's life became a nightmare. His office was watched, his phones were tapped and police followed him everywhere. He was forced to meet his henchmen in building and hotel lobbies, on subway platforms and in restaurant washrooms.

"I sneak away from the cops... I lose them... mostly in the subway," he explained to Paul Berger, one of his labor organizers.[30]

Adding to Lepke's troubles, the federal government began to investigate his involvement in drug trafficking.

Unable to find relief, Lepke went into hiding in 1937. "Things are getting too hot here," he told Berger. "I'll have to lam. Be careful."[31]

A warrant was issued for his arrest, but he eluded his pursuers for two years. Albert Anastasia, one of the Mafia's prized executioners, and Abe Reles hid Buchalter in a secret apartment above the Oriental Palace, a cheap dance hall in Brooklyn. While the authorities combed the United States for him, a disguised Buchalter lived under their very noses.[32]

While in hiding, Lepke tried to protect himself against informers by having Abe Reles, Harry Strauss, Buggsy Goldstein and the rest of Murder, Inc. kill anyone and everyone who could finger him. Brooklyn became a slaughterhouse.

As the terror spread, the law applied more pressure. The authorities questioned every underworld figure of note in their search for Lepke. A special federal grand jury in Newark subpoenaed Longy Zwillman to ask if he knew where Lepke might be hiding.

"I know Lepke a long time," Zwillman admitted, "but I haven't seen him in three-four years. So far as I know, he was a pleasant fellow... and clean morally." Zwillman received a six-month jail sentence for refusing to answer the grand jury's questions.[33]

Bugsy Siegel was asked whether he had spoken to Lepke. Siegel replied that he could not remember. Judge John Knox ruled that Siegel's alleged lapse of memory was "frivolous and contumacious" and sent him to jail pending a return of memory.[34]

Desperate to find Lepke, the federal government and New York State put out a $50,000 reward for his capture and published his picture on handbills, movie screens and in newspapers. He became the most wanted man in the country, perhaps in the world.

The last of the wanted circulars distributed by the New York police contained the following description of Lepke's "peculiarities": "Eyes, piercing and shifting; nose, large, somewhat blunt at nostrils; ears, prominent and close to head; mouth, large, slight dimple left side; right-handed; suffering from kidney ailment. Frequents baseball games."

The New York underworld was in turmoil, threatened by Dewey on one side and menaced by Buchalter on the other. It couldn't go on like this. The manhunt for Lepke was ruining their business. It

Jacob Shapiro

became obvious to the crime bosses that the only way to keep their operations from being destroyed was for Lepke to surrender.

According to Lucky Luciano, he, Thomas "Three Finger Brown" Lucchese and others discussed the problem at Dannemora Prison. Luciano modestly claims he solved it.

The idea was to make it appear to Lepke that a deal had been worked out with J. Edgar Hoover. "If he'd give himself up to the FBI and take the narcotics rap, he'd have Hoover's guarantee that he wouldn't be turned over to Dewey, and by the time he finished the federal stretch, the Dewey case would probably've caved in.

"I knew that Lep was scared to death of Tom Dewey, especially after what the prick done to me," said Luciano. "Of course we didn't make no deal at all with Hoover, but it had to look damn sure to Lepke like we did."[35]

Whether Luciano conceived the plan or not, it worked. Meyer Lansky sent Moe "Dimples" Wolensky, Lepke's trusted lieutenant and friend, to tell Buchalter that a deal had been made with J. Edgar Hoover. Hoover promised not to turn Buchalter over to Dewey, said Wolensky. Once Lepke was in jail, the "heat" would be off the bosses and everything would return to normal. After serving a "short" sentence of ten to twelve years, he would be free.

Lepke remained suspicious. He told Abe Reles, "Those bastards are more interested in their own take than they are in my hide."[36]

He was right. But he also realized that unless he complied, his criminal associates would take matters into their own hands, just as they had done with Dutch Schultz. Nothing personal, but business is business.

Buchalter agreed to the plan.

On August 5, 1939, Walter Winchell, the famous gossip columnist and news broadcaster, received an anonymous call that Lepke "wants to come in," but was afraid he would be shot before he could surrender.

Winchell was a close friend of J. Edgar Hoover. The two men often shared the same table at New York's Stork Club and each helped the other in important ways. From his extensive files, Hoover illegally supplied Winchell with secret tidbits on the private lives of famous people. In return, Winchell willingly served as Hoover's biggest fan, press agent and booster.

Winchell contacted Hoover, who assured him that Lepke would be arrested and not shot. During one of his broadcasts, Winchell relayed Hoover's assurance of a safe-conduct to a federal jail for Lepke.

On the evening of August 24, 1939, Lepke came out of his hideout in an apartment on Foster Avenue in Brooklyn and got into a waiting car. Behind the wheel sat Albert Anastasia who drove the automobile over the bridge into Manhattan. At a predetermined spot he stopped the car. Buchalter got out and walked over to a car with two men parked nearby. The door opened and Lepke got in.

"Mr. Hoover," said Walter Winchell, who was the driver, "this is Lepke."

"How do you do," said Hoover, who sat in the back.

"Glad to meet you," said Lepke. "Let's go."[37]

With Winchell driving, and surrounded by a fleet of other cars filled with FBI agents, they took Lepke straight to prison.

From the moment he entered the car, Lepke sensed that he had been double-crossed. There was no fix, no deal. By then it was too late.

Lepke's federal narcotics trial took place in December 1939. Lepke, together with several co-defendants, was convicted of

"Conspiracy to Unlawfully Import, Possess, Conceal, Transport and Sell Narcotics." In January 1940, Buchalter received sentences totalling 192 years. Since most of the sentences ran concurrently, the actual time involved was 14 years.[38]

The terror Buchalter inspired was evident at his trial. One of the witnesses against Lepke was a middle-aged convict named Solomon Stein who, at the time of the trial, was serving a seven-year sentence for larceny. Stein had worked in Buchalter's narcotics smuggling operation and identified Buchalter as his boss.

The judge asked Stein to identify Buchalter by placing a hand on his shoulder. Stein took a few steps toward Buchalter, then stopped. Buchalter glared coldly at him. Stein turned pale and started trembling. Speaking in Russian through an interpreter, Stein said he was afraid and would go no closer. He asked the judge if he could point to Buchalter. The judge, seeing Stein's distress, agreed. Stein then pointed his finger at Buchalter.[39]

After his conviction, Buchalter was held for a time in the Federal Detention Headquarters in New York pending the outcome of the proposed action against him by the State of New York. Buchalter's attorney filed an action for a stay of execution of the state's writ, but the Court of Appeals denied this. Successive appeals to higher courts affirmed this decision. Buchalter was then turned over to Thomas Dewey for trial.

In April 1940, he was found guilty of extortion in the bakery and trucking rackets and received thirty years to life. This sentence was to begin after he had completed his federal jail term.[40]

When Buchalter boarded the train which would take him to prison, he talked to reporters. "I may have done a hundred things wrong, but my conscience is clear," he said. "I never did one-millionth of the things they said I did."[41]

"Those politicians had to have something to talk about, so they picked on me. Dewey is running for president because he picked on me. Why don't they go ahead and investigate those politicians? Why don't they investigate Dewey?"[42]

When he arrived at Leavenworth, Lepke continued railing. "So they call this justice," he said. "They double-crossed me.

"When I gave myself up, I was promised the world. They told me what a great guy I was and that I was doing the right thing and that the whole affair would blow over in no time. Well, boy, did I get the greatest double-cross ever."

When asked about the Brooklyn murder mob, Lepke said "Why, I haven't been in Brownsville in twelve years. I'd be afraid to walk the streets there. Anyone that does is crazy."[43]

On June 20, 1940, Lepke wrote to James Bennett, Director of the Federal Prisons, complaining of his treatment in prison. For "security reasons," Lepke had been put in a single cell and his movements severely restricted. He couldn't stand the isolation.[44]

"May I take the liberty of explaining my present predicament," wrote Lepke, "and ask of you your kind consideration in this matter.

"I am not going into the full details of my case because I believe your honor knows as much about it as I do. However, I am to serve 14 years in a federal prison. My conduct in New York while awaiting trial, and the time spent until I was sent here, will speak for itself. Since I have been here I have lived up to all rules and regulations. I was put to work after my quarantine period and after several weeks for some unknown reason, I was put back into my cell. I am being kept there for twenty-four hours a day, without any exercise whatsoever.

"Mr. Bennett, all I ask is to alter this for me and put me back to work, it doesn't matter what it may be, and let me prove to you and the officials here that I am worthy of this kind consideration.

"I faithfully promise that I will not betray any trust that you may bestow upon me. Hoping you give this some consideration and may I hear from you soon. Respectfully, Louis Buchalter."[45]

The authorities were not finished with Lepke yet. On May 28, 1940, the Grand Jury of the County of Kings, State of New York, presented a "true bill for murder in the first degree" against Buchalter, charging that he, with others, had "shot and killed one Joseph Rosen with revolvers on September 13, 1936, in the County of Kings."[46]

Rosen owned a small trucking company. He had been forced out of business in 1932 because he refused to join Lepke's truckers' union. He blamed Lepke for his unemployment and his family's ensuing destitution, and threatened that unless Lepke took care of him, he would go to the authorities. Lepke obliged. He had Rosen killed.

On December 1, 1941, Buchalter was found guilty and sentenced to die in the electric chair.[47]

At his sentencing, Buchalter identified himself thusly: "I am 44 years of age. I was born in New York City; I reside at 427 West Street. I am retired. I am married. I can read and write. I am a public school graduate. I am a Hebrew, irregular attendant. My mother is living. I am temperate. I do not use drugs."[48]

His attorneys appealed the sentence to the Supreme Court, but that body upheld the lower court's decision. After a series of delays, Buchalter was transferred to Sing Sing Penitentiary at Ossining, New York on January 21, 1944.

In an effort to gain a last-minute reprieve, Lepke's wife and son implored him to ask U.S. Attorney James B.M. McNally in New York to listen to his story of a widespread coalition between crime and politics.[49]

"He'll listen to you, Lou," Mrs. Buchalter pleaded. "God knows you can tell him enough to save you."

Buchalter merely shook his head. "Look," he said. "Suppose I did talk to him. Suppose he asks for a reprieve. What's the best I could expect? I'll tell you: they'd give me another six or eight months — at the most a year. No Betty," he finished. "If that's the case, I'd rather go tonight."[50]

Lepke was placed in a death row cell to await his execution. At 11:30 P.M. on March 4, he was taken from his cell and led to a small room. Inside, bolted to the floor was the electric chair. Buchalter said nothing. He walked quickly across the chamber and almost threw himself into the seat.

He sat rigidly as restraining straps were quickly tightened around his arms, chest and abdomen. The attendants fastened the electrodes, making sure that one electrode was attached to his leg through a slit in his trousers.

As the head electrode was lowered into place, Lepke looked up at it. That was the last thing he saw.

A mask was placed over his face to hide the facial contortions from the witnesses when the current was turned on. The mask was made especially tight around the eyes to keep them from popping out of their sockets.

Buchalter's heart raced and he gasped for breath.

Everyone moved clear of the chair.

Warden Snyder dropped his hand. Unseen, Joseph Francel, the official executioner, pulled the switch. There was a whir of motors. Twenty-two hundred volts slammed into Lepke's body, heaving him against the bindings. His hair stood up and his flesh turned beet-red. Foam seeped out from behind the hood.

Another massive jolt was delivered. Then the whirring stopped. The attendants bared Lepke's chest and Dr. Charles Sweet, the prison physician, stepped forward and applied a stethoscope.

"I pronounce this man legally dead," he said.

Attendants loaded Lepke's body onto a stretcher and rolled it into the autopsy room.

"You look at the face... you cannot tear your eyes away," wrote Frank Coniff the next day in the *New York Journal American*.

"Sweat beads his forehead. Saliva drools from the corner of his lips. The face is discolored. It is not a pretty sight."[51]

Lepke was the only big-time American gangster to die in the electric chair.

Chapter Six

The Hit Parade

Once, in an expansive mood, Bugsy Siegel told Del Webb, the contractor who built the Flamingo Hotel, "that he had personally killed twelve men." Webb turned pale.

Noticing the change in his friend's face, Siegel laughed and said that Webb had nothing to worry about. "There's no chance that you'll get killed," he said. "We only kill each other."[1]

And so they did. Oftentimes, mobsters posed a greater menace to each other than did the police.

After putting Waxey Gordon away for income tax evasion, Thomas Dewey turned his sights on Arthur "Dutch Schultz" Flegenheimer. He began to probe Schultz's tax reports and to investigate other aspects of his underworld empire. Using a vast network of illegal wiretaps and intimidation of witnesses, Dewey made the Dutchman's life miserable.

Schultz became furious and began suggesting things like "Dewey's gotta go," and "We gotta knock off Dewey."[2]

Eventually he brought an assassination proposal to his associates, Lucky Luciano, Meyer Lansky, Bugsy Siegel, Longy Zwillman and Lepke Buchalter. They tried to dissuade him. Killing Dewey, they explained, would bring the heat and the feds down on all of them. It would wreck their rackets and launch a nation-wide war on crime.

"All of us was very worried," Luciano later explained.

"We didn't kill nobody but our own guys, if they give us too much trouble... I just couldn't see how we'd be able to buy our way out of trouble if we let Dewey get knocked off."[3]

Buchalter registered the strongest veto, saying: "This is the worst thing in the world. It will hit us all in the pocketbook because everybody will come down on our heads."[4]

Dutch was not deterred. "I still say he ought to be hit," he raged. "If no one else is gonna do it, I'm gonna hit him myself." He then stormed out of the meeting.[5]

Schultz signed his own death warrant with this outburst,. The contract was given to Charlie "the Bug" Workman, referred to by Allie Tannenbaum, a Murder, Inc. colleague, as "one of the best killers in the country."[6]

On the night of October 23, 1935, Schultz went to his favorite restaurant, the Palace Chop House and Tavern in Newark. With him were two bodyguards, Abe Landau and Bernard "Lulu" Rosenkrantz, and his bookkeeper, Otto "Abbadabba" Berman. Later in the evening, as they sat around the table, Schultz got up and went into the men's room.[7]

A moment later, Bugs Workman and Mendy Weiss entered, walked over to the table and began shooting. Landau, Rosenkrantz and Berman never had a chance. Workman looked around for Schultz and, noticing the men's room door, walked over to it and pulled it open.

Seemingly oblivious to the shooting, Schultz was standing at the toilet urinating. Workman aimed and fired, putting one bullet in the Dutchman. He then turned and walked quickly out of the tavern.

Mortally wounded, Schultz staggered out of the toilet and slumped at a table. The single bullet had hit him just below the left chest and tore through the abdominal wall into the large intestine, gall bladder and liver before lodging on the floor near the urinal.

Jacob Friedman, the owner of the Palace Chop House, had dropped to the floor when the shooting started. He got up only when the killers bolted out the door.

"The first thing I noticed was Schultz," he later recounted. "He came reeling out like he was intoxicated. He had a hard time staying on his pins and he was hanging on to his side. He didn't say a cockeyed thing. He just went over to a table and put his left hand on it, kind of to steady him, and then plopped into a chair just like a souse would.

"His head bounced on the table and I thought that was the end of him, but pretty soon he moved. He said 'Get a doctor, quick.'

"But when he said it, another guy gets off the floor. He had blood all over his clothes but gets up and comes over to me, and he looked like he was going to cry. He throws a quarter on the bar and he says, 'Give me change for that,' and I did."

The man was Lulu Rosenkrantz. Having probably learned his parsimony from Schultz, he hung on to the bar while waiting for his change.

After getting his change, he wobbled unsteadily toward the phone. Sagging against the wall, he managed to dial O and gasp, "I want the police. Hurry up."

Patrolman Patrick McNamara at police headquarters heard a faint, faltering voice say, "Send me an ambulance, I'm dying." But the only sound that came back when he asked where the call was

Marty Goldstein (left), detective (center), and Harry Strauss (right)

coming from was that of the receiver banging against the wood below the coin box.

McNamara, who had already received a call about the shooting at the Palace, immediately sent a squad car and an ambulance to that address.

Police, detectives and three ambulances arrived on the scene, where they found Schultz still alive. One of the detectives asked him who shot him.

"I don't know who shot me," said Schultz.

"You've got a serious wound," said the detective. "Why don't you tell us who did it."

"I don't know," replied Schultz. "I know I got bad cramps. Do something."

The police brought Schultz a drink and loaded him, still slumped in the chair, into the ambulance.

Once at the hospital, Schultz was given a dose of morphine to kill the pain, and questioned by deputy police chief John Haller.

"What happened, Dutch?" asked Haller.

"All I know," said Schultz, "is that I saw fire and sort of lost track of everything. Now I've told you the truth."

"You haven't told us who shot you," Haller said.

"I've told you everything I know," replied Schultz. "I don't know nothin'. I was in the tavern and some fellows came in shooting."

Under guard, Schultz was moved to a vacant four-bed ward on the second floor of the hospital to await surgery. Patrolman Timothy O'Leary sat next to him.

"Anything you want me to get for you," asked O'Leary.

"Yes," said Schultz. "I want a priest."[8]

This seemed a strange request coming from the son of German-Jewish parents. Yet some years earlier Lucky Luciano had noticed Arthur's interest in Catholicism. Once, Schultz had dropped in to visit Luciano during a meeting with Vito Genovese. "And I'll be damned if he didn't start to talk about the Catholic religion," recalled Luciano. "He wanted to know what it was like to be a Catholic; whether Vito and me ever went to confession, if we knew what a guy had to do to switch into Catholicism from bein' a Jew.

"I almost fell over when he told us that... in all his spare time he was studyin' to be a Catholic. I swear, from that minute on, the Dutchman spent more time on his knees than he did on his feet.

"It's funny. When I first started hangin' around with Jewish guys like Meyer and Bugsy and Dutch, them old guys Masseria and Maranzano and lots of my friends used to beef to me about it. They always said that some day the Jews was gonna make me turn and join the synagogue.

"So what happens? It ain't me that gets turned, it's the Dutchman. That's some joke."[9]

Schultz wanted to see Father Charles McInerney, a prison chaplain Schultz had met while in the Hudson County jail.

During Schultz's operation, McInerney sat on a bench in the corridor with the gangster's mother, Emma Flegenheimer, his sister Helen and Helen's husband Henry, who was called "Peanuts" because he took care of the vending machines in Schultz's speakeasies.

After surgery, Schultz rallied briefly but then began to decline. He became delirious and ranted incoherently, but in a lucid moment, he called for Father McInerney.

When the priest came in, Schultz asked to die a Catholic. McInerney baptized him and gave him the last rites of the Catholic Church.

Some hours later, Schultz fell into a deep coma. He died in the evening of October 24, 1935.

Immediately thereafter, Dr. Earl Snavely, the superintendent of the hospital, went into an adjoining room where the family waited. Walking directly to Arthur's mother, who rose as he approached, the doctor said, "Mrs. Flegenheimer, your son has died."

Schultz's mother fainted into the arms of her daughter.

Schultz was buried at the Gate of Heaven Cemetery in Westchester County. Father McInerney officiated and performed a fifteen-minute Catholic service, omitting the eulogy.

Schultz's mother waited until everyone had left, then took a Jewish prayer shawl and placed it over the coffin.[10]

By killing Schultz the syndicate saved Dewey's life. Dewey later showed his gratitude by prosecuting Buchalter and Luciano.

Jacob "Little Augie" Orgen was an early labor racketeer in New York who got his training as a slugger in the pre-World War I labor wars. In 1919, Jacob organized his own gang of musclemen, which included the young Lepke Buchalter and Legs Diamond, and fought a running battle with the forces of the much larger Nathan "Kid Dropper" Kaplan organization.

Kid Dropper was quite a character. When he began his criminal career, he was a sloppy and slovenly dresser. Once he became a gang leader, however, he dressed commensurate with his position, appearing along Broadway and the Lower East Side in a belted checked suit, narrow, pointed shoes, and shirts and neckties of weird designs and loud, garish colors. In summer he wore a straw hat with a narrow brim and brightly colored band. In the winter he wore a derby which he pulled rakishly over one eye. He let it be known that he preferred to be called Jack, and he named his gang "The Rough Riders of Jack the Dropper."

The two sides slaughtered each other, especially for control of the wet wash laundry workers. From 1922 to mid-1923 their war resulted in 23 murders.

In August 1923, Kid Dropper was arrested on a concealed weapons charge. As he entered a police car to be transferred to another court, a minor hoodlum named Louis Kushner jumped forward and shot him through the windshield.

Kushner nursed a grudge against Kaplan because Kid Dropper had attempted to blackmail him out of $500. Kid Dropper had damaging information about Kushner beating up a strike-breaker. Kushner, who was none too bright, also dreamed of being a great killer and seeing his name in the newspapers. He shot Kid Dropper for revenge and glory.

Kaplan collapsed inside the car while his wife fought through the police to reach her husband. "Nate, Nate," she cried. "Tell me that you were not what they say you were."

The Kid looked at her and gasped, "They got me," and died.

"I got him," crowed Kushner. "I'd like a cigarette."[11]

Kushner was convicted of murder and sentenced to serve from twenty years to life. He died in jail.

Little Augie immediately took control of Dropper's enterprises and was crowned "King of the East Side Gunmen." He retained the crown for only a few years.

On the evening of October 15, 1927, Orgen and his bodyguard Jack "Legs" Diamond were strolling along Norfolk Street on the Lower East Side. A black touring car with four men inside drove up alongside them. Lepke was behind the wheel; next to him, pistol in hand, sat Gurrah Shapiro. They were after Orgen only. Shapiro jumped out of the car, yelling for Diamond to move. Jack hugged the wall of a building as Shapiro fired. Little Augie fell to the ground, dead, a bullet in his head.

Diamond didn't move fast enough and was wounded in the arm and leg. After this brush with death, he felt it would be healthier to stay out of the labor rackets. When he recovered from his injuries, Diamond made peace with Lepke and Gurrah and concentrated on bootlegging and the narcotics trade.

Orgen was buried in a cherry-red coffin lined with white satin. On the lid gleamed a silver plate which read: "Jacob Orgen, Age 25 Years." His real age was thirty-three. But eight years had passed since he assumed active leadership of his gang. That same day his father, a religious Jew, had declared him dead.[12]

Lepke then took over New York's labor rackets.

Since Lepke was a leading exponent of contract killing, an explanation of this underworld enterprise is in order. "Contract" is a common English word which, in the underworld, means one thing — murder by hire. Once a contract is ordered, the procedure follows certain rules. To protect the person ordering the hit, he is isolated from the trigger man, never saying a word to him about the job. The contract is passed to a second party who selects the killer. Often the order will be passed on to yet another party. Since all the negotiations are handled on a one-to-one basis, it doesn't matter if someone along the line of command eventually talks. In order to make a conviction, the authorities need the corroboration of someone who knows the entire setup.

The actual killers are given the identity of the victim, background on his habits and a place where he can most likely be found. Sometimes they are given a spotter who points out the victim. Once the deed is done, the gunmen vanish, notifying no one but the person who gave them the specific orders. The information is then relayed up the line to the one who originally ordered the murder.

Frequently the hitmen are from out of town, making it harder for the local authorities to trace them. The police are left with a killing, few clues and no likely suspects, because often the killers do not even know their victim.

Authorities frequently learn the details of contract murders through informers, but this rarely leads to a conviction. For example, there were approximately 1,000 gangland executions in

Chicago from 1919 to 1967, but in only thirteen cases was there a conviction.[13]

Despite the portrayals in over-romanticized Hollywood gangster films, hitmen rarely make a deal with their intended victim. This would destroy their professional standing and reputation.

Gangland lore is filled with examples of men who were specialists in this line of work. Israel "Ice Pick Willie" Alderman got his moniker because he was supposed to have perfected this method of execution.

Ice Pick was a Minnesota mobster who was a close friend of Meyer Lansky in his bootlegging days and was later one of the first investors, along with Lansky, Bugsy Siegel and Moe Sedway, in Las Vegas gambling.

Willie ran a second story speakeasy in Minneapolis. He boasted of having committed eleven murders with his trusty ice pick there.

The ice pick method was favored by many hitmen because it made the victim's death appear to be the result of natural causes. Generally, the victim was cornered in some out-of-the-way place, and while two or three hitmen held him, the executioner jammed the ice pick through the eardrum into the brain. The pick produced only a tiny hole in the ear and a minute amount of bleeding which could be carefully wiped away. After examining the corpse, doctors generally concluded that the cause of death was a cerebral hemorrhage. Only a meticulous and expert medical examination could reveal the truth.

According to one source, Willie would engage his intended victim in a conversation and ply him with drinks. When the man was properly inebriated, Willie would shove the ice pick in his ear, then take his victim into a back room and dump his body down the laundry chute. The body would be disposed of later that evening.[14]

Another consummate professional hitman was Samuel "Red" Levine who achieved notoriety for a reason other than his work. Red was an Orthodox Jew, a strange man, devoted to his religion and his family but at the same time a killer. Born in Toledo, Ohio, Levine was hand-picked by Meyer Lansky and Lucky Luciano to kill Luciano's nemesis, Salvatore Maranzano, in 1931. After this killing, Luciano and his generation of gangsters took over and dominated the New York underworld.

Luciano called Red "the best driver and hitman I had." Luciano recalled that at home Levine always wore a skullcap, and if he was going to do a job during the Sabbath, from sundown Friday to sundown Saturday, he always wore a skullcap under his hat.

Whenever possible, Red tried not to kill anyone on the Sabbath. If he had no choice and had to make a hit on that particular day, he would put a talith (prayer shawl) over his shoulders and pray before doing anything.[15]

Perhaps the most famous professional killer in American gangster history was Harry "Pittsburgh Phil" Strauss. Phil killed more than 100 (some said over 400) men from the late 1920s to 1940, making him the most prolific killer New York, and perhaps syndicated crime, had ever produced.[16]

The Brooklyn-born Phil was so good that when an out-of-town mob needed someone eliminated, they almost always asked for him. Phil packed his briefcase with a shirt, a change of socks and underwear, a gun, a knife, a length of rope to tie or strangle his victims and an ice pick. He then hopped a train or plane to his destination, pulled the job and caught the next connection back to

New York. Often Phil didn't even know the name of the person he had killed, and he usually didn't care enough to find out.

Killing never seemed to bother Phil, but he did worry a great deal about his own health. Once, in the middle of beating a hood by the name of Puggy Feinstein, the victim, fighting for his life, bit Phil on the finger.

"The bastard bit me in the hand," yelled Phil, as he and his associates garroted Feinstein.

After the job was done, Strauss and some of the boys took Puggy's body to an empty lot, poured gasoline over it and set it ablaze. All the while Phil whined about the bite. "The son of a bitch give me some bite," he said.

The group adjourned to a local restaurant for a fish dinner. Phil, however, could not enjoy his meal. "Maybe I'll get lockjaw from being bit," he fretted. Despite assurances he would not, Phil could barely finish his meal.[17]

The autopsy report on George Rudnick shows the kind of work Phil was capable of. Rudnick was a small-time hood who Lepke Buchalter suspected of being an informer. Taking no chances, Buchalter wanted him eliminated and gave the contract to Pittsburgh Phil.

On May 11, 1937, Phil and some of his colleagues snatched Rudnick as he loitered on Livonia Avenue near Midnight Rose's store. A few hours later Rudnick's body was found in a stolen car at the other end of Brooklyn.

According to the medical examiner, "There were sixty-three stab wounds on the body. On the neck, I counted thirteen stab wounds between the jaw and collarbone. On the right chest, there were fifty separate circular wounds.... His face was intensely cyanic, or blue. The tongue protruded.... When the heart was laid open, the entire wall was found to be penetrated by stab wounds."[18]

Tall and handsome, with an athletic build, Phil was an elegant dresser with a special fondness for expensive suits. Lewis Valentine, New York City's police commissioner during the 1930s, once spotted Phil in a police lineup. "Look at him," exclaimed Valentine. "He's the best dressed man in the room and he's never worked a day in his life."

Phil had one redeeming quality: he was in love. The object of his affection was a beautiful Brooklyn girl named Evelyn Mittleman.

Longy Zwillman

Evelyn was dubbed "The Kiss of Death Girl," a sobriquet newspapers apply to women whose lovers appear to die at a much faster rate than is normal. Phil eliminated anyone he thought could be a rival for her affections.

It appears, however, that Evelyn had earned this nickname before Phil met her. Evelyn was a luscious blond who seemed to attract violent men. In 1933, at the age of eighteen, she was at a dance with her then current boyfriend, Hy Miller, when another man was taken by her looks. He tried to cut in and Miller objected. A fight ensued and Miller was killed. A couple of years later Evelyn was dating one Robert Feurer, when she caught the eye of a Brownsville gangster named Jack Goldstein. When Feurer objected to Jack's advances, Goldstein killed him. Goldstein became her new boyfriend.

One day in 1938, they happened to pass a Brownsville pool hall where Pittsburgh Phil saw them. Phil liked what he saw, and said so. Goldstein took offence at the remark and told Phil to buzz off. Phil went inside the poolhall, got a cue stick, and beat the daylights out of Goldstein. He then supplanted Goldstein as Evelyn's new paramour.

Goldstein was later killed by Phil, but not because of Evelyn. A contract was put out on Jack because of his racket activities, and a number of hitmen, led by Phil, were assigned the job. The men hammered Goldstein into unconsciousness, but did not kill him. Instead, they brought him directly to Phil, who insisted on drowning Goldstein personally.

Pittsburgh Phil was Evelyn's final victim. She was the last person to visit him in his death cell before he was executed for murder in 1941. Evelyn left off consorting with mob figures, married and faded from view.[19]

Phil had been put on death row by his erstwhile pal and fellow killer-for-hire, Abe Reles. Reles had been arrested in February 1940, along with several other Brooklyn hoodlums, for allegedly murdering a petty burglar and small-time crook named Alexander "Red" Alpert.

At the time he was picked up, Reles sported a rap sheet that contained 42 arrests, accumulated over a sixteen-year period, for robbery, assault, burglary, possession of narcotics and homicide. He never served time for any major charge.

Abe was squat and ugly, with thick, powerful fingers which he used to twist the necks of his victims. This skill earned him his underworld nickname, "Kid Twist."[20]

Kid Twist started in racketeering in 1927 as a hooligan. He began murdering in 1930 when he put together his own gang to take over in the Brownsville section of Brooklyn. He never stopped racketeering and he never stopped killing. According to his own account, he committed eleven murders, not counting the times he participated but didn't pull the trigger, or the times where he held one end of the strangling rope but, as he claimed, "had not yanked it."

Nothing fazed Abe. In 1934, he was sentenced to three years for assault, breaking a bottle of oil over the head of a garage attendant who hadn't gotten to his car fast enough. Before pronouncing sentence, the judge admonished Reles severely.

"Reles is one of the most vicious characters we have had in years," he said. "I am convinced he will eventually either be sentenced to prison for life, or be put out of the way by some good detective with a couple of bullets."

Reles listened with a sneer on his face. When the judge finished,

Abe leaned over and whispered in his lawyer's ear. Reles' attorney repeated his client's message to the court.

"I will take on any cop in the city with pistols, fists or anything else," Reles said. "A cop counts to fifteen when he puts his finger on the trigger before he shoots."

Abe never counted.

When the police arrested him in 1940, Reles proved to be a tough cookie. The police had little hope of making him crack. Luckily for the authorities, one of the men picked up with Reles began to talk and Reles feared he would be implicated. In addition, Reles's wife Rose was pregnant. She implored her husband to cooperate with the authorities to save his life so the baby would have a father. He agreed.

Reles's wife went to assistant district attorney Burton Turkus. Weeping, she cried "I want to save my husband from the electric chair. My baby is coming in June." Recovering her composure, she added, "My husband wants to talk to you."[21]

Reles made a deal. If he was not prosecuted for any of the murders he had participated in, he would talk. The District Attorney swallowed hard and agreed, and Reles began to sing. He told the police about fifty homicides he and his friends had committed in New York, New Jersey, Detroit, Louisville, Los Angeles and Kansas City. At the end of twelve days of testimony, the prosecutors had twenty-five notebooks filled with stenographers' shorthand record. Later investigation proved Reles' information to be entirely accurate, down to the last detail.

Abe became one of the most famous stool pigeons in criminal history, furnishing prosecutors with the particulars of 85 New York murders and hundreds more nationwide. Not only did he put his friends Pittsburgh Phil, Happy Maione, Dasher Abbandando and

Buggsy Goldstein in the electric chair, but he provided prosecutor Burton Turkus with insight into the workings of the Brooklyn-based gang of murderers for hire.

An incredulous Turkus finally asked Reles how he brought himself to take human life so casually. "Did your conscience ever bother you?" asked Turkus. "Didn't you feel anything?"

"How did you feel when you tried your first law case?" countered Reles.

"I was rather nervous," Turkus admitted.

"And how about your second case," asked Reles.

"It wasn't so bad, but I was still a little nervous," said Turkus.

"And after that," asked Reles.

"Oh, after that, I was alright. I was used to it," answered Turkus.

"You answered your own question," said Reles. "It's the same with murder. I got used to it."[22]

Just how matter-of-fact Reles could be about killing is illustrated by a story that Itzik Goldstein, a Newark bar owner and driver for Doc Stacher, swears is true. Reles and his pal Buggsy Goldstein were sitting in Midnight Rose's candy store when a fellow named Johnny approached them and asked, "Do you know if Angelo hangs around here?"

"Yeah, he hangs around," said Reles, "but I don't know where he is. Would you like to leave a message?"

"Yeah. Tell him Johnny was here."

Unbeknownst to Johnny, Reles had a contract to kill him.

"This was on Friday afternoon," says Itzik, "and Reles used to go to his mother's house every Friday evening to have a traditional Sabbath meal of gefilte fish, chicken soup with noodles and boiled chicken.

"So he says to this fellow Johnny, 'Why don't you come up to the house and have something to eat. In the meantime, maybe we will run into your friend."

Having nothing better to do, Johnny accepted.

Reles and Goldstein escorted Johnny to Reles's mother's home where she made dinner for the three of them. Reles then sent his mother to the movies.

When she was gone, Reles and Goldstein bludgeoned and strangled Johnny. "They carried his body into the bathroom," says Itzik, "and dumped it in the bathtub. They chopped the body into pieces and put it into bags." Then they dragged the bags down to Goldstein's car. Goldstein took the bags to an unknown destination and incinerated them.

Meanwhile, Reles quickly but carefully cleaned up the bathroom and waited for his mother to return. When she came home, he joined her in a cup of tea and a piece of honey cake.[23]

Reles's testimony helped build a successful case against Lepke Buchalter, as well as two of Lepke's aides, Louis Capone and Mendy Weiss, who were convicted of killing truck company owner Joseph Rosen.

By this time, Lucky Luciano, Frank Costello, Albert Anastasia, Bugsy Siegel and other top mob figures began to worry. Reles knew too much and no one knew where this would end. "If he keeps on goin'," Costello told Luciano, "they're gonna get everybody for murder."[24]

Reles had to be stopped. The problem was how. To secure their star witness, the police had put Reles under protective custody on the sixth floor of the Half Moon Hotel in the Coney Island section of Brooklyn. He was guarded around the clock by two policemen and three plainclothes detectives.

Sometime before seven o'clock in the morning of November 12,

1941, the hotel's assistant manager heard a "thud" on the extension roof beneath Reles's room, but he ignored it. When the room was checked, Reles was missing. His fully dressed body was found on the ground more than twenty feet from the wall of the building. Two knotted bedsheets were laying nearby.

Theories on how it happened abounded. The police said Reles must have tried to escape by twisting bedsheets together and using them for a rope. However, the knotted bedsheets gave way and he fell 42 feet to his death. Another theory was that Reles became conscience-stricken over his past and fearful of his future, and committed suicide.

Neither of these, or other theories, explain how the 160-pound Reles landed twenty feet from the wall. He only could have done so if he had wings.

Lots of people wanted Reles dead. His closest pals relished seeing him in a coffin. Buggsy Goldstein's only objection to dying in the electric chair was that he couldn't hold Reles's hand when it happened.

Pittsburgh Phil told an attorney he wanted to get into the same room with Reles just so he could sink his teeth in his jugular vein. "I didn't worry about the chair," he said, "if I could just tear his throat out first."

In 1961, Lucky Luciano told his biographer that it cost upwards of $50,000 to get rid of Reles. "The whole bunch of cops was on the take," he said. "Reles was sleepin' and one of the cops give him a tap with a billy and knocked him out. Then they picked him up and heaved him out the window. For Chrissake, he landed so far from the wall he couldn't't've done that even if he had jumped."[25]

No one was ever prosecuted for Reles's death, and the entire underworld heaved a collective sigh of relief.

There have been few hoodlums in American history more infamous than Bugsy Siegel. By the age of twenty-one, his police charge sheet included assault, white-slavery, dope dealing, bootlegging, hijacking, rape, extortion, robbery, bookmaking, the numbers racket and murder. He was ruthless and wild, with a reckless disregard for danger. His fits of temper became an underworld legend.

In 1981, NBC-TV produced a miniseries titled *The Gangster Chronicles,* supposedly based on the lives of Meyer Lansky, Bugsy Siegel and Lucky Luciano. Meyer Lansky, retired in Florida, enjoyed watching the program with his friends. The men and their wives kept up a running commentary on the actions portrayed on the screen.

One of Lansky's pals, Benny Sigelbaum, took exception to the depiction of Bugsy as a violent and unthinking hoodlum.

"The television company should be sued," he said.

"What are you going to sue them for," Lansky asked, laughing. "In real life, he was even worse."[26]

Benny Newman's barbershop in Newark often served as a meeting place for Longy Zwillman and his associates.[27] Itzik Goldstein remembers going into Newman's barbershop one day in 1938. "When I'm walking in, Benny walked over to me and says, 'Itzik, you know that fella sitting on that chair?'

"I says, I don't know him. I says, why do you ask?

"He says, 'Look, he's sitting there naked. Took off all his clothes.'

"At that time, they didn't have no air-conditioning. I said, I don't know him. So I sat down. I was waiting for Doc [Stacher] to come in.

"So Doc came in and Longy came in and they went into the back

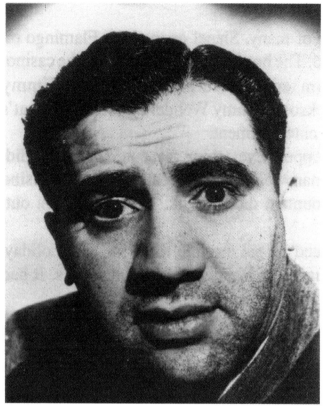

Abe Reles

room. And this fella, they were probably just about through shaving him, gets up. And he was looking in the mirror, standing there naked.

"I was looking at him. He was nice looking, a handsome looking fella. I didn't know who he was.

"He puts on his pants, and a jacket and a tie, and he went in the back. Then he comes out and leaves.

"Now, I get in the car with Doc and I was driving. I says to Doc, 'Who was that fella sitting there naked? Benny Newman told me he walked in there and took off all his clothes.'

"Doc says, 'That's Bugsy Siegel.'

"I said, 'Really.'

"He says, 'Don't you recognized him?'

"I says, 'I never met him.'

"He says, 'Well, they had his picture in the paper. I thought maybe you recognized him from the paper.'

"I says, 'No. That was Bugsy Siegel?'

"He says, 'Yeah. If you ever meet him, don't call him Bugsy, call him Ben, 'cause he'll get mad. He don't like the name Bugsy.'

"That was funny, him sitting there naked, just with his shorts on, getting a shave.

"Maybe that's why they called him Bugsy, 'cause he was crazy. Who knows.

"But he had a lot of nerve to walk into a strange barbershop and take off all his clothes."[28]

Dating back to Prohibition, Siegel was good friends with Meyer Lansky, Lepke Buchalter, Lucky Luciano, Abner Zwillman, Frank Costello, Joe Adonis, Johnny Torrio, Al Capone, Jake Guzik and Tony Accardo, to name just a few of America's better-known mobsters. Everyone who knew Ben either admired or feared him, sometimes both.

Siegel had an advantage over his compatriots. He was handsome and a sharp dresser. His taste ran to broad snapped-brim hats, pin-striped suits with high-waisted trousers and pegged cuffs, exquisitely tailored overcoats with fur-lined collars, hand-crafted shoes with pointed toes, and handmade silk shirts. Everything was monogrammed, right down to his tailored silk shorts

Bugsy also pursued a high-class life. He moved into a suite in the Waldorf Astoria, rode around in a bullet-proof, chauffeur-driven limousine and was accompanied by two bodyguards wherever he went. Siegel dined in the finest restaurants and spent his evenings frolicking in nightclubs and speakeasies.[29]

Dinner with Bugsy was sometimes more than just a pleasant meal.

Beatrice Sedway, the wife of Bugsy's pal, Moe, remembers the time she and her husband dined with Siegel and some friends at an Italian restaurant. "We had a big table spread out, and there was windows, big windows," she said.

"All of a sudden a car comes around and starts machine-gunning the window, and Ben yells, 'Down!'

"There was a ladies' room back of us. I started slithering on my tummy. And there was a space above the ladies' room where the entrance was, and I went in and stood up on the seats so nobody could see my feet, and I just stayed there.

"I saw Ben and the boys tip up the table for protection and duck. In a little while Moe came to the door and he said, 'Honey, you can come out now'."

Beatrice came out not knowing what to expect. She was relieved to find that no one had been hurt. "The table was all set again with new antipasti, and nothing was ever mentioned. That was it."[30]

In 1937, Bugsy's associates sent him out to Los Angeles to consolidate and expand their business on the West Coast. They couldn't have chosen a better ambassador. Before long, the charming Mr. Siegel was hobnobbing with the Hollywood elite and having well-publicized affairs with some of the film industry's most beautiful women. His growing notoriety made Siegel's associates back east nervous and they began to worry.

Ben calmed their fears by doing a splendid job for them. He formed a coalition of top mobs and brought order to what had been a chaotic situation. He made the local Mafia chieftain, Jack Dragna, his lieutenant and together they reorganized the narcotics, prostitution and bookmaking rackets. Bugsy also spent thousands of dollars buying politicians and police. By the end of 1945, Siegel had the California crime situation well in hand and turned his attention to another state, Nevada.

Nevada had legalized gambling, but its two largest cities, Reno and Las Vegas, were little more than desert watering holes. Siegel visited Las Vegas in 1941 and was struck by its potential as a gambling center. He envisioned the place as eventually encompassing dozens of hotels and casinos that would serve the country's high rollers. It could be a bonanza for the underworld.

Few shared his enthusiasm. Many years later, Meyer Lansky recalled his visits there during the 1940s. "It was in sorry shape," said Lansky. "Living conditions were bad. No one wanted to go to Vegas to gamble. Air connections were bad. And the trip by car was bothersome. It was so hot that the wires in the car would melt."[31]

But Bugsy had a dream. He wanted to own the grandest, most magnificent gambling casino in the world. It would not be just a casino, but a luxurious hotel with a nightclub, bars, swimming pools, fountains, landscaped gardens, and the finest service available.

His enthusiasm was contagious and his partners back east agreed to finance his dream. In 1946, Siegel moved to Las Vegas. His wife Esta went to Reno and got a divorce.

Siegel and his partners bought a two-thirds interest in a financially troubled hotel being built by Billy Wilkerson, the owner of the *Hollywood Reporter* and the man who had created a number of successful Hollywood night spots. The name of the hotel was the Flamingo.

Ben set a deadline for the completion of the hotel: Christmas

1946. He hired the Del Webb Construction Company of Phoenix, Arizona and began to build. Siegel demanded the latest innovations and used the most expensive materials. Since postwar steel, copper and other items were scarce, Siegel went to the black market, sparing no expense. The cost was originally calculated at $1.5 million, but it quickly doubled to $3 million.

To the surprise of many, Siegel opened the Flamingo on December 26, 1946. The hotel wasn't finished, but the casino, lounge, showroom and restaurant were all open for business. Jimmy Durante, Eddie Jackson, Tommy Wonder and Xavier Cugat's band provided the entertainment.

Still, the opening flopped. Everything that could go wrong, did. Bad weather kept many celebrities from attending. The casino lost money. The fountain didn't work. The lights went out. And Bugsy had a fit.

Bad luck plagued Siegel throughout the New Year holiday. At the end of January, the Flamingo closed its doors, having been open less than a month.

Siegel asked his friends for more money. They grumbled, but Meyer Lansky and Frank Costello gave him the money he needed to finish the hotel.

The Flamingo reopened in March 1947 and Siegel was told in no uncertain terms that this time the hotel had better show a profit.[32]

It did, but not fast enough to suit Ben's partners. Moreover, they began to suspect Bugsy of cheating them. Meyer Lansky allegedly learned that Siegel's paramour, Virginia Hill, was making regular trips to Switzerland, buying fancy clothes and depositing money in a numbered bank account. If Siegel was in financial straits, where was Virginia getting the money from?[33]

A meeting was held to discuss "the Siegel Situation." According to Lucky Luciano, Meyer Lansky said, "there's only one thing to do with a thief who steals from his friends. Benny's got to be hit." A vote was taken and the result was unanimous.

Bugsy was as good as dead.

On the night of June 20, 1947, Siegel was sitting on the chintz-covered sofa in Virginia Hill's home on North Linden Drive, Beverly Hills, reading the *Los Angeles Times*. Siegel's close friend Allen Smiley sat across from him. Charles Hill, Virginia's brother, was in a bedroom upstairs with his girlfriend.

Someone rested a .30 caliber army carbine on the latticework outside the window and squeezed the trigger.

The first bullet crashed through the window into Siegel's head, blowing his right eye out. It was later found fifteen feet from his body. Another shot smashed his left eye, broke his nose and shattered a vertebra in the back of his neck. There were seven more shots, all of which missed.[34]

Siegel never knew what hit him.

Bugsy always said, "Live fast, die young and have a good-looking corpse." He looked anything but good when he died.

About twenty minutes after the shooting, and just as the police began to arrive, Gus Greenbaum and Moe Sedway strode into the Flamingo and announced to the staff that the hotel was under new management.[35]

Meyer Lansky always denied having anything to do with the killing. "Ben Siegel was my friend until his final day," he told Israeli journalist Uri Dan. "I never quarreled with him. If it was in my power to see Benny alive, he would live as long as Methuselah." Meyer believed that Lucky Luciano ordered the hit. Despite Lansky's denials, however, the rumor persists that Siegel would not have been killed without Meyer's okay.[36]

Only five mourners attended Siegel's funeral: Esta Siegel, his ex-wife; Millicent and Barbara, his teenage daughters; his brother Dr. Maurice Siegel, a respected Beverly Hills physician; and Bessie Soloway, his favorite sister. To observers, it seemed odd that none of Siegel's friends or associates came to pay their last respects.[37]

Bugsy's killers were never found.

By 1954, Abner "Longy" Zwillman was a tired man. He had spent most of his adult life bossing crime in New Jersey, and now he wanted out. In 1951, the televised Kefauver Crime Committee hearings exposed Longy as one of "the top gangsters in America" and, in one swoop, the facade of respectability he had built up over the years fell away. He was never again the same person. Photographs taken of Longy after the hearings show him looking sullen and worried.

He had turned his organization over to his Italian lieutenant, Gerry Catena, and planned to enjoy a life of leisure with his friends and family. Or so he thought.

In 1956, after two years of investigation, the Internal Revenue Service brought Longy to trial for evading income taxes in the years 1947 and 1948. After a month-long trial, the jury reported that it was hopelessly deadlocked. No new trial date was set. It appeared that Longy could retire after all.[38]

But in 1959, the FBI arrested a number of Longy's associates for "offering money to... influence the decision of the jury in the Zwillman tax-evasion case."[39]

The FBI had installed a microphone in the office of Herman Cohen, one of Longy's close associates and friends. In January of that year, the agent monitoring the bug heard Cohen discussing how the jurors were bribed. Sam Katz, Longy's confidante, chauffeur and bodyguard, was mentioned as one of the payoff men.[40]

The authorities arrested Katz, but he never stood trial. He plea-bargained, pleading guilty, and received six years in prison. He could have gotten out in two if he had implicated Longy. His friendship with Zwillman and his personal code of honor kept him silent.

Years later Katz described how one went about finding the right juror to bribe.

"You have to be scientific about it," he said. "You hire private dicks sometime. You go to the man's neighborhood. You check with neighbors, friends, relatives. You claim you're a private eye, and you need information because the person you're checking may come into a large sum of money. That ain't a lie is it?

"When you get a line on somebody — he needs money badly, he has a mistress his wife doesn't know about, he gambles or drinks, something — you have a lever."[41]

Katz's arrest and the ongoing IRS and FBI probes of his affairs troubled Longy and allowed him no rest. Subpoenas, indictments and litigation were nothing he looked forward to.

In addition, Longy had been experiencing severe chest pains for more than a year. They began to concern him and he consulted his personal physician, Dr. Arthur Bernstein. After examining him, Bernstein told Longy that he suffered from a serious heart ailment and high blood pressure. Bernstein remembers Longy becoming depressed.[42]

Meanwhile, the underworld was awash with rumors that Longy would talk to save his skin.

On the morning of February 26, 1959, West Orange Police Chief Thomas F. Mulvhill got a call that there had been "an accident" at

Mickey Cohen

Longy Zwillman's home. He dispatched Lt. George Bamford to investigate.

Bamford took one look at the "accident" and called the prosecutor's office and the medical examiner.

He had found Longy hanging by a plastic electric cord, grasping one part of the cord in his left hand. He was dressed in a checked bathrobe, striped pajamas, brown leather slippers and socks. The pocket of his robe contained twenty-one tablets of the tranquilizer Reserpine. A half-empty bottle of Kentucky bourbon stood on a table near the body.

After an investigation, the prosecutor ruled Zwillman's death "a suicide due to temporary insanity." Nevertheless, questions remain.

Longy's body showed unexplained bruises, and there were strong indications that his hands had been tied with some kind of wire. To kill himself, Zwillman would have had to tie one end of the cord around his neck, throw the other end over an exposed beam in the ceiling, and slump downward while holding the loose end in his hand until he suffocated. Very difficult and cumbersome to say the least.

Longy's friend Itzik Goldstein does not believe this verdict.

"They claim he committed suicide," says Itzik. "I doubt it.

"I met him in a steak joint up in West Orange. It was a Monday or Tuesday. He was sitting in a booth, him and his wife and another couple. I told the maitre d' to give that party there a drink. He came back and said they're leaving right away.

"Abe got up and said 'Hello, Itzik, how are you.'

"I said, 'All right.'

Then Goldstein recounts, "I was hanging around in a place off

Springfield Avenue, in a club. And a guy calls me up and says, 'Itzik, they just killed Longy.' This was on a Wednesday or Thursday.

"I said, 'You're full of shit. I just seen him the other day.'

"I put the radio on. Sure enough. They found him hung in his basement.

"Now me, personally, I think he was killed. Abe didn't drink no bourbon. He hated bourbon. He used to drink brandy. They found two, three glasses, and a bottle of bourbon there.

"Somebody must have come in, must have said listen, if you don't do what we tell you to do, we'll go up and kill your whole fucking family. He had his wife and kids there.

"They went down the cellar and they strung him up. That's what I think."[43]

Lucky Luciano also expressed skepticism about Longy's suicide.

"Suicide over tax problems? That's bullshit," Luciano said. "They murdered Longy. He tried to put the arm on Carlo (Gambino) after Vito (Genovese) got his sentence. What the hell, the poor guy was part of us for a long time and there was enough money around to give him a hand.

"But the guys in Brooklyn was afraid he'd do a Reles. So they beat him up and trussed him up like a pig and hung him in his own cellar."[44]

Meyer Lansky believed that Vito Genovese had Zwillman killed. "Genovese was behind that killing," said Lansky. "He just ordered his killers to make it look like Zwillman had taken his own life."

According to Lansky, many people at the time believed that Zwillman killed himself. "Longy was in trouble with the tax people," said Lansky, and was worried about the effect of the publicity on his family. The theory was that Longy committed suicide in order to spare his family from additional publicity and embarrassment. Lansky adamantly discounted this.

"It was a Genovese murder. I know," he said.[45]

Zwillman's funeral took place twenty-four hours after he died. It was a simple ceremony held in a funeral parlor a few doors down from his boyhood home in Newark's Third Ward. Rabbi Joachim Prinz, president of the American Jewish Congress, officiated.

In brief remarks, Rabbi Prinz called for "understanding, comfort and love" for members of the Zwillman family. He termed Longy a "loving husband, a devoted father and a kind son."[46]

About 350 people crowded inside the funeral parlor while another 1,500 stood outside.

One hundred red roses covered Longy's coffin. As the casket was wheeled out, Longy's 80-year-old mother sobbed, "Abele, Abele, my son, my son."

Zwillman was buried at B'nai Abraham Memorial Cemetery, in Union, New Jersey. After the *kaddish*, the traditional mourner's prayer, was recited, Longy's coffin was lowered into a concrete vault in the ground.[47]

Yet despite the mob bosses' apparent success in hitting their man, they did not always accomplish their goal. Mickey Cohen is a case in point.

Cohen was born in Brooklyn in 1913, the sixth child of poor Russian Jewish immigrants. Mickey's father, a produce worker, died when he was two months old. Seven months later his mother moved to California, taking Mickey and leaving her other children with relatives.[48]

Mickey started selling newspapers at the age of eight and began hanging around a gym. He got a job as a sparring partner, dropped out of school in the sixth grade, and began fighting as a bantamweight at thirteen.

When his mother remarried, Cohen ran away to Cleveland to be a boxer. The "natural step" for a washed up pugilist in those days, he said, was "to wind up in the racket or gambling world." By the time he was nineteen, he was running with an outlaw gang in Cleveland.[49]

In 1938, Cohen transferred his illegal activities to Chicago, then to Los Angeles, where he worked in Bugsy Siegel's bookmaking operations. After Siegel's death in 1947, Cohen tried to continue Bugsy's business and to emulate his lifestyle.

Mickey lived in Brentwood, California in a $120,000 mansion surrounded by an electric fence and spotlights, and containing closets filled with expensive suits and shoes. In 1948, he bought a clothing store on Santa Monica Boulevard called "Michael's Exclusive Haberdashery," invested in a supermarket chain and promoted prizefighters. Mickey traveled everywhere in a Cadillac, followed by another car carrying his armed "helpers," and enjoyed escorting beautiful showgirls to Los Angeles nightspots.[50]

The Los Angeles Mafia boss, Jack Dragna, had deferred to Bugsy Siegel, but he was not about to do the same with Cohen. He made numerous attempts to kill Mickey, but each one failed.

In 1949, Dragna's men bombed Cohen's home twice, once with a torpedo and once with dynamite. The first attempt failed; the second shattered every window in the house and blew a huge hole in his bedroom wall. Mickey, his wife, his dog and his maid were shaken but unharmed. What upset Mickey most of all was that more than forty suits, each costing $300, were shredded into rags.

On another occasion that year, a Dragna gunman blasted away

at Mickey with both barrels of a shotgun as he drove home late one night. The car was peppered with shot, but Mickey was untouched.

Mickey survived another shooting in August 1949, when two gunmen opened up at him with shotguns as he was leaving a restaurant with a group of friends. Mickey bent over to examine a scratch on his car just as they squeezed the trigger. His bodyguard and a movie starlet were seriously wounded. Mickey took a slug in the shoulder and survived.[51]

None of this surprised Mickey. "Throughout my career in the racket world, the element of force and violence was something that was expected of you. You didn't ask any questions when you were told to do something, you just did it," he said. "But whenever you're asked to do something against somebody, it was always somebody in the racket world who had an in for you. And that guy would do it to you just as fast as you would do it to him."[52]

He knew Jack Dragna was behind the attempts on his life, but did not hold it against him. It was all part of the "line of work" they were in. "I don't call a man a son of a bitch who's in a walk of life that calls for him to be a son of a bitch," he said.[53]

During the Kefauver Committee hearings on organized crime in 1950, the committee's counsel, Mr. Halley, asked Cohen whether it was not a fact that he lived "surrounded by violence."

"What do you mean, that I am surrounded by violence," sputtered Cohen. "I have not murdered anybody. All the shooting has been done at me. What do you mean, I am surrounded by violence, because people are shooting at me?" he asked indignantly.

"People are shooting at me," Cohen said, turning to the committee, "and he (Halley) is asking me if I am surrounded by violence."[54]

Jack Dragna never got Mickey, but the Internal Revenue Service did. He served four years the first time in 1952, and ten years of a fifteen-year sentence the second time in 1962.

Mickey emerged from prison in 1972, partially paralyzed as a result of being hit over the head by a convict wielding a lead pipe in 1963. Mickey claimed he didn't know why the man tried to kill him.

Cohen spent his last years in reduced circumstances in a rented apartment in West Los Angeles. He died in 1976.[55]

Despite all its so-called glamour and the lure of the good life, most gangsters paid a terrible price for doing what they did.

Appearing before the parole board in 1933, Jack Guzik said that he had "a hard life."

"What do you mean, dragging down $25,000 and $50,000 a month," asked Arthur Wood, chairman of the parole board. "That isn't very hard."

"The gambling life is a hard life," answered Guzik.

"How so?" queried Wood.

"Nervous, dangerous," answered Jack.

"Dangerous, what do you mean," asked Wood.

"You are liable to be held up," said Guzik. "Lot of things can happen."

The fear of "things" happening led Guzik to carry large sums of money with him, sometimes as much as $25,000, wherever he went. "With a roll like this," he explained, "I don't have to worry about getting kidnapped. I just give the dough to the guys who want to snatch me and they go away satisfied."[56]

Doc Stacher was another one who took precautions, albeit of a different sort, to protect himself. Doc had a fear of being "hit" while he slept, so he continually invited friends to spend the night with him. Once he asked Itzik Goldstein to sleep over. Itzik was warned by his friend Hymie Kugel, who knew Stacher well and had himself slept there, not to do it.

"Don't sleep there, Itzik," said Hymie, "because you won't have a minute's rest. All night long Doc'll ask you what time it is and keep coughing and hocking."

"Well, the next day," recalls Itzik, "Doc says, 'Listen, why don't you move in here?' I couldn't say no, so I slept there one night.

"He had a folding bed. There was a foyer. You had to walk in this way and there was this bedroom over there.

"I said, 'Where do I sleep?'

"He says, 'Move that bed over by my door.'

"I stuck the bed by his door. He's got the door open. 'Here,' he says, 'put it closer to my door.'

"I didn't sleep all fucking night. They're killing people, and this cocksucker wants me to sleep by his door. In case they do come in, he'll jump out the window.

"I said, 'Listen Joe, I'd like to sleep here, but my mother's all alone.'

"Hymie told me right. All night long, at least half a dozen times, he asks, 'What time is it, Itzik?' Then I hear, 'Hock, spit. Hock, spit. ' Hocking like that all night.

"He was a nice fellow, but he was worried someone would knock him off."[57]

All of this uncertainty and tension could make a weaker man nervous and ill. That's what it did to Moe Sedway, whose real name was Morris Sidwirtz. He was a long-time associate and front man for Bugsy Siegel, and became a vice-president of the Flamingo Hotel after Siegel was killed.

Moe was born in Poland in 1894 and came to the United States with his parents in 1900. He grew up on the lower East Side of New

York where he attended public school till the age of fifteen. Moe began his criminal career working for Waxy Gordon. His rap sheet included arrests for assault, robbery, vagrancy, and conspiracy.

FBI files describe Moe as "a dwarf Jewish boy with all the worst traits of his nationality over-emphasized… Prone to be a snappy dresser, vain to the point of being boresome and in his own mind a terrific woman killer. Being deprived of physical power, Sedway relies upon his natural tendency to bargain and frequently follows the bribery theory. During periods of stress he wrings his hands, becomes wild-eyed and resembles a small dog about to be subjected to the distasteful procedure of being bathed. Sedway's obsessions are monogrammed silk shirts and silk underwear, as well as well-manicured hands."[58]

This characterization says as much about the predilection of J. Edgar Hoover and his attitude toward Jews as it does about Sedway.

Testifying before the Kefauver Committee, Sedway complained that he had "three major coronary thromboses, and I have had diarrhea for 6 weeks, and I have an ulcer, hemorrhoids, and an abscess on my upper intestines."

After listening to this list of ailments, Senator Tobey asked Sedway, "If you had your life to live over again, would you play the same kind of a game again?"

"No, sir," said Sedway.

"You are in cahoots with a lot of people like Bugsy Siegel," said Tobey, "and you wonder whether it pays or not or what it amounts to, and why men do these things."

"Senator, you see what it got for me," replied Sedway, "three coronaries and ulcers."

"What does it all amount to?" asked Tobey. "Why do men play

the game this way? What makes it attractive to them? What is the matter with men?"

"Just go into that type of business and you get into it and you stay in it," answered Sedway.

"When decent men want to make a living, these men peel it off," said Tobey. "They may have money, but that is all they have got."

"We don't get as rich as you think we do," said Sedway. "This is hard work. I work pretty hard in this business."

"But you get the rich end all the time," said Tobey. "If you put the same talent you have got toward constructive things in life, producing something that makes real wealth and human happiness, men would arise and call you blessed."

"You asked me if I would want to do it over again," said Sedway. "I would not do it over again. I would not want my children to do it again."[59]

This attitude, of not wanting one's children to follow in one's footsteps, characterized the Jewish gangster. For him, like other Jewish parents, the family always came first.

Chapter Seven

The Family
Came First

*"T*he people in my walk of life that I've been associated with throughout... the top Jews... they always had a very, very strong family tie," said Mickey Cohen. "Even if they had an outside broad they fooled with, they only looked upon her as a broad. They still kept the highest regard and respect for their family.... We had a code of ethics like the ones among bankers, other people in other walks of life, that one never involved his wife or family in his work."[1]

As ruthless and violent as they may have been, Jewish gangsters adhered to this code throughout their lives.

Dave Berman was a good example of this. Born in Russia in 1904, he came to the United States with his parents one year later and grew up in Ashley, North Dakota, and Sioux City, Iowa.[2]

Very early, Dave displayed the aggressiveness and toughness that characterized him all his life. Those who knew him remember that "he was always looking for an angle" to make extra money. Like so many other children of immigrants, Davie sold newspapers, buying the papers for a penny apiece and selling them for two cents, or three for a nickel. He turned all the money he earned over to his mother.

His fearlessness led him to become the protector of the Jewish newsboys. Once, when he and the other newsboys were in a drugstore drinking sodas, two big, strapping farm boys walked in. One of them glared at the Jewish boys, and in a loud voice announced that "for a penny, I'd kill a Jew today."

Davie went to the cash register and got change for a nickel. He then walked over to the much bigger boy, dropped a penny on the counter in front of him and said, "I'm a Jew, take me on."

In a flash, both boys were on the floor, punching, biting and kicking each other. The bigger boy's friend jumped in, followed by the newsboys, battering each other with their fists and chairs. Blood was everywhere. When it looked like the bigger boys might kill the smaller ones, Davie pulled a knife and the farm boys fled.

Davie's friends regarded him with awe. As he put the knife away, he remarked, "You've got to use what you have to get by." This became his lifelong motto.

He soon discovered that he would never earn the kind of money he wanted by selling papers or working in a shop or store. Looking for another career, he chose gambling. Berman began hanging around the Chicago House Hotel, running errands for local and visiting gamblers. They liked Davie and taught him the tricks of their trade.

Berman was a good pupil and rapidly mastered the art of rigging and cheating. He learned how to mark cards, to conceal tiny mirrors in the palm of his hand and to use loaded dice in crap games. At fifteen, Davie could beat anyone in Sioux City at pool, poker and shooting dice. Seeing a bright future for himself in his chosen profession, he dropped out of school.

By the age of sixteen, Davie was working full-time for Sioux City's gamblers. Because he was tough and good with his fists, they used him as a debt collector. Berman saw his opportunity and took it, putting together a gang of local hoodlums and hiring them out to gamblers. After the boys administered their first few beatings, the mere threat to send Davie and his friends to see someone was enough to get the debts paid.

Before he was seventeen, Berman had his own apartment and wore fashionable clothes. He was tall, at 5 feet ten inches, lean and with high cheekbones. His friends referred to him as "Dave the Dude."

Davie never forgot his parents. He kept them supplied with the finest cuts of kosher meat and a steady supply of fresh fruit and vegetables. He bought his mother beautiful clothes and regularly gave his father money. His parents accepted his generosity.

When Prohibition came, Berman became a bootlegger. Still a teenager, Davie rode shotgun in the back of cars and trucks transporting illegal booze to and from Iowa.

Almost every night, lines of black automobiles filled with whiskey moved along Highway 75 north from Sioux City to Winnipeg, Manitoba, in Canada. The trip took three days and hijackings became an almost daily occurrence.

Between 1922 and 1926, over two hundred Sioux City bootleggers lost their lives in the city's "Beer Wars." Berman took part in many of the battles and his reputation as a gunman grew.

After a year of working for others, Berman became self-employed. By 1921, he operated twenty distillery plants. Using muscle and guns, Berman and his gang absorbed smaller bootlegging enterprises until he commanded the largest bootlegging syndicate in Iowa. Dave protected his operation by paying off the local politicians and police.

His family still had no idea of what he did for a living. All they knew was that he was in some kind of "business." Davie's parents saw less and less of their son, but he still supported them generously. Berman also distributed money to his relatives, and when his sister Lillian married, he paid for a huge and lavish wedding.

In 1923, just before his twentieth birthday, Berman was caught holding up a poker game at the Grand Hotel in Watertown, South Dakota and was arrested for the first time. He was sentenced to eight months in jail.

Berman's parents couldn't believe it was true. Davie said it was all a mistake and refused to let them visit him in jail. After his release, he returned to Sioux City with his status enhanced.

In 1925, Berman branched out from bootlegging to robbing banks and post offices, leading an ethnically mixed gang of Irish and Jewish hoodlums. One of the Irish members once described Berman as the bravest man in the gang. "You knew he'd take the rap first if we ever got caught. And Davie was fair," he said. "He carried an equalizer (gun), but nobody ever wanted to push him to use it."

Berman's technique for robbing a bank or post office was the same. He would take one trusted man with him and drive to a small town far from Sioux City. Arriving at night, he would drive around until he spotted the local law officer. Berman would pretend to have car trouble and when the officer came to help, would capture him. He would then force the policeman to "escort" him to the bank or post office. Once there, Berman broke in with a crowbar or sledgehammer, taking the money and leaving the unfortunate cop tied up inside.

Robbery proved to be a lucrative sideline. From 1925 to 1926, he stole $180,000 in cash from a bank in Laporte, Indiana; $280,000 in bonds from the Northwestern National Bank in Milwaukee; and $80,000 in registered mail from a post office in Superior, Wisconsin. He was never convicted in any of these cases.

Along the way, Berman acquired notoriety for guts. "If anybody gets arrested or shot," he said, "It'll be me first."

One of Davie's bankrobbing pals remembers Berman as being totally unafraid. "I never saw courage like that," he said. "When he went in, he went in to win. You were safe with him, he wasn't crazy like some of the guys. He was calm and steady. He was just after the money.

"Other gangs were afraid of him. He didn't talk much, but you knew he was smart. I once asked him if he was ever afraid he would be killed. He just smiled, his eyes got kind of cold and he said, 'When your number's up, it's up'."[3]

Davie was also considerate of those he robbed. After the Wisconsin post office heist, the New York Times called Berman "a gentlemen yegg (robber) by his courtesy for his captive."

A confederate in one of Berman's robberies remembers a time the gang unexpectedly encountered a night watchman. The men were just putting the money into bags when the watchman appeared holding a gun. "He told us to line up against the wall. Davie walked behind him and kicked the gun out of his hand. He didn't kill him, just tied him up. We all had our caps pulled way down over our faces. We didn't want to get no murder rap," he said. "We just needed the dough."

In 1927, Berman ventured to New York to work in a new racket. New York mobsters retained him to kidnap wealthy men engaged in illegal activities and hold them for ransom. Since the men were

Meyer Lansky

criminals, they would not readily complain to the police. It seemed like a perfect setup.

In May 1927, Davie and his associates kidnapped a bootlegger named Abraham Scharlin and held him for $20,000 ransom. A few days later police arrested Berman for the kidnapping in a shootout near Central Park.

Berman and a co-conspirator, Joe Marcus, were lounging on West 66th Street when they saw two detectives approach. Berman had a pistol tucked in his belt, but a detective grabbed him before he could draw it. Marcus was not so lucky. He drew his gun, but not fast enough. The detective shot him dead.

The police grilled Berman, but he wouldn't talk. One of the detectives told him that if he pleaded guilty he would go free. Berman looked at him and said, "Hell, the worst I can get is life."[4]

Dave's defiance made headlines and New Yorkers loved it. For weeks people went around saying, "Hell, the worst I can get is life."

The police finally found Scharlin hidden in Brooklyn, but he refused to identify Berman as the kidnapper. The authorities charged Davie with attempted felonious assault and violation of the Sullivan Law. Berman still kept mum.

In November 1927, Davie was sentenced to twelve years in Sing Sing. While in prison he developed ulcers that would plague him all his life. The police never found out who Berman's accomplices were.[5]

Dave proved to be a model prisoner and was released after seven and a half years. The warden made a special request to have him freed, citing Berman's exemplary behavior, high IQ and "total rehabilitation."

As soon as he got out, the "rehabilitated" Berman solidified his links with organized crime. He moved into New York's Mayflower Hotel and began a life-long affiliation with Bugsy Siegel, Meyer Lansky, Lucky Luciano and Frank Costello.

With their encouragement and backing, in 1934 Berman relocated to Minneapolis, where his brother Chickie and his mother lived. He concentrated on gambling and built a city-wide Jewish gambling syndicate. According to the FBI, Berman's bookmaking establishments were popular because "he always located them near Hebrew cafes which served excellent Hebrew food." The menus of these restaurants listed delicacies such as, tongue, flanken, boiled chicken, goulash, kreplach, kneidlach, knishes and potato pancakes, most of which were cooked in chicken fat.

Minneapolis contained other criminal syndicates as well. An Irish combination dealt in liquor, and another Jewish syndicate, led by Isidore Blumenfeld, ran a variety of illegal businesses, including gambling. In 1941, Marvin Kline, a Berman-supported candidate, won the mayoralty race. Shortly thereafter, Davie replaced Blumenfeld as the city's gambling czar.

A 1939 FBI memo described Berman as "tall, lean, giving the appearance of a great quantity of nervous strength. Quiet to the point of being noticeable. High cheekbones tended to accentuate the peculiar steadiness of the eyes. Berman in his conversation, as well as mannerisms, clearly reflected that he spent a great deal of his adult life in prison confines... Inasmuch as he had tasted confinement for a considerable length of time, he is a most dangerous type of law violator, due to the great price he is willing to pay in order to avoid another taste of confinement. Had a great ability to control his emotions, and where prior to being sent away to Sing Sing Prison for a lengthy term he was considered tough, subsequent to his release he was considered vicious."[6]

When the United States entered World War II, Berman wanted to enlist and "kill ten Nazis for every Jew." Rejected by the U.S. Army because he was too old and a convicted felon, Davie joined the Canadian Army in 1942. He was wounded in action on the Italian front and honorably discharged in 1944.

Minneapolis had changed during the war. Reform-minded mayors such as Hubert Humphrey, cleaned up the town and abolished gambling. They put pressure on gamblers and "encouraged" them to take their operations somewhere else. Davie decided it would be wise to leave.

In 1945, Berman moved west to Las Vegas, a place he had visited before. He borrowed a million dollars from his mob contacts and purchased the newly refurbished El Cortez Hotel. His co-owners were Bugsy Siegel, Moe Sedway, Meyer Lansky and Ice Pick Willie Alderman, an old associate from Minneapolis.

In Las Vegas, Berman became known as "the Mob Diplomat." Everyone trusted his integrity and he set up liaisons between aspiring opportunists and East Coast gangster bosses. After Bugsy Siegel's death in 1947, Berman became one of the owners and operators of the Flamingo Hotel and, later, the Riviera Hotel. He died of a heart attack, after surgery, in 1957.

Berman had married twenty-year-old Gladys Evans, a professional dancer, in 1939. Berman adored their daughter Susan, born in 1945, and until his death he did everything in his power to shield her from knowing about the life he led.

She writes, "He told his friends that I must never know the secrets of his past because the knowledge might destroy me."

Susan's mother, Gladys, "remained fanatical about keeping me away from anything that might mention my father — newspapers, detective magazines, books."

Her mother's friend, Ethel Schwartz, remembers that she used to say over and over again, "But what if Susie reads something one day on her own?"

Once Susan bought her father some detective magazines, which he enjoyed reading, for his birthday. Her mother "admonished me severely and told me never to purchase such a magazine or look at one again."

One issue of the *New Yorker* contained a "Talk of the Town" column which said that Las Vegas was run by former bootleggers. "My parents took no chances," remembers Susan. "My father had all the issues on sale bought out so that there would be no chance I could see it and make a connection."[7]

Their vigilance bore fruit. Susan knew nothing about her father's mob connections and activities until she reached young adulthood.

As a result, she never questioned what she later came to see as "unusual" precautions taken for her safety while she was growing up. "We had kidnap drills," she says. Berman told her, "If anyone asks if you're Davie Berman's daughter, say no, run, scream, yell, use whatever you have to get away."

"We carried no house key," she says, "because someone was always home. Several men lived with us who my father said were 'friends'. I never knew they were bodyguards."

Consequently, Susan's memory of her father was of a man who read to her, hugged her and played with her. She enjoyed a wonderful, albeit sheltered, childhood.

"He lived in the midst of a world that was dangerous, violent and severe," she says. "But he fabricated a childhood for me that seemed all-American and completely normal, disguising his real career as carefully as he managed it."

When she grew to adulthood, Susan became a journalist, writer and editor. She became renown for being able to get the "impossible" interview.

Many years after Davie's death, Susan finally learned who and what he had been. It was painful for her, but she still remembers him as a loving and wonderful father "who was a gangster, not a gangster who was a father."[8]

For more than thirty years, Abner "Longy" Zwillman was one of America's leading gangsters. Longy had connections everywhere, from his home base in Newark, New Jersey to Las Vegas, Los Angeles and Hollywood. And he was on intimate terms with America's top mobsters, Jews and Italians alike. Despite this, he kept his family totally separated from and uninvolved in his illegal businesses.

Longy is a prime example of the way Jewish gangsters kept their children and relatives isolated from their criminal activities. Longy's Italian mobster friends, on the other hand, often brought their offspring and relations into the business. This was a major difference between the two ethnic groups.

Like the Jews, Italian syndicate leaders were proud and devoted fathers. They, too, wanted their children to marry well and attain success. They, too, wanted their children to be accepted in the legitimate world. So they sent them to the best schools and paid for their studies in law, medicine or some other prestigious profession.

At the same time, they wanted to maintain control of their criminal business within the biological family. If this was not possible, they made an effort to keep it within their extended family of nephews, cousins and other relatives. If necessary, they brought in outsiders through marriage and godparentage.

For example, the children of three of the five "bosses" of New York crime families, Carlo Gambino, Tommy Lucchese and Vito Genovese, married into each others' families. In Detroit, mob boss Joseph Zerilli's daughter Rosalie married Dominic Licavoli, the son of Peter Licavoli, who headed another Detroit Mafia faction. Zerilli's son married the daughter of Joseph Profaci, boss of a New York crime family. Zerilli's sister, Rosalie, married William Tocco, a Mafia associate of Zerilli in Detroit. Their son, Anthony, married Carmella Profaci, another daughter of Joe Profaci. And so it went.

Of the more than sixty Mafia bosses who attended the famous meeting in the tiny upstate New York town of Appalachin, in November 1957, almost half were related by blood or marriage.[9]

This is why Italian-American criminal syndicates are referred to as "families." They are tied together by marriage and kinship.

This tradition was totally absent among Jewish gangsters. None of their children married the offspring of other Jewish gangsters. And none of their relatives "inherited" their business. Jewish mobsters knew that what they did was not an "honorable" occupation, and they did not want to pass it on to their loved ones. This is why the activities of the Zwillmans, Lanskys and Buchalters lasted a single generation. It lived and died with them. [10]

Longy had three sisters and three brothers, Barney, Harry and Irving. According to Itzik Goldstein, who knew Longy very well, Longy was wonderful to his family.

"The only thing is he never wanted his brothers to be connected to the mob," says Itzik. Longy controlled Local 244 of the Motion Picture Machine Operators Union through an associate, Louis Kaufman. Longy used his influence with the union to get jobs for his relatives.

"Irving was a motion picture operator (projectionist), Harry was a motion picture operator," says Itzik. "Barney had a shoe store. As the years went by he went into the liquor business. He had a couple of liquor stores."

As long as he lived, Zwillman supported his relatives. He continually gave them money and found jobs for them. Although they were not part of Zwillman's operation, the family sometimes encountered whisperings and slights from "respectable" citizens of Newark because they were Zwillmans. Nonetheless, the family continued to love and respect him.

"His mother was a wonderful woman," remembers Itzik. "I used to go to their house. They lived on Hansberry Avenue. Wonderful people.

"Longy used to come there every Friday with a half dozen fellows. His mother used to cook Jewish food, kreplach, gefilte fish.

A few Italianas (Italians) used to come. They never ate so good, them assholes."[11]

In 1939, Longy married Mary Mendels Steinbach, a divorced woman with a son, John. The wedding and reception took place on a Saturday afternoon in July, at the Chanticleer Restaurant in Newark. The Zwillman party took over the premises for the day.

The guest list for the wedding reception included Wall Street financiers, government officials, including former New Jersey governor Harold Hoffman, Democratic and Republican politicos, and nationally-known gangsters. Longy's best man was Joseph Sisto, a Wall Street financier, head of J.A. Sisto and Co., and chairman of the board of Barium Steel Corporation, a company in which Longy held a controlling stock interest.

Outside, some uninvited observers, including FBI agents, prosecutor's investigators and state troopers, checked the comings and goings of the guests.

Longy adored his wife and raised her son as his own. The boy loved Zwillman and the two became inseparable. Longy took the youngster with him wherever he could even to "business" meetings. This alarmed some of Longy's colleagues, who worried that the child might remember some of the things he heard.

As the boy grew up, this changed. Longy's bodyguard remembers that when the boy was a teenager, Longy would "ask him to leave the room when a meeting began."

Despite their father-son relationship, Longy never legally adopted John. "If I adopt you," Longy told the youngster, you'll carry my name. You'll be marked for life, and that won't be an advantage. No matter what you do, how well you behave, you'll be pointed out as a Zwillman. I've seen it happen to the rest of my family," said Longy, and I don't want it to happen to you."[12]

It didn't. John married in 1958 and led a respectable life without anyone connecting him to the Zwillman era.

Waxey Gordon grew up tough. As a young man he was a terror on the streets and later ruthless as a bootlegger. However, his wife and three children meant more to him than anything else. Throughout his criminal career he shielded them from the uglier aspects of his life. His conviction for income tax evasion shattered the illusion of respectability he sought to create, exposing him for what he was. His wife, Leah, the daughter of a rabbi, was forced to endure the shame.

Waxey's beloved eldest son, Theodore, was a nineteen-year-old pre-medical student at the University of North Carolina at the time of the trial. Waxey often boasted to his friends about Teddy's aptitude for study, his love of books and his devotion to his parents.

During his father's trial in December 1933, Teddy remained in New York to be with his mother. He returned to school after Waxey's conviction. A few days later, Teddy received a call from his uncle, Nathan Wexler, urging him to return to New York and go to the judge and Thomas Dewey in order to plead for a reduction of his father's ten year sentence, and to ask for Gordon's release on bail pending appeal.

"But uncle, I have an exam in the morning," the boy said. "Can't it be put off for a day?"

His uncle told him that haste was important. Teddy went straight to his car and started back to New York. It began to snow and sleet and he was tired, so he asked a friend of his to drive for him. The boy fell asleep at the wheel and the car went off the road and crashed. Teddy was killed.

A few hours after the accident, Waxey was told of his son's death.

"That boy was my one hope," Waxey told his attorney. "I counted on him. Everything I did centered around him."

Gordon asked the court for permission to attend his son's funeral, and prosecutor Thomas E. Dewey granted his request. Teddy was buried in the Mount Hebron Cemetery, in Flushing, New York. Gordon, tears streaming down his face, stood in the sunlight. Mourning beside him stood his wife and their other children, Paul, fifteen years old, and Beatrice, eleven.

Rabbi A. Mordechai Stern led the *kaddish* and Gordon followed, muttering like a man in a dream. Afterwards, he stood as if in a daze as the clods of earth rained down on the coffin. "I would rather have taken any sentence, even life," he said, "than to have this happen to Teddy."

Weeping bitterly, Gordon was led away.[13]

Charley "The Bug" Workman was a short, curly-headed and casual killer, one of the Brooklyn underworld's most valuable gunmen. It was said that he killed twenty men, all criminals, during his career. Because he was so expert at assassination, Lepke Buchalter gave Charley the contract to kill Dutch Schultz.

Charlie was born on New York's Lower East Side in 1908, the son of Samuel and Anna Workman. Bad from the beginning, he quit school at seventeen to become a thief and slugger. His first arrest, for robbery, came at eighteen. The next year the police picked him up for shooting a man behind the ear in an argument over $20. He beat the case when the victim thought it healthier to develop amnesia and could not identify who shot him.[14]

Over the next twelve years, from 1927 to 1939, Charley was

arrested, but not jailed, for a variety of offenses, ranging from carrying concealed weapons to bashing in the face of an off-duty cop in a traffic argument. By then he had graduated from being a mere bruiser for the mob to a full-time spot on Lepke Buchalter's payroll, available at all times to the Brooklyn gun-for-hire ring called Murder, Inc.

Charley earned the usual fee of $125 per week, which was not a bad salary during the Depression. He supplemented this by sweeping out the pockets of his victims for loose cash and change. Charley became one of the gang's better marksmen, ranking right alongside Harry Strauss, Abe Reles and Buggsy Goldstein. Lepke, who liked Charley very much, used to say that he had so much guts he was "bugs" (crazy). The appellation fit and from then on Charley was called "the Bug." He went by other underworld nicknames as well, among them "the Powerhouse."

Author Paul Sann, once asked a police inspector how he would characterize the Bug. He replied, "The same as a regiment."[15]

And Burton B. Turkus, the assistant district attorney who, in 1940, prosecuted Harry Strauss, Buggsy Goldstein and the other sterling characters of the so-called Murder, Inc. execution cartel and later wrote a book about it, called Charley "one of gangland's most deadly executioners."[16]

Despite his underworld reputation, Workman kept his occupation hidden from his family. While they may have suspected something, neither his parents, brothers or wife knew exactly what Charley did for a living. They only discovered it after Charley was arrested for killing Dutch Schultz.

This seems hard to believe. But those in the know kept their knowledge to themselves. Given who Charley was, it seemed the prudent thing to do. Workman's secret career became public when

Abe Reles began to sing. When Reles's information was corroborated and embellished by another sterling hitman and Workman pal Albert "Allie" Tannenbaum, Charley's fate was sealed.

Tannenbaum had been born in Nanticoke, Pennsylvania, in 1906, but the family moved to the Lower East Side when he was three. From there they moved to Brooklyn. Allie quit school at seventeen and went to work in the garment center, later becoming a salesman for a paper jobber. Allie's father acquired the Lock Sheldrake Country Club in the Catskills and Allie helped him out on weekends and summers.[17]

It was there, in 1931, that Allie met Jacob "Gurrah" Shapiro, a guest at the resort. Shapiro was impressed with Allie's brawn and intelligence, and introduced him to his Brooklyn mob pals. Allie found the boys and their work far more fun then selling. So at the age of twenty-five he became an enforcer and hitman.

Tannenbaum's testimony was crucial because Workman told him everything.

Allie hadn't seen Charley for several days after the Schultz shooting, When he did see him, he asked Workman, "Where were you the last couple of days?"

"Gee, what an experience I had," the Bug was supposed to have replied.

Then, according to Tannenbaum, Workman described to him in great detail how he killed Schultz. Workman supposedly ended his account by claiming "It looked like a Wild West show." Tannenbaum never clarified what Workman meant by that.[18]

Workman's trial was held in June 1941. Charley was a very tough and uncompromising defendant. His facade began to crack, however, when his emotion-wracked parents came into the courtroom. It was obvious to everyone that Workman could not bear to see them there. He decided to spare them and his family further shame and disgrace and switched his plea to *non vult*, which meant that he would not offer a defense. In Workman's case this was tantamount to a confession of guilt.

Charley said he changed his plea because he did not want "members of my family and others to be subjected to humiliation on my account."[19]

Charley knew the difference between right and wrong. He also knew that thieves and killers were not valued members of the Jewish community. Growing up among Jews in Brooklyn, he knew how his parents and their friends viewed Jewish crooks. Charley knew that the parents of wayward boys suffered terrible guilt, feeling they were somehow to blame for their son's evildoing. He also knew that these parents suffered from the disdain of their neighbors. Charley realized that he had brought all of this on his own parents, who did not deserve it. Remorse for what he had done to his family eventually broke his will.

Workman was sentenced to life at hard labor. Before he was led away, Charley was allowed a brief visit with his younger brother, Abe. Abe threw his arms around Charley and wept uncontrollably.

Detectives guarding Workman heard him give this advice to Abe. "Whatever you do, live honestly. If you make 20 cents a day, make it do you. If you can't make an honest living, make the government support you. Keep away from the gangs and don't be a wise guy (troublemaker). Take care of Mama and Papa and watch Itchy (a younger brother). He needs watching."[20]

After Workman was sentenced, a Bronx detective who knew Dutch Schultz's mother, called to tell her that the man who killed her son was going to jail for a long time.

Max (Boo-Boo) Hoff

"I'm so glad to hear about it," she said. "Thank God, thank God."[21]

Charley Workman went to Trenton State Prison to begin serving his sentence. He was a model prisoner and earned a transfer to the Rahway State Prison Farm in 1952. Charley behaved so well that he became a trusted member of the prison's operation.

"If I had a thousand inmates like him," said Warden Warren Pinto, "I wouldn't have to worry with this job. He's just like an ordinary guy, not one of the 'big shots' who try to gain special favors. He never asks for anything."

The prison psychologist listed Charley as "a reasonably stable individual." He kept physically fit by playing handball, and he became thrifty as well. Warden Pinto noted that Workman had managed to accumulate a few U.S. Savings Bonds from his 18-cents-a-day prison salary.

Charley's family never abandoned him, and his wife, Catherine, visited him regularly.

In March 1964 Charley won his parole. He was now 56 years old and a grandfather. His wife, who waited for him outside the prison, had not missed more than two Sunday visits in all those years.

Workman and his wife walked away from the prison and got into a blue Thunderbird driven by his brother Abe. Home after 22 years in jail, Charley got a job selling zippers and other items to dress manufacturers and was never heard from again.

Workman died content, surrounded by his family and loved ones. But history would always remember him as the man who, in his own words, "went into the shithouse" and killed the Dutchman.[22]

Meyer Lansky loved his two sons and daughter, and kept them away from his criminal activities. Doc Stacher, who knew Lansky well, said that "Meyer was close to his children, crazy about them."

Lansky's first wife, Anna, was "opposed to everything Lansky stood for, but there was nothing she could do about it. She was terrified that the children would follow in his footsteps." Despite Lansky's repeated assurances to Anna "that he wouldn't let the children get involved," she continually worried.[23]

But Meyer meant it. His first child, a son Bernard, nicknamed "Buddy," was born in 1930. The boy was cheerful and even-tempered, but had a damaged spinal cord and would always be a cripple. Meyer was committed to Buddy and supported him all his life.

Meyer's second son, Paul, was born in 1932. He grew up normal and healthy. Lansky wanted his younger son to be completely integrated into American society. In 1950, Paul Lansky was accepted to West Point on the basis of his own ability, without his father pulling any strings. Lansky was forever proud of Paul's achievement and never ceased talking about it.[24]

Meyer loved driving up to visit his son at the United States Military Academy, and he took the family there for picnics. His son's graduation from the Academy gave him the feeling, as perhaps nothing else could, that he had made it in America.

This feeling was reinforced for him in 1952 when Dwight Eisenhower became president. The father of one of Paul's roommates was a close friend of Eisenhower's, and Lansky received an invitation to Eisenhower's inauguration. Lansky thought this was a mistake. He wrote the man a letter thanking him, but hinting that some of the dignitaries at the ceremony might find his presence objectionable.

The man wrote back telling Lansky not to forget to come. He

disclosed that his club used the same slot machines that Lansky had in his casinos, and during Prohibition he and his friends used to drink Lansky's bootleg whiskey. Lansky was surprised and flattered, but still declined to attend.[25]

Paul graduated from West Point in 1954 with a commission as a captain and a degree in engineering. In 1962, he went to Vietnam for a year, one of the first American advisors sent by the Kennedy administration. By then he was married and had a child. Keeping a promise he made to his wife, he resigned from the army when his tour ended. He moved with his family to Washington State and worked for a logging company and then for Boeing Aircraft. Later he worked for the Defense Department in Washington. In the late 1980s he retired from government service and went to live near Carson City, Nevada. He never had anything to do with criminal activities.[26]

Moses "Moe" Annenberg enjoyed the highest income of any American, including Henry Ford, during the Depression. During that time of unemployment and breadlines, Moe netted more than $6 million a year. He controlled the race track wire service, without which no bookie could operate.[27]

"Our position is similar to that of the English nation," he once confided to one of his sons-in-law. "We in the racing field own three quarters of the globe and manage the balance." No one ever accused Moe of having an inferiority complex.[28]

It has been said that Moe was to the bookies of America what Arnold Rothstein was to the bootleggers and narcotics peddlers. He put the racket on a businesslike basis.

Moe was born in East Prussia in 1877. His father, Tobias, immigrated to Chicago alone in 1882 and found work as a peddler. Three years later, he brought his wife and seven children to America and found them a home in a second-floor apartment over a junk shop on South State Street. Eventually, Tobias ran a junkyard on South Dearborn Street.[29]

Moe quit school at the age of twelve, completing the fifth grade, and went to work selling papers. He grew to be tall and rangy, with a long jaw and horse-like face. A tough kid, he got a job at eighteen as a subscription solicitor for the *Chicago Examiner,* one of William Randolph Hearst's newspapers.

Moe became involved in the Chicago circulation wars which pitted Hearst's *American* and *Examiner* against the *Tribune.* Both sides hired ex-boxers, sluggers and gangsters to persuade newsstands to feature one or the other newspaper. Delivery trucks were seized, bundles of papers destroyed and people killed. Moe got a good education and held his own with the best of them.

"I was a hungry wolf," he said. "I had a large family. I had to hunt or starve. I learned how to hunt. And I kept it up."[30]

He hunted so well that Hearst made Moe circulation manager for the *Examiner.*

In 1907 Moe moved to Milwaukee, where he handled circulation for several of Hearst's newspapers and bought a newspaper of his own. He stayed in Milwaukee until 1920, when Hearst brought him to New York as circulation manager for the entire Hearst chain.

Moe always wanted to be self-employed and in 1922 he bought his first racing sheet, the *Daily Racing Form.* It did so well that he quit working for Hearst and bought into another paper, the *Morning Telegraph.* He expanded to Chicago in 1930 and started a bookie wire service, the Nationwide News Service.

Of every four dollars bet on horses, three were handled by illegal bookmaking operations all across the United States. These bookies needed the race results as they happened. The Nationwide News Service provided these reports from observers stationed at twenty-nine different race tracks. These men reported back by telephone and telegraph to 15,000 bookies in 223 cities in 39 states. Moe Annenberg became the fifth largest customer of American Telephone and Telegraph.

Moe charged his customers about $50 million a year for this service.

He bought out his rivals and partners, and used muscle and guns in New York, Chicago, Philadelphia and Houston to gain control of the nation's wire service market. Moe did business with Longy Zwillman, Meyer Lansky and other mobsters. In Chicago, he reportedly paid Al Capone a million dollars a year for protection and enforcement services.

The Chicago district attorney called Annenberg "a murderer and a thief." He once told Moe's tax attorney that he could give him "the names of three people he had killed in the city of Chicago in the last five years. He ought to be hung," said the DA.[31]

Moe had seven daughters and one son, Walter. When Walter turned twenty-one, Moe gave him a harmless job in the family business. Although he employed some of his sons-in-law in the more dangerous and sinister aspects of the operations, he kept Walter out of it. Moe wanted Walter to have a wholesome and legitimate career.

In 1939, the government indicted Moe for massive income tax evasion. Walter was charged with aiding his father. Moe was devastated. He would do anything to keep his son out of jail.

Moe agreed to plead guilty to one count of income tax evasion. As part of the deal, all charges against Walter would be dropped. Moe received three years in prison and a fine of $8 million. At the time, this was the largest single fine ever paid by an individual tax evader. With Moe gone, Nationwide News folded.

Suffering from cancer, Moe was released from prison in 1942. He died that same year.[32]

Walter took over his father's newspaper empire and added to it *Seventeen* magazine and *TV Guide*. As if to atone for his father's crimes, Walter became a philanthropist, donating hundreds of millions of dollars to schools, hospitals and the Republican Party.

In 1969, Richard Nixon appointed Walter Annenberg ambassador to Great Britain. Thus, his father's analogy comparing his empire to that of England was not far-fetched.[33]

Even the vicious and violent Lepke Buchalter was a doting husband and father. Buchalter married Betty Arbeiter Wasserman, a widow with one child, in 1931. Following his marriage to Betty, Buchalter adopted her son, Harold. Lepke made certain the boy never knew what his father did for a living.

According to an FBI report, Lepke did not drink or gamble, and "apart from his criminal activities, Lepke appears to have been content to lead a quiet home life in the company of his family to whom, regardless of his other traits, he appears to have been genuinely devoted."[34]

This affection was genuine. Some years later, Harold remarked that "Louis was better to me than my own father could have been."[35]

Betty's first husband had left a small trust fund for their son. Buchalter, however, would never allow his wife to draw any of the income from the trust fund, insisting that the monies accrued be used later for Harold's college education. It was.

Jewish gangsters revered their mothers. In this, they were little different than other second generation American Jews. Among them, the immigrant East European Jewish mother, the "Yiddishe Mama," achieved mythical status, symbolizing the parent who sacrificed everything for her children.[36]

In dozens of stories, plays and films, the Yiddishe Mama is depicted as going to irrational lengths to provide her children with the best and freshest food, the best medical care, the warmest clothing, all at the sacrifice of other needs, especially her own.

The canonization of this image occurred in 1925 when entertainer Sophie Tucker, "the Last of the Red-Hot Mamas," introduced the song "My Yiddishe Mama" to audiences. This paean to the long-suffering immigrant Jewish mother took the American Jewish community by storm and became a national hit. The song could not have reached the popularity it did among Jews (it's still being recorded today) if it did not contain truths and strike a responsive cord.

"My Yiddishe Mama" had an English and a Yiddish version, both calculated to evoke the past and tug at the audience's heartstrings. The Yiddish version contained the following verses:

As I stand here and think my old mother comes to mind.
No made-up, well-dressed lady, just a mother,
Bent over from great sorrow, with a pure Jewish heart
And with cried-out eyes.
In the same little room where she's gotten old and gray
She sits and cries and dreams of long gone days
When the house was full with the sound of children's voices....
You can be sure our house did not lack poverty,
But there was always enough for the children.

She used to voluntarily give us bread from her mouth
And she would have given up her life for her children as well....
A Yiddishe mama, oh how bitter when she's missing.
You should thank God you still have her with you
You don't know how you'll grieve when she passes away.
She would have leaped into fire and water for her children.
Not cherishing her certainly the greatest sin.
Oh, how lucky and rich is the person who has such a beautiful gift
   from God:
Just an old little Yiddishe mama, my mama.
Nur an alte, kleyne yiddishe mame, mayn mame[37]

Jewish gangsters frequented nightclubs and heard the song. In fact, Jewish underworld figures owned many nightspots and speakeasies. In New York, Dutch Schultz owned the Embassy Club. Charley "King" Solomon owned Boston's Coconut Grove. In Newark, Longy Zwillman owned the Blue Mirror and the Casablanca Club. Boo Boo Hoff owned the Piccadilly Cafe in Philadelphia. Detroit's Purple Gang owned Luigi's Cafe, one of the city's more opulent clubs.[38]

Jewish singers and comedians such as Al Jolson, Eddie Cantor, Fanny Brice and Sophie Tucker played in the mob clubs and they sang "Yiddishe Mama." Oh, how they sang it. The song always brought the house down. More than one observer noted how these hardened Jewish mobsters would break into tears when they heard "My Yiddishe Mama."

Despite their notoriety, most of these gangsters managed to keep their mothers blissfully unaware of their underworld activities and treated them with gentleness, respect and affection.

Meyer Lansky adored his mother. He remembered how she

gladly sacrificed herself for her children. While still a youngster he swore that when he grew up he would be very rich, "and I'd make sure that for the rest of her days my mother had only the best."[39]

As he rose in the world of crime, Meyer settled his parents in an elegant apartment, complete with maid, in a fashionable section of Brooklyn. When his mother had eye surgery in the late 1930s, Meyer got her a full-time private nurse to stay with her in the hospital. The nurse remembers Meyer showing "much compassion" for his mother. He came to visit every day, sitting at her bedside for hours, talking and listening. Before he would leave, he always asked the nurse if there was anything else his mother needed.

After his mother came home, Meyer asked the nurse to stay on till his mother was completely recovered. He continued to visit his mother every day, talking with her in Yiddish. From time to time he called home so his children could speak to their grandmother. The nurse who cared for Lansky's mother was struck by the closeness between mother and son.

In later years, Meyer settled his mother in a retirement apartment near the sea in Hollywood, Florida and visited her regularly. As his mother grew frailer, Meyer made sure that she had the very best in medical care.

To the end, Meyer remained an affectionate and devoted son. He had made good on his childhood vow that for the rest of her days his mother should have only the very best.[40]

Longy Zwillman bought his mother a beautiful home in the Weequahic section of Newark and visited her often. Longy's mother constantly worried about her son, but not because he lived in a violent world. She never knew what he did for a living. She fretted about him because he was not married and had no one to care for him.

She frequently admonished Sam "Big Sue" Katz, Longy's boyhood friend, sometime chauffeur, and bodyguard, to "watch out" for her son. "You hear, Sam? Take care of my Abe," she would say.[41]

When Zwillman's mother learned that he was finally getting married, she cried with joy. She told everyone that maybe now she would become a grandmother.

In 1944, Longy's daughter Lynn was born and his mother's wish came true.

Detroit Jewish mobster Maxie Hassel venerated his mother. Whenever he remembered or spoke about her, he would choke up and tears would come to his eyes. Once, during the Depression, when broke and wanted by the Detroit police in connection with a gangland killing, he had to leave town, and fast.

Maxie's father, Jake, had immigrated to the United States from Russia in 1910. Jake was an Orthodox Jew who peddled junk for a living. Jake wanted nothing to do with Max, considering him a bum and no good. Maxie's mother, Gita, loved her son and never abandoned him.

Maxie asked his mother to help him. "It was the Depression," he said. "My father would get up at four thirty in the morning, stoke the furnace, say his prayers and go off to work. He came home at eight or nine at night. He was careful with his money and gave Ma a few dollars a week. With this she had to feed my six brothers and sisters and run the house.

"She couldn't manage and took a job plucking chickens for a kosher butcher. She saved her pennies and kept it hidden somewhere in the house.

"I was desperate, so I went to her for help. I'll never forget what she did as long as I live.

"She gave me $3 tied in a handkerchief. It was all the money she had. But it was enough to get me out of town. She saved me."[42]

Despite the strong tradition of keeping their family uninvolved in their business, there was an occasional gangster who did not oppose his son's going illegal.

Mervin's (whose identity must be kept secret) father was in the rackets during the 1930s and 1940s, but he "insisted on me going to college after my brother. And I really had no great ambitions whatsoever, but I only followed suit because my father insisted on us having a college education. In view of the fact that I was not college material, he still encouraged me to go to school."[43]

When he graduated, Mervin became involved in illegitimate activities, primarily gambling. Mervin remembers his father's reaction. "He said to me, I chose my life, you choose your life."

Mervin admits that his father would have preferred he go into some lawful profession. If his father was upset that he didn't, he never showed it.

With regard to his own son, Mervin says that he would not oppose the boy being involved in illegal activities, but with limits. "The only thing is that whatever you choose to do, I would say to him, you gotta put on tefillin (phylacteries) every morning, you gotta eat kosher meat, you have to maintain certain principles. That means you have to keep your word. A word is a bond.

"After that, whatever a person chooses to do, that's his business. But no acts of immorality. When I say immorality, I mean pornography, drugs and prostitution.

"If a man deals in drugs, he sells death. Maybe he sells death and children buy it.

"As far as illegality is concerned, since that changes every day of the week, just like the weather, I'm not in a position to say what's illegal."[44]

In 1932 Jack Guzik went to prison for evading income taxes. While there, he corresponded regularly with his family. Books and articles portray Guzik as an immoral and unsavory character; the letters show another side to the man, that of a dutiful son, and a loving and concerned father and grandfather.[45]

Guzik married at age twenty and had a son and a daughter. By 1932 his daughter was married and had two children.

The family never forgot a holiday, Jewish or secular, birthday or anniversary. Their letters express great affection for each other.

In November 1935 Guzik wrote to his grandson Billy Jack on the boy's birthday. "Please accept my sincerest congratulations on your fifth birthday anniversary. Sorry I cannot attend, but will surely celebrate your sixth. Give my love to your mother and grandmother. Wishing you all health and happiness in the world and sending you so much love. Yours devotedly. Grandpop."[46]

On Rosh Hashanah [Jewish New Year]1935, Jack's brother Joe wrote him, "May you be inscribed in the book of life."[47]

Jack's sisters and brothers wished him "every joy and happiness for the coming year. May it bring your wife and family all you have ever wished for. Hope you are well. Love and kindest regards."[48]

In September 1935 a hurricane threatened the coast of Florida. Guzik's daughter was there at the time and he was very worried. He sent her a telegram expressing his unease. "Received your wire," he wrote. "Sure hope it's a false alarm." However, take no chances whatever. Would suggest you move inland to Coral Gables till it blows over.

"Wire me and mom by Western Union developments. Am awfully uneasy about that. Have already written you. Don't forget. Watch yourself closely. Awaiting and watching news. Much love, Pop."[49]

In February 1935 his daughter wrote him, "Dearest Dad: Valentine greetings to the sweetest sweetheart of them all. We are all great. Have been writing to you right along. Hope you have received all mail. Did you get our pictures. Did you like them? All our love Valentine's Day. Jeanette, Mother, Charles and Billy Jack."[50]

Jack wrote his daughter on her birthday in 1935: "Dear Jeanette. I am wishing you my finest and sincerest thoughts of love, happiness and health on your birthday and forever after. Take care of yourself and our Billy Boy. How is Rosie ? Give her and Charles my love. Hope you have a wonderful time on your birthday. Lovingly, Pop."[51]

On the anniversary of his mother's death, Jack received a letter from his son. "Have appropriate services said for anniversary of your mother's death Wednesday evening to Thursday evening. Mom will burn candles for you."[52]

On his wedding anniversary in 1934, Jack sent his wife a telegram. "My best wishes of love, good health and happiness to my dear old girl on our twenty-seventh anniversary and hoping we spend together many, many more happier anniversaries.

"I hear from our children and they are fine. Just don't worry about anything, as I am feeling good and taking good care of myself. Best to Frank and Lou, also Harry and Erma. Lovingly, Jack"[53]

The Guzik family correspondence notwithstanding, once most

families discovered that a relative was in the rackets they experienced humiliation and anger.

Longy Zwillman's daughter, Lynn, displayed artistic talent. But whenever she applied to art schools she was refused admittance. Longy had the problem investigated and discovered that Lynn was turned down because of his reputation.

Longy loved his daughter with a passion, but Lynn never returned his affection. She could never accept Zwillman for what he was, and blamed him for the rejections. As Longy grew older, his daughter's remoteness affected him greatly.[54]

Brothers and sisters of mobsters also often suffered because of their notorious siblings. At the time that Harry and Irving Kushner of Detroit's Purple Gang received life sentences for murder, their younger brother was a student in a Hebrew day school.

The trial caused a sensation in the city's Jewish community. One afternoon, as the younger Kushner sat in class, his teacher began to shout at him. "You... Your family is bringing shame on the Jewish people."[55]

The youngster jumped up and ran out of class and never returned to Hebrew school. In adulthood, he changed his name, became a successful attorney and a judge. But he never got over this incident from his early life.

Sam was another Purple Gangster who was convicted of murder and received a life sentence. His sister Sarah remembers the shock and shame the family suffered. "My mother and father sat around the table at night whispering about my brother so we children wouldn't hear what they were saying. When I found out about my brother from kids at school, I was traumatized. I couldn't believe it, I wouldn't believe it."

She remembers how difficult it was for her to go to school and face "all the stares and know that everyone was talking about my family."

For years Sarah refused to believe that her brother was a killer. She decided to devote herself to proving him innocent. Later, while a student at Wayne University in Detroit, she dated a law student who wanted to marry her. Sarah agreed, but made him promise that he would help free her brother. He kept his word.

After thirty-five years, Sarah's efforts were rewarded and her brother was paroled. She and her family drove up to Jackson State Prison to bring him home. When he came out, she could hardly contain her joy.

As they walked to the car, her brother took Sarah aside. "I want you to know how much I appreciate what you've done for me," he said. "But I have to tell you. I was guilty."

Sarah was devastated and never fully recovered from the shock of this revelation.[56]

After the disclosure that Jews worked as hitmen for the so-called Murder, Inc. gang of killers-for-hire, the New York Jewish community was in an uproar. In March 1940, the *Jewish Daily Forward* sent a reporter into Brooklyn to talk to the man-on-the-street and to interview the parents of the convicted killers.

The reporter was struck at how humiliated all the parents were. Some mourned as though their son had died. Others searched for some explanation to the tragedy that had befallen them. A few were too shocked and embarrassed to speak.

The mother of Abraham "Pretty" Levine expressed her dismay to her interviewer. She wailed to him, "All my other children are good and decent. All studied, all work. All have married, lead good family lives and are a comfort in our old age. All except for one. Except for him."[57]

Yet, some relatives recall the the gangster members of their family with affection and view them as something akin to folk heroes.

Dorie Shapiro Grizzard, the granddaughter of Gurrah Shapiro, is a case in point. When she speaks about Gurrah, she does so with affection, and even pride. In her grandfather's time, she says, men like him did not indulge in random acts of violence. "They had a code of honor. They only hurt people they knew." Gurrah "killed for a reason. He killed somebody that bothered him or did something to him. Not a stranger."

She also notes that being the relative of a gangster could have its advantages.

"Anytime I would go out with somebody, and it wasn't working, I just told them who I was, and you would see an instant change in their personality. I mean, they were so nice to me. They were like my best friend.

"If I couldn't get a job or something like that and I hinted who my grandfather was, I had the job the next day. Regardless of whether I could spell or I could read, they gave me the job."[58]

George Tane was a bootlegger who controlled Green Bay, Wisconsin. After Prohibition, he owned all the houses of prostitution in the city. Every November George would go through Chicago on his way to Florida. He usually came driving a brand-new Packard sedan and with a brand-new "wife."

His niece Dena remembers her parents telling her that "Uncle George is a gambler and he goes to Florida to gamble." George "always arrived laden with presents and each of the thirteen nieces and nephews would get a dollar bill."

During World War II, when many of Dena's cousins were in the armed services, it was Dena's job "to mail a $20 bill to each of them from Uncle George."

In the spring, George "would return from Florida, always with an entourage, and the gorgeous little blond who was always introduced as his wife," remembers Dena. "He was married to several showgirls, for a few years each," she says.

"He was warm and full of fun. The entire family would gather and he would tell wonderful stories, enchanting us all.

"He always said he came to Chicago to see his mother. He treated her like a queen. His three sisters adored him, and so did all the children in the family," says Dena.

"Many years later," relates Dena, "I learned that he was known as 'Silky,' because he always wore custom-made silk shirts. I remember that he wore nothing but custom-made imported shoes, smoked cigarettes with a gold cigarette holder and always smelled beautiful.

"In later years he married the woman who had been his bookkeeper for years," says Dena, "and lived out his life between Green Bay and a little hunting lodge he had in Mountain, Wisconsin.

"He was buried on the day American astronauts landed on the moon."[59]

As they say, you can choose your friends, but you can't choose your relatives. So it was that some Jewish families of the inter-war years had a father, a brother, an uncle or a cousin who was adept at using guns in illegal enterprises. Jews were not unique in this, other ethnic groups did it as well. This was all part of being an American.

Meyer Lansky was once asked if he had his life to live over again, would he live it another way.

After thinking for a while, Lansky remarked that when he was young he thought that Jews should be treated like other people. He remembered that after a pogrom, a young soldier in Grodno, the town where Lansky was born, said that Jews should stand up and fight.

"I guess you could say I've come a long way from Grodno and a long way from the Lower East Side," Lansky said. "But I still believe him. I wouldn't have lived my life in any other way."[60]

Chapter Eight

Defenders of
Their People

C hicago gangster Samuel "Nails" Morton (born Markowitz) was a stellar member of the Dion O'Banion mob and one of the gang's few Jewish recruits. Morton was a stylish dresser who lived the high life and loved horseback riding. One fine Sunday morning in May of 1923, while cantering through Lincoln Park, a stirrup strap broke and Morton tumbled to the ground. The horse, later described as "particularly nervous and mettlesome," lashed out, kicking Nails in the head and killing him.

Morton's grief-stricken buddies demanded revenge. Led by Two-Gun Louis Alterie, a zany and pathological killer and Morton's closest friend in the outfit, they broke into the stable and kidnapped the guilty horse. The group led the horse to the spot where Morton died and solemnly "bumped him off," each man pumping a bullet into its head. Alterie then telephoned the stables. "We taught that goddamned horse of yours a lesson," he said. "If you want the saddle, go and get it."[1]

The O'Banion gang then staged a lavish gangster funeral. The funeral cortege was two miles long, and it took six limousines to carry the flowers. Five thousand Jews, including rabbis, turned out to pay tribute to Nails.

Local reporters were shocked. Why would so many law-abiding Jews attend the funeral of a gangster? When the story came to light, it showed that Morton had another side to his life that few outsiders knew about. From the time he was a teenager, Morton had protected and defended Jews from attacks by anti-Semites. Attending the funeral was the community's way of showing its gratitude.[2]

Morton grew up on Chicago's Maxwell Street, the heart of the city's East European Jewish quarter. The immigrant Jews who lived in the district faced a daily battle for economic survival, as well as constant harassment from Jew-baiting Polish gangs who enjoyed going down to "Jewtown" to beat up Jewish kids, steal from pushcarts and create mayhem. As a young man, Morton organized a defense society to drive these gangs from the west side.[3]

In one incident, several Jewish youngsters were assaulted as they passed through the Polish neighborhood. When Morton heard about this, he assembled a gang of Jewish toughs and headed for the Polish district to retaliate. They went to the street corners indicated by the boys who had been attacked and started a free-for-all fight. After administrating a sufficient amount of physical punishment, the Jews withdrew.[4]

When the United States entered the First World War in 1917, Morton enlisted in the 131st Illinois Infantry that went overseas with the famed "Rainbow Division."

Nails rose through the ranks to become a first lieutenant, and received the *Croix de Guerre*, France's highest decoration for bravery, for capturing a German machine gun nest despite being wounded. He returned to Maxwell Street a hero, became a bootlegger, and put his training in warfare and weapons to practical use.

After his death, Nails was characterized as a man who led a number of lives. To one set of acquaintances he was a gallant soldier. To another, a dauntless defender of Jewry. And to the police, a notorious gangster.[5]

Morton was not unique. During the early decades of the twentieth century, Jewish districts and immigrant Jews were often victimized and attacked by young hoodlums from other ethnic groups. Jewish gangsters frequently protected their neighborhoods from these racist gangs. It was not simply an aspect of protecting one's turf against rivals, but part of a deeper commitment to the safety of one's people.

This protection extended to individual Jews as well. Alex Levinsky was the first Canadian Jew to play professional hockey. He began his career in 1932 playing for the Toronto Maple Leafs. In the mid-1930s, Toronto traded him to the Chicago Black Hawks. While playing for Chicago, opposing fans harassed him verbally, and opposing players verbally and physically, because he was a Jew. After one blatantly anti-Semitic assault on the ice, a group of Chicago Jewish mobsters contacted Alex and offered to protect him on and off the ice whenever he traveled to other cities to play. Levinsky thanked them, but declined their proposal.[6]

Levinsky closed his hockey career by coaching the New York Rangers and winning two Stanley Cup championships.

Some mobsters even considered protecting Jews to be one of their gang's functions. When one such Chicago gangster was told that there were no Jewish gangsters in Milwaukee, his first question was, "Do the Jews get pushed around much in Milwaukee?"[7]

This role brought the mobsters a measure of admiration and

status among law-abiding members of the Jewish community. For instance, Jews on the Lower East Side of New York accorded a grudging respect to the notorious killer Max "Kid Twist" Zweibach because he kept Italian and Irish gangs, or as he called them, "the wops and the micks" from invading their neighborhood.[8]

Zweibach's sometime rival and successor, Big Jack Zelig, was another gangster who kept other ethnic hoodlums out of the Jewish neighborhood.

In 1912, the New York Jewish community hired Abe Shoenfeld, an experienced detective, to investigate crime and vice on the Lower East Side. For five years, Shoenfeld diligently gathered information and compiled intelligence reports on the location, management and clients of gambling resorts, brothels and gang hangouts. He offered a perceptive evaluation of Zelig.[9]

Shoenfeld never minimized Zelig's criminality. But he also noted that Zelig performed a valuable service for the Jewish community, because "he has rid the East Side of Italian pimps and thieves."

According to Shoenfeld, Zelig was angered by the Italian gangs who invaded the Jewish quarter, looking for Jewish women to seduce into prostitution and businesses to rob. Zelig and his henchmen, Louis "Lefty Louie" Rosenzweig, a dead shot with his left hand, and Jacob "Whitey Lewis" Seidenshner, who could not shoot straight, but was a "frisky scrapper," opened fire on some armed Italians who attended a dance sponsored by a local group of prostitutes and procurers. They killed the leader of the gang and sent his comrades scattering into the streets.

After that, Italians dared not strut in the Jewish district escorting a Jewish girl, and they stopped patronizing the local dance academies.

Shoenfeld was no admirer of Jewish gangsters. Nevertheless, he credited Zelig with ridding the East Side of Italians who robbed gambling houses and legitimate businesses. "He has prevented more hold-ups and things of a similar nature in his career than one thousand policemen," wrote Shoenfeld.

The East Side Jewish community was so appreciative of Zelig's efforts that when he sponsored a ball at Arlington Hall, not only did the underworld community attend, but legitimate businessmen came as well. They came, said Shoenfeld, "to pay tribute to Jack Zelig."

At Zelig's demise from an assassin's bullet in October 1912, thousands of people gathered at his house to get a glimpse of the coffin and to pay their final respects.

"The streets all around Broome Street were jammed," wrote Shoenfeld. "A choir consisting of twelve singers conducted by Cantor Goldberg of Newark, New Jersey sang their Jewish hymns as the procession proceeded down Delancy Street to the bridge.

"There was an unbroken line of people covering the sidewalk watching the funeral. Only the funeral of Rabbi Joseph [a revered spiritual leader] surpassed this, the funeral of Jack Zelig."

Fifty years after Zelig's death, historian Arthur Goren asked Judge Jonah Goldstein, who had been a young lawyer at the time and involved in local politics, why so many Jews attended Zelig's funeral. Did the East Side look upon Zelig as a hero, Goren asked. The judge replied that "going to Coney Island, you take the street car at the Brooklyn Bridge. Jack Zelig and a couple of his thugs would hire some Jews with beards to ride on the open trolley cars. Then some good-for-nothing loafers would come along and pull the Jews' beards. They'd give it to those who pulled the beards. They didn't want a Jew's beard pulled. They had never been educated in

Hebrew, didn't go to shul [synagogue], but they weren't going to have a Jew tossed around because he was a Jew. They made it possible for the Jews not to get tossed around."[10]

As a youngster, Abner "Longy" Zwillman earned the gratitude of local Jewish peddlers because he and his gang, the "Happy Ramblers," defended them from assaults by Irish thugs. Old-time Jewish residents of Newark still recall that whenever the Irish came into the Jewish district to create trouble, the cry "Ruff der Langer" ("Call the tall one") went up. And quick as a flash, Zwillman and his pals would stop whatever they were doing and rush to help. As a result, Longy acquired a reputation for assisting Jews that remained with him all his life.[11]

One of Zwillman's most loyal lieutenants, Max "Puddy" Hinkes, protected elderly Jews when he was a young man. A friend of Puddy's remembers him as "a tough kid who liked to fight. He was a prizefighter and he had a mean streak.

"When the goyim, particularly the Irish toughs, would come into the Prince Street area, where the Jews congregated in Newark, and they would beat up elderly Jews or belittle them and pull their beards, the old Jews would holler for Puddy. And Puddy provided physical protection for these old-timers. It was Puddy's great pleasure to take a stick and beat a bunch of guys and break heads. He loved a good fight.

"Puddy came from a good Jewish home. His mother was president of the synagogue sisterhood. Puddy was devoted to his parents and he would never allow anyone to badmouth Jews.

"Once he was at the fights in Laurel Gardens on Springfield Avenue in Newark, and some local Jewish kid was fighting that night. Somebody sitting in front of Puddy kept hollering 'Hit that Jew, kill 'em.'

"Puddy was smoking a Havana cigar and was rather reluctant to use it for purposes other than personal enjoyment. However, he finally made the supreme sacrifice of his personal pleasure. He tapped the guy in front of him on the shoulder. When the guy turned around to see who was tapping him, Puddy stuck the lit cigar right in his eye, badly injuring the man. Although his enjoyment of the cigar was ruined, Puddy got pleasure from hurting the anti-Semite."[12]

Another Zwillman associate, Hymie Kugel, would also tolerate no slurs against Jews. Though a small man, standing only five feet two inches, Hymie was fast, tough as nails and afraid of no one. They called him "the Weasel." His son Jerry knew with whom his father associated, but still loved and admired him, especially because Hymie would tolerate no slurs against the Jews.

Itzik Goldstein remembers one time he and Hymie happened to be in the Ideal Restaurant, when "three Pollacks came in and ordered meat. They were making a party. They started to abuse the owner, Izzy the Chink. 'You Jew bastard,' they said.

"Hymie came out. He went upstairs. I happened to be sitting in the front reading the paper. This is maybe twelve, one o'clock, maybe later," recalls Itzik.

"Hymie went over by the stove and he took the top of the stove, that plate that goes on top of the stove. He says to me, 'Grab something.'

"So I grab a celery tonic bottle.

"'You don't do nothing until they come outside,' he says.

"So I see he goes inside and he's talking to these guys, moving his hands. Finally Hymie and the three Pollacks walk out.

"So he says, 'Listen, Sonny, they don't serve meat in there. This is a Jewish restaurant. So why don't you fellas be nice and go home.'

"While he's talking to them he takes the steel plate and hits a guy across the face. And I hit one of the guys with the bottle. One of the guys ran down the street. And these two guys are laid out right in front of the restaurant.

"So Hymie and I ran upstairs of the Old Vienna. We went up on the second floor. So we're looking out the window and the guy that ran away comes back.

"In the meantime, Chink called the police. They came down with the patrol wagon and locked the three of them up. They picked up the two guys that were beat up and the guy that ran down the street.

"Before he got in the wagon, I heard him say 'they went upstairs there.'

"We hid. The cop comes up looks around. 'Nobody up there,' he says.

"Before they put this guy in the patrol wagon, he went to lock his car.

"Hymie says, 'Ooh, he's got a car here.'

"Well what Hymie did to that car. He got a meat cleaver and he jumped on the hood. He put holes in that car."

Hymie's son remembers the time his father, his sister, his mother and his mother's sister and husband went to eat at Child's Restaurant on Market Street. "It was raining. We come in and we had umbrellas. You know, when you put in an umbrella, you shake it out," he says.

"Some guy's paying the tab, and my aunt accidently shook her umbrella all over this guy. She apologized.

"This guy says, 'These Jews, they don't know their place.' And he's rattling off.

"At each cashier's desk there used to be a big ashtray. My father picks up the ashtray and smashes the guy in the face with it. He destroyed him. Knocked his tooth out.

"The place had revolving doors. And my dad runs out, waits a couple of minutes, and then comes back in. Like he doesn't know anything.

"He says, 'What happened?' He was cute. He said, 'What happened here?'

"Then he helps the guy up!"

"I loved my dad. He was quite a guy."[13]

Among Jewish youngsters growing up in the ghettos, respect for the gangster as a tough and fearless protector of his ethnic group became something akin to idolization. Television talk-show host Larry King admitted that when he was a boy in New York, "Jewish gangsters were our heroes.... Even the bad ones were heroes to us."[14]

Chicago Jewish mobster Davey Miller recognized the source of this adulation. He and his three brothers, Herschel, Max and Harry, ran a family business of slugging, thieving, extortion and bootlegging. They held one of the biggest gambling concessions in Chicago during the early 1920s. It embraced the entire length of Roosevelt Road, which contained the greatest concentration of Jewish merchants in the city. Chicago's corrupt mayor, William Hale "Big Bill" Thompson, sold it to them.[15]

But the Miller gang had another side: that of defending Jews against anti-Semites. Davey once explained his role in this to a reporter. "What I have done from the time I was a boy was to fight for my people here in the ghetto against Irish, Poles, or any other nationality," he said. "It was sidewalk fighting at first. I could lick any five boys or men in a sidewalk free-for-all.

"Maybe I am a hero to the young folks among my people, but it's not because I'm a gangster," he said. "It's because I've always been ready to help all or any of them in a pinch."[16]

The sense of obligation to protect the Jewish community led some Jewish mobsters to fight against American Nazis and their sympathizers during the 1930s. The Great Depression and the rise of Hitler and Nazism in Europe spurred an increase in anti-Semitism in the United States. The violent and hate-filled rantings of men like Detroit radio priest Father Charles E. Coughlin; the quasi-fascist fundamentalist Protestant preacher Gerald Winrod; and the head of the German-American Bund (referred to as the Nazi Bund), Fritz Kuhn, worried American Jewish leaders, but they were uncertain how to respond.

Concerned about "what the gentiles thought" and fearful of stirring up even more anti-Jewish sentiment, the American Jewish establishment's response was often tentative and disorganized. One group of American Jews which did not trouble themselves about what the gentiles thought and had no compunctions about meeting the anti-Semites head-on were Jewish gangsters.

Nazi Bund rallies in New York during the late 1930s created a terrible dilemma for the city's Jewish leaders. They wanted the meetings stopped, but could not do so legally. Nathan Perlman, a New York judge and former Republican congressman, was one Jewish leader who believed that Jews "have to demonstrate a little more militancy."[17]

Perlman surreptitiously contacted Meyer Lansky and asked him to help. He assured Lansky that money and legal assistance would be put at his disposal. The only stipulation was that no Nazi

Bundists were to be killed. Beaten up, yes. Terminated, no. Lansky reluctantly agreed. No killing.[18]

Always very sensitive about anti-Semitism, Lansky was acutely aware of what the Nazis were doing. "I was a Jew and I felt for those Jews in Europe who were suffering," he said. "They were my brothers."[19]

Lansky refused the judge's offer of money and assistance, but he did make one request. He asked Perlman to insure that he would not be criticized by the Jewish press after he went into action. The judge promised to do what he could.

Lansky rounded up some of his friends and members of Brooklyn's Murder, Inc. mob, and went about New York disrupting pro-Nazi meetings. Young Jews not associated with him or the rackets also volunteered to help, and Lansky and others taught them how to use their fists and handle themselves in a fight.

Lansky's crews worked very professionally. Nazi arms, legs and ribs were broken and skulls were cracked, but no one died. The attacks continued for more than a year.[20]

Judd Teller, a reporter for a Yiddish daily newspaper, characterized one of the actions in New York's Yorkville, the center of pro-Nazi sympathy, as a miniature reenactment "of the night when God struck all the firstborn in Egypt." According to Teller, some gangsters infiltrated the meeting while others waited outside. At a prearranged time, the men inside the hall bounded from their seats and charged the speakers, while their confederates outside rushed the sentries guarding the door and burst inside. A third group of invaders climbed the fire escapes and clambered through the windows.

The mobsters worked expertly and swiftly, and it was all over in a matter of minutes. There were no fatalities and no permanent injuries, only dislocated limbs, bloodied heads and noses, and damage requiring dental work. "Like commandos, they were gone before the police arrived," writes Teller.[21]

Years later, Lansky recounted one of the onslaughts in Yorkville to Israeli journalist Uri Dann. "We got there in the evening and found several hundred people dressed in their brown shirts," he said. "The stage was decorated with a swastika and pictures of Hitler. The speakers started ranting. There were only fifteen of us, but we went into action.

"We attacked them in the hall and threw some of them out the windows. There were fistfights all over the place. Most of the Nazis panicked and ran out. We chased them and beat them up, and some of them were out of action for months.

"We wanted to teach them a lesson," Lansky said. "We wanted to show them that Jews would not always sit back and accept insults."[22]

For months afterward, whenever the Nazis held rallies, they demanded police protection. Mayor Fiorello LaGuardia, whose mother was Jewish and who spoke Yiddish, complied with their request. To ensure the Nazis' safety, he confined the Bundist parades and rallies to Yorkville and forbad them to wear their uniforms or sing their songs. As an additional measure, he sent Jewish and black policemen to guard their meetings.[23]

Reflecting on his role in these episodes many years later, Lansky fumed that though he helped the Jewish community, all he got for his trouble was abuse. He believed the city's Jewish leaders were pleased with the actions, but they failed to stop the Jewish press from condemning him. When the press reported the anti-Bund incidents, they referred to Lansky and his friends as "the Jewish gangsters." This infuriated Lansky.

"They wanted the Nazis taken care of but were afraid to do the job themselves," he said. "I did it for them. And when it was over they called me a gangster. No one ever called me a gangster until Rabbi Wise (Stephen Wise) and the Jewish leaders called me that."[24]

Lansky never forgot the slight.

The Nazi Bund was also active across the river in New Jersey, especially in Newark which had a large German-American community. As a Jew, Longy Zwillman was not about to allow the Nazis to operate with impunity. He delegated Puddy Hinkes to handle the problem.

In 1938, with Zwillman's encouragement, Hinkes joined a group of Newark Jews who called themselves the "Minutemen," borrowing the name from the Minutemen of Revolutionary War fame. The original Minutemen were members of the farmer-militia in Massachusetts who fought the British at Lexington in 1775. They were named Minutemen because they were expected to be ready to fight at a minute's notice.

Newark's Jewish Minutemen had been organized by a Jewish ex-prizefighter by the name of Nat Arno. They saw to it that no Nazi Bund meetings were held in the New Jersey area, particularly in Newark and the small towns surrounding it. Arno and his men monitored the movement of the Nazis and, finding out where their meetings were held, broke them up.

Arno received financial and political support in these forays from Longy Zwillman. In those days, Zwillman controlled Newark's police and government. Whenever the Bund met, the police informed Longy of the time and place and conveniently abandoned their posts so that the Nazis were left unguarded.[25]

The Minutemen's most famous exploit occurred at Schwabben

Hall on Springfield Avenue, bordering the German neighborhood in Irvington. According to Hinkes, "The Nazi scumbags were meeting one night on the second floor. Nat Arno and I went upstairs and threw stink bombs into the room where the creeps were.

"As they came out of the room, running from the horrible odor of the stink bombs and running down the steps to go into the street to escape, our boys were waiting with bats and iron bars. It was like running a gauntlet. Our boys were lined up on both sides and we started hitting, aiming for their heads or any other part of their bodies, with our bats and irons.

"The Nazis were screaming blue murder. This was one of the most happy moments of my life. It was too bad we didn't kill them all.

"In other places we couldn't get inside, so we smashed windows and destroyed their cars, which were parked outside. The Nazis begged for police help and protection; however, the police favored us."[26]

Heshey Weiner, another participant in the fracas, remembers that one of the Nazis, who came running down the stairs, had the indiscretion to shout "Heil" and was met with a chorus of lead pipes. Heshey claims that after this attack, he "never heard any more of Bund meetings by the Nazis in our area."[27]

In 1992, in recognition of these actions, the Synagogue of the Suburban Torah Center in Livingston, New Jersey, sponsored a dinner to honor Hinkes as a man who "wreaked havoc and destruction" on those "that would wish to do harm to Jewish lives."[28]

In Chicago, blond, blue-eyed Herb Brin, who worked as a crime reporter for the City Press, joined the local Nazi party as a spy for the Anti-Defamation League of the B'nai B'rith. "I joined the Nazi party at the Hausfaterland, on Western Avenue across from Riverview Park. It was a hotbed of Nazi activity," he recalls.[29]

From 1938 through 1939, he kept the ADL informed about Nazi activities. What the ADL did not know was that Brin also fed information about Nazi marches and rallies to Jewish gangsters.

"I marched with the Nazis," recalls Brin, "but I came back later with Jewish gangs and we beat them up good."[30]

Minneapolis, Minnesota was also a hotbed of anti-Semitism during the 1930s, only here, the problem was William Dudley Pelley's pro-Nazi Silvershirt Legion. A California native, Pelley was a former screen writer, crime reporter, novelist and magazine journalist. He hated President Roosevelt and wanted to rescue America from an international Jewish-Communist conspiracy. Pelley created his Silvershirts, he said, to "save America as Mussolini and his Blackshirts saved Italy and as Hitler and his Brownshirts saved Germany."[31]

Minneapolis had a long history of anti-Semitism and was one of the few American cities to successfully bar Jews from the service clubs (Rotary, Kiwanis and Lions) and civic welfare organizations. Because of Minneapolis' anti-Jewish tradition, Pelley felt it would be easy to gain a foothold there.[32]

At the time, the city's gambling czar was Davie Berman, an associate and sometimes rival of Isidore Blumenfeld. Berman despised anti-Semites and determined to destroy the Silvershirts. He found out where they met and prepared his men for a raid.

One evening the call came to Berman's bookmaking operation at the Radisson Hotel. "Tonight there's a Silvershirt meeting at the Elk's Lodge at eight P.M.," said the caller.[33]

Berman immediately called his men. "Be at the office at seven P.M. and bring anybody and everything you've got," he said.

When his men arrived, Berman distributed brass knuckles and clubs. He and his men then drove in a convoy of Cadillacs to the Elk's Lodge and waited for the right moment to attack.

The hall inside was decorated with Nazi banners and portraits of Hitler, and the crowd waited expectantly for the meeting to begin. As soon as the Silvershirt leader mounted the podium and began shouting for an end to "all the Jew bastards in this city," Berman's lookout signaled to him.

Berman and his men charged through the door and began beating every Silvershirt within reach. The meeting turned into pandemonium, with the audience screaming and running for the exits followed by every Silvershirt still able to stand.

The attack lasted ten minutes. When it was over, Berman, his suit covered with blood, took the microphone. "This is a warning," he said in a cold controlled voice. "Anybody who says anything against Jews gets the same treatment. Only next time it will be worse." He then took out a pistol and fired a shot into the air.

After this, he and his men left the hall. It took two more such attacks to frighten off the Silvershirts. Berman and Blumenfeld paid off the police and there were never any arrests connected with the incident.[34]

The Silvershirts and Nazi Bundists were also active on the West Coast, especially in Los Angeles. Although few in number, they were noisy and brazen and alarmed the city's Jewish community. During the height of Nazi activity in the summer of 1938, Mickey Cohen happened to be serving a short sentence in the Los Angeles County jail. He was reading a newspaper in the bullpen (the barred enclosure where prisoners are kept temporarily), waiting to go to court, when Robert Noble, a notorious local Nazi Bundist, and another Nazi colleague were brought in for questioning. Cohen knew what Noble was and Noble knew who Cohen was. The police made the mistake of seating the anti-Semites near Mickey and leaving them alone.

The two Nazis tried to move away, but Cohen grabbed them before they could. "I started bouncing their heads together," relates Cohen. "With two of them, you'd think they'd put up a fight, but they didn't do nothing.

"So I'm going over them pretty good. The windup is that they're climbing up on the bars, both of them, and I'm trying to pull them down. Now they're screaming and hollering so much everybody thinks it's a riot.

"The jail chief at that time was a guy named Bright. So a riot call goes out, and Bright comes running down himself with a group of sheriffs. Bright's all excited. He's trying to open the bullpen door, but he can't get in. These two guys are still up on the bars screaming about their rights and, 'Why did ya throw us in with an animal, with a crazy man?'

"By this time I've gone back to my corner and picked up the newspaper. So I'm reading when Bright finally gets the door open.

"He comes over and says, 'You son of a bitch, what happened now?'

"I says, 'What are you asking me for? I'm sitting here reading the newspaper. Them two guys got into a fight with each other. I don't know what happened. I didn't want to mix in with them.'

"He says, 'You're a lying son of a bitch.'

"Actually I didn't know them at all except they were anti-Jew. But I sorted that one out, and boy, I felt so good about it.[35]

"After this got heard about, I'd get calls from places like the Writer's Guild to help with their problems with Nazi bastards. One time there was even a judge that called me about a German Nazi Bund meeting. I told him all right, don't worry about it."

Cohen gathered together some of his Jewish mobster friends and raided the Nazi meeting. "So we went over there and grabbed everything in sight, all their bullshit signs, and smacked the shit out of them, broke them up as best we could.

"Nobody could pay me for this work. It was my patriotic duty. There ain't no amount of money to buy them kind of things," said Mickey.[36]

Perhaps the most famous gangster-Nazi story concerns Benjamin "Bugsy" Siegel. In 1938, Joseph Goebbels, Hitler's Minister of Propaganda, and Hermann Goring, head of Germany's air force and Hitler's designated successor, were visiting Mussolini and staying at the Rome villa of Count Carlo Di Frasso and his wife, Dorothy.

Dorothy Di Frasso had met Siegel in Hollywood and the two were in the midst of a torrid affair. The countess brought Siegel to Rome at the same time the two Nazis were there. Siegel did not like what he had heard about Nazi anti-Semitism, and when he discovered that Hitler's henchmen were nearby, he became livid. He announced his intention of liquidating them both.

"You can't do that!" protested the countess.

Misunderstanding her concern, Siegel replied, "Sure I can. It's an easy setup the way they're walking around here."

Siegel abandoned his homicidal intentions when the countess pointed out that her husband would be held responsible. According to Siegel's friends, the gangster always regretted not killing Goebbels and Goring when he had the chance.[37]

Buried in the FBI archives is an even more startling story.[38]

On March 29, 1933, Homer Cummings, the Attorney General of

the United States, received an intelligence report from Secretary of State Cordell Hull about an alleged threat by American Jews to assassinate Adolph Hitler.

Six days earlier, the German Ambassador to Washington, Friedrich Wilhelm von Prittwitz-Gaffron, had received a letter from an individual by the name of David Stern, in which Stern warned that unless there was "an immediate and complete end of the persecution" of Jews, he would "go to Germany and assassinate Hitler."[39]

Was Stern a crackpot? Was the letter a hoax? Given the well-publicized attacks and demonstrations against Jews that began as soon as Hitler became Chancellor of Germany in January, a threat by an American Jew to kill him could not be discounted.

Von Prittwitz asked the State Department to look into the matter. Hull quickly contacted the Attorney General and requested that he conduct an investigation and report back to him.[40]

Any threat to assassinate a foreign dignitary — even outside the United States — had to be taken very seriously by American authorities. Not only were there grave international repercussions to conspiracies hatched in the United States against foreign leaders, but such plots could easily turn against an American leader. This had been dramatically demonstrated on February 15th in Miami, when an unemployed bricklayer named Giuseppe Zangara fired six bullets at President-elect Franklin Roosevelt. The bullets missed Roosevelt, but struck and killed Mayor Anton Cermack of Chicago who accompanied him. Zangara later told police that he purchased the pistol in Italy in order to kill King Emanuel. Then he changed his mind and went after Roosevelt.

Zangara said that he did not hate Roosevelt personally. He hated all presidents, no matter what country they came from, and he hated all officials and everybody who was rich. Zangara was executed in the electric chair.

Zangara was certainly unbalanced. But so might be the man who now threatened to kill Hitler. And he, too, might turn on an easier target — one closer to home. In addition, given the anger of American Jews toward the Nazis, any threat on Hitler's life by a Jew had to be taken seriously.

After Hull contacted him, Cummings called J. Edgar Hoover and asked him to find Daniel Stern and stop him. Hoover assigned one of his best agents, Dwight Brantley, to coordinate the national investigation. Brantley promptly alerted Division of Investigation field offices across the country to the news of the plot to kill the Fuhrer.[41]

Throughout the remainder of the spring and summer, and into the fall of 1933, Hoover's G-men searched for Daniel Stern. Their search led them from Washington to Chicago and then to Philadelphia, Detroit, Arizona and New York.

One avenue that Hoover initially adopted in the hunt for Stern and any of his confederates was to question members of the Jewish underworld. If Stern was a professional killer and not just some kook, then he might be known to other Jewish mobsters such as Max Hoff in Philadelphia, Meyer Lansky, Bugsy Siegel and Lepke Buchalter in New York, and Longy Zwillman in Newark. They might, in some way, be connected with Stern, or they may have been approached by someone to do the job. If so, they could provide leads in the case.

Agents in Philadelphia turned to Max Hoff for help. R.G. Harvey, the agent in charge of the Division's Philadelphia office, interviewed Hoff and scores of his associates. They all claimed they had never heard of Daniel Stern or of any plot to kill Hitler, or any other Nazi for that matter. But almost all of them, Harvey reported, were impressed by the plot and thought it was a great idea!

G-men interviewed the German consul in Philadelphia and examined his files. The consul stated that he had not been advised of any plot to kill Hitler. He also said that, in all probability, the letter from Stern was written by "some crank, who is a sympathizer of the Jewish element." He told agent Harvey that he was often "besieged by individuals who make threats upon him, but that they are all of the crank type and he dismisses them and pays no attention to them, as he does not consider their threats serious."[42]

The most promising lead reached the Justice Department from a source in Tucson, Arizona. There, a man reported that, on the evening of May 19, 1933, he was in the San Carlos Hotel when he overheard a Yiddish-speaking group whom he described as "stout men in their fifties," including a rabbi, discussing "a plan to murder Chancellor Hitler." He immediately informed the German Embassy in Washington.

According to this informant, the men initially talked about conditions in Germany and the Nazi persecution of the Jews. Then, "one of the speakers told the others that Hitler would not last long; that a number of Jews in New York were sending someone to Germany to assassinate Hitler."[43]

The FBI quickly dispatched agents from Los Angeles to Tucson. They interrogated everyone working in the hotel and combed the hotel registry for names. Every clue turned into a dead end.

On August 19, 1933, Special Agent J.M. Keith sent a progress report regarding "Daniel Stern and the threat to assasinate German chancellor Hitler" to Hoover. Keith summarized the investigations in Philadelphia, Arizona, Detroit and New York and conceded that the Bureau had failed to locate Stern or to uncover any plot to kill

Hitler. He concluded his report by saying that "this case has been reassigned and in the future will receive appropriate attention."[44]

Nothing more was done.

Finally, on September 2, 1933, Acting Special Agent Dwight Brantley submitted his own final report to Hoover, writing that "all outstanding leads have been completed without any definite information having been obtained." Accordingly, he wrote, "this case is closed." Brantley assured Hoover that the case would be "reopened in the event further information is received by the German Chancellor."[45]

Was there really a plot hatched by someone to murder Hitler in early 1933?

Daniel Stern was never found, nor could he be accurately described.

More than fifty years later "Dutch," a former New York mobster, recounted how, in the early spring of 1933, "someone respectable" had approached him about "bumping off" Hitler. He was asked to take the request to some of his "associates" who might show an interest in the undertaking. When he asked for more details on the project, Dutch was told that "there are people in Germany who are ready to assist us."

Dutch said he "talked to some of the boys about it. And they were willing to go to Germany to do the job." They all spoke Yiddish, he said, and so believed they could get around any language problems in Germany. But before the contract could be formalized any further, "Hoover's men started snooping around and asking questions." "The boys" thought it wiser to drop the matter.

Reflecting on the plot, Dutch concluded, "We shoulda done it.

Too bad we didn't do it. So many Jews woulda been saved. They woulda given us all medals. We woulda been heroes. Imagine."[46]

Just as gangsters were admired for their defense of their community, so, too, were they honored for their philanthropy. The Jewish leadership averred it never took contributions from criminals. A prominent Chicago Jewish communal leader, Dr. S.S. Hollender, claimed that while he was general chairman of the Chicago United Jewish Appeal campaign in 1951, Jack Guzik "came to see me with $5000 in cash and I turned it down. We just didn't want to take tainted money."[47]

Yet Jewish organizations and charities did accept gangster contributions, rarely inquiring as to the source of the money; neither did they discriminate among donors. Meyer Lansky donated large sums of money to his synagogue, Temple Sinai in Hollywood, Florida; to Brandeis University; and to causes related to Israel.

Shepard Broad, one of Miami Beach's most eminent Jewish activists, remembers that when it came to Israel, "You did not have to ask Meyer Lansky twice. Not like some. He was always waiting for me in the lobby with a check."[48]

In his later years, Moe Dalitz also became something of a philanthropist whose contributions were accepted by one and all. At a dinner in Las Vegas in 1970, Moe received the City of Peace Award of the State of Israel, "in recognition of distinguished service to the people and the State of Israel." The governor of Nevada, United States senators, judges and other public officials attended the event. Six years later the American Cancer Research Center acknowledged Moe's support by presenting him with its "Humanitarian Award." And in 1985, the Anti-Defamation League of the B'nai B'rith, a national Jewish defense and human rights organization, awarded Moe its Torch of Liberty award in "deep appreciation" of his financial contributions over the years.[49]

Moe Sedway, a former associate of Bugsy Siegel and one of Dalitz's Las Vegas partners, revealed to the Kefauver Committee that he had served as chairman of the Nevada United Jewish Appeal in 1947.[50]

When Jake Guzik died, Rabbi Noah Ganze of the Chicago Loop Synagogue eulogized him as a man who had generously helped hundreds of people. "His charities were performed quietly," said Ganze. "And he made frequent and vast contributions to my congregation."[51]

In Newark, New Jersey, Longy Zwillman's generosity was legendary. He provided needy Jews with food during the Jewish holidays and distributed truckloads of food and toys to the Christian community every Thanksgiving and Christmas. One of Zwillman's friends estimated that it cost Longy about $10,000 for Thanksgiving and as much as $15,000 for Christmas.[52]

During the Depression, Longy contributed $1,000 per week to a soup kitchen established by the city's Catholic diocese in the basement of St. Patrick's Cathedral on Mulberry Street. The sign over the entrance proclaimed, "All needy regardless of race or creed are welcome to the free dinners served here every day from 11 A.M. to 2 P.M."[53]

When word leaked out that the soup kitchen's benefactor was a notorious gangster, some Catholic laymen demanded an explanation. One of them approached the city's archbishop, the Reverend Thomas J. Walsh and complained about the soup kitchen receiving "sinful" money. The archbishop replied that "$50,000 of that money is blessed."[54]

Longy also financed the college education of young people in

Newark, New York, Cleveland and Chicago, even sending a number of them through medical and law school. Two of the young men were the sons of waiters at Toots Shor's restaurant in New York. Shor was a friend of Zwillman's and Longy often ate at his restaurant when he came to New York.

A list of Longy's charitable contributions was presented to the court during his trial for income tax evasion. In 1947-1948, Zwillman donated money to the United Jewish Appeal, the *Newark News* Christmas fund for the needy, the National Conference of Christians and Jews, the National Probation Association, the Catholic Actor's Guild, Congregation Beth Torah, Sinai Congregation, the Newark Welfare Federation, the Policeman's Benevolent Association and the East Orange General Hospital.[55]

Most of the time, Zwillman gave his aid directly to the individuals or charitable organizations. Sometimes, however, he proffered his charity in strange ways. One year, for example, between the Jewish New Year and the Day of Atonement, Zwillman invited Rabbi Isaac Unterman of Jersey City to his office.

Unterman was nervous because he did not know what Zwillman wanted. When they met, Zwillman said, "Rabbi, I understand you're the only honest man in the Jewish community. It's before Yom Kippur, so here's $50,000. Give it to any charity you want." Whereupon he handed Unterman $50,000 in cash.[56]

Philanthropic activity by mobsters and its acceptance, even solicitation by the legitimate community, was not a phenomenon unique to Jews. Italian Mafia figures also contributed to charity. Mafia bosses made regular donations to their local Catholic parish and their children's private schools, and their contributions were made openly, with no attempt at secrecy. The Catholic Church and

Catholic charities were aware of where the money came from and they displayed no qualms about accepting it.

In 1949, Frank Costello held a $100-a-plate dinner for the Salvation Army at the Copacabana nightclub in New York, a gala event attended by mob figures, churchmen and judges. Joe Bonanno, the head of one of New York's five leading crime families, boasted that he belonged to innumerable civic and charitable organizations. "I am a life member of the Elks, as well as a perpetual member of the Society for the Propagation of the Faith," he said. "I'm a member of the Knights of Columbus... I've contributed to St. Mary's Hospital. I can't begin to count the money I've donated to the Roman Catholic archdiocese in Tucson."[57]

Thus in both the Jewish and Italian communities, occasions arose when underworld figures became acceptable.

Commenting on this aspect of Jewish communal life, one underworld figure declared that "There was never once, when I gave *tsedakah* [charity] that somebody said to me, 'From whence comes this source of money?' Never once did anybody ever say that. And everybody knows who I am."[58]

Jewish gangsters also assisted in the creation of the State of Israel by providing much needed aid in its war against the Arabs. After the Holocaust, Zionists viewed the establishment of a Jewish state as a matter of life or death. This led them to solicit and accept help from any and every quarter.

In 1945, the Jewish Agency, the pre-state Israeli government headed by David Ben-Gurion, established a clandestine arms purchasing and smuggling network throughout the United States. The operation was placed under the aegis of the Haganah, the underground forerunner of the Israel Defense Forces, and involved

Isidore (Kid Cann) Blumenfeld

American Jews and non-Jews from every walk of life, including the Jewish underworld.[59]

Yehuda Arazi, a long-time gunrunner for the Haganah, came to the United States to assist in the arms purchasing effort. Known as a loner with his own method of operation, Arazi made contact with former members of the notorious Murder, Inc. gang of killers for hire and asked for their assistance. As he explained, "In my business we can't be too fussy who we do business with. Sometimes they're not nice people."[60]

At the time, the government of the United States maintained an arms embargo against Israel. This embargo did not apply to the Arab states, which could always import military hardware.

Arazi knew that the Mafia controlled the port in New York. He approached Meyer Lansky and asked him to find out what weapons passed through the port targeted for Arab countries and, if possible, prevent them from reaching their destination. Lansky said he would handle it.

Lansky contacted Albert Anastasia, who controlled the longshoreman's union and the docks. Anastasia's men made certain that weapons destined for the Arabs mysteriously got lost, fell overboard or were mistakenly loaded onto ships bound for Israel.[61]

New York and New Jersey longshoremen also helped Israeli agents conceal the arms they purchased for Israel. Illegal consignments of military hardware, some of it brand-new and still packed in oil and straw, were secreted onto ships and sent directly to Israel.

At their own initiative, a delegation of Jewish gangsters from Brooklyn met with Teddy Kollek, who orchestrated the arms smuggling venture from a two-room suite on the second floor of the

Hotel Fourteen in New York City. The men offered to help in any way they could. One of them said, "If you want anyone killed, just draw up a list and we'll take care of it." Kollek politely refused.[62]

Reuven Dafni, another Haganah emissary, was sent to Miami. While there, he met with a leading Miami Jewish gangster, Sam Kay.

"The contact was made for me by a Jewish lawyer whose office was in the same building as the gangster's," says Reuven. "The lawyer felt it was worth seeing the man, since we had nothing to lose. He called the gangster's office and I was invited upstairs.

"When I entered, I faced his secretary. It was like something out of a movie. She was blond, wore a low cut dress with her bosom half out, and was chewing gum and filing her nails. She never even looked at me, but said 'Go in, he's expecting you.'

"When I went in, all I saw were someone's feet on the desk, a newspaper and cigar smoke curling up from behind the paper. After standing quietly for a few minutes, I cleared my throat a couple of times. The paper was lowered and Sam said, 'Sit down and tell me what you want.' So I told him. When I finished he said okay, he would help.

"Now this Sam was good friends with the president of Panama. They were very close. And Sam contacted him for us. From then on, all our ships carrying weapons to Israel were registered in Panama and flew under the Panamanian flag. This was a very, very big help to us."[63]

A few months later the Haganah sent Reuven to Los Angeles. One day he received a curious phone call from a man who identified himself as "Smiley" and requested a meeting. When they met, Smiley asked Reuven to "Tell me what you're doing. The boss is interested." The "Boss" turned out to be Bugsy Siegel, and Smiley was Allen Smiley, his right-hand man.

Smiley arranged a meeting between Siegel and Reuven at the LaRue restaurant on La Cienega Boulevard. At the appointed time, Smiley and Reuven went into an empty room at the rear of the restaurant. After a few moments, Smiley left, leaving Reuven alone.

Soon, two tough-looking goons entered and searched the room. When they were satisfied it was safe, they left. Shortly thereafter, Siegel came in.

Reuven told him his story, the Haganah's need for money and weapons with which to fight. When he finished Siegel asked, "You mean to tell me Jews are fighting?"

"Yes," replied Reuven.

Siegel, who was sitting across the table, leaned forward until the two men's noses were almost touching.

"You mean fighting, as in killing?" he asked.

"Yes," answered Reuven.

Siegel looked at him for a moment and said, "I'm with you."

"From then on," recalls Reuven, "every week I got a phone call to go to the restaurant. And every week I received a suitcase filled with $5 and $10 bills. The payments continued until I left Los Angeles."

Reuven estimates that Siegel gave him a total of $50,000.[64]

In part, this episode reflects Siegel's attitude and past activities as a gunman and mob killer. Bugsy always remained enthusiastic about violence. Even after he became a major crime boss, he wanted to do the killing himself rather than simply arrange matters. This may explain his willingness to help Israel once he learned that Jews were willing to kill to achieve their state.

Murray Greenfield, an American who had been part of Aliya Bet, the "illegal immigrant" movement bringing Holocaust survivors to Palestine, was sent to the sporting division of the United Jewish

Appeal in Baltimore in 1949, and given the name of a local contact. Greenfield went to the man's house and was told to come back at midnight.

"I thought it strange," he remembers. "But if it helped Israel, I would do it."

When he arrived late that evening, Greenfield was ushered into the basement recreation room and told to wait. At about 12:30 A.M. the door opened and "the strangest group I had ever seen entered. The men were all short and stocky; their female companions were all blonds. The men sat on one side of the room, the women on the other."[65]

The host then asked Greenfield to tell his story. When he finished, his host said, "Okay, you guys know why you're here and what you have to do."

Then he looked around the room and said, "Joe, you're giving $5,000; Max, you're giving $5,000; Harry, you're giving $10,000; and so it went.

One of the participants complained that "business is tough because of the cops," and said he couldn't contribute so much. Another indicated that "I can't give you a lot of cash, but don't forget I helped you last year when you needed guns."

Undeterred by all the grumbling, Greenfield's host, formerly one of Baltimore's leading Jewish mobsters, continued dunning. In no time, more than $90,000 was collected. The money, in cash, was put in a paper bag and handed to Greenfield.

"There I was," he recalled, "in Baltimore at two o'clock in the morning holding thousands of dollars in a paper bag."[66]

In Los Angeles, Mickey Cohen held a fund-raising affair for the Irgun (the underground Jewish organization led by Menachem Begin) in 1947. Leading underworld figures from California and Las

Vegas attended and, according to Cohen and other sources, thousands of dollars were raised. The money, claimed Cohen, was used to purchase weapons and have them shipped to Israel.

Jimmy "The Weasel" Fratianno, a top Mafia killer who later turned informer, attended the party, which he recalls being held at Slapsy Maxie's restaurant. "The place's packed. I've never seen so many Jewish bookmakers in one place in my life... They're all there. Famous actors, producers, bigshots in the community. It's a full house. The entertainers are Lou Holtz, Ben Blue, Martha Ray, Danny Thomas. Sitting at our table's the chief of police of Burbank and his wife."[67]

To start things off, Mickey Cohen pledged twenty-five thousand dollars. "After that," remembers Fratianno, "forget about it. Everybody's pledging thousands. Even the bookmakers are pledging five and ten grand. They know Mickey's running the show and they're going to have to pay off."

Nevertheless, Fratianno remained suspicious.

His suspicions increased when a story in the *Los Angeles Herald* reported that an unnamed ship carrying arms for the Jews in Israel had sunk in the Atlantic Ocean during a storm.

Fratianno knew Cohen very well. When he wasn't socializing and working with Mickey, he was trying to kill him.

Fratianno maintains that Cohen kept the money for himself, insisting Cohen would never let hundreds of thousands of dollars slip through his fingers.

According to Fratianno, Cohen had a girlfriend who worked at the *Herald*. "And this broad would walk on hot coals for Mickey. The way I see it," says Fratianno, "Mickey called her and made up a story about buying guns and ammunition for the Jews with the million raised at the benefits and then told her the boat sank. A few unknown people died, some were saved, and she prints it on his sayso."

Fratianno confronted Mickey with his suspicions. "I says, 'Mickey, congratulations. You've just pulled off the biggest, cleanest fucking score I've ever seen made.' And he looks at me, just squinting, you know, and for a split second there's this big shit-eating grin on his face.

"But he says, 'Jimmy, you've got me all wrong. The story's right here in the paper.'

I says, 'Mickey, with your bullshit you better hold on to that paper, it might come in handy when you've got to wipe your mouth'."[68]

Other sources, including Yitzhak Ben-Ami, dispute Fratianno's allegations. Ben Ami headed the Irgun's European-based illegal immigration operations. In 1947, the Irgun sent him to the United States to assist the American League for a Free Palestine, the Irgun's funding and propaganda arm in the United States.

Ben-Ami helped organize the fund-raising affairs Fratianno spoke about. He claims that "between $50,000 and $60,000 was raised," and not the hundreds of thousands that Fratianno mentions.

"The 'Jewish underworld' contributed all together about $120,000," for the Irgun, says Ben-Ami.[69]

The funds were transferred to New York, partly for the outfitting of an LST vessel, renamed "Altalena," the pen name of writer Vladimir Zeev Jabotinsky, the leader of Revisionist Zionism.

Carrying 900 people and a cargo of 5,000 rifles, 450 machine guns and millions of rounds of ammunition, the "Altalena" sailed to Israel from France on June 11, 1948. When it reached the coast of Tel Aviv, David Ben-Gurion, the prime minister of Israel, ordered it fired upon, believing the weapons, designated for Menachem Begin's Irgun forces, posed a threat to the new Labor-led Israeli government.

The "Altalena" burst into flames. Forty persons perished and many of the weapons were destroyed.[70]

This was most likely the ship referred to in the *Los Angeles Herald* article.

Ben-Ami regards Fratianno as Mickey's enemy. Spreading a false story about the Irgun money was his way of denigrating Cohen, and since Mickey was dead, he couldn't refute the charges.

Herb Brin also discounts Fratianno's version. He knew Cohen and believes Mickey told the truth about buying weapons with the money he raised.

"I knew who he was and what he was," says Brin. "But when we talked about Israel, he was a different person. He had tears in his eyes once when we talked about Israel."[71]

Why did these gangsters help the Jewish community? Some saw themselves as defenders of the Jews, almost biblical-like fighters. It was part of their self-image.

Herb Brin believes they helped their people because in each of them there was a "pintele Yid," a spark of Jewishness.[72]

Although he did not believe in God and was uninterested in religion, Meyer Lansky said he felt obligated to help the Jewish community and Israel because he was a Jew. Perhaps this was a way of compensating for his other, less heroic, life.[73]

In their later years, some gangsters simply sought the respect and legitimacy denied them in their youth. The way to acquire communal recognition and approbation was through Jewish philanthropy and devotion to "Jewish causes."

Other mobsters sought respectability so as not to embarrass their children and grandchildren, and thus jeopardize their chances for success in the legitimate world.

Reuven, the Haganah emissary, believes that Sam, the Miami gangster, assisted the Haganah for just this reason. "He had a daughter of marriageable age, but she had a difficult time meeting Jewish boys because of what her father was," he says. "I think he helped us because it was a way to gain acceptance in the Jewish community.

"Once it became known that he was helping us, the Jewish community's attitude toward him changed. His daughter began dating Jewish boys and eventually married one."[74]

Be that as it may, helping Israel may be seen as a later version of the Jewish gangster's tradition of protecting his neighborhood from anti-Semites. After World War II, the Jewish state symbolically came to represent the Jewish neighborhood. In defending Israel against her enemies, the Jewish gangster was still defending his people against the Jew haters.

Nevertheless, not every Jewish gangster was so altruistic toward the Jewish community or Jewish interests. Some of the same Jewish hoodlums who later claimed to have defended their neighborhood and Jews aginst anti-Semites, got their start in crime by preying on fellow Jews. Mickey Cohen, who boasted that he "would do anything for a cause that was right, particularly Jewish causes," and who said that "Jews should behave differently and more correctly," threatened and extorted Los Angeles Jewish businessmen left and right.[75]

Other Jewish criminals thought nothing of working against Israel's interest if they could profit by it doing so. In 1951, two Detroit Jews, Arthur Leebove and Sam Stein, were convicted for conspiracy to smuggle 21 American warplanes from Newark, New Jersey to Egypt during the Arab-Israeli hostilities in 1948.[76]

Their scheme was to purchase surplus military aircraft, load them with British crews in Newark and fly them to England. Once there, an Egyptian crew would be brought on board and the planes flown to Egypt. The syndicate bought AT-6 airplanes and one B-25 bomber.

The plot came to light in December 1948 when the B-25 bomber was forced to return to Newark because of bad weather. The planes were then seized by federal agents before they could be delivered.[77]

For men such as these, protecting and helping Jews was fine as long as it did not interfere with business. When the two clashed, making money superseded ethnic loyalties.

Although the activities of the Lanskys and Siegels embarrassed the Jewish community, they could provide what respectable Jews could not: physical protection for the community and arms for an Israel struggling to survive. These men were not latter-day Robin Hoods and should not be glorified as such. Yet in their time, they contributed to their people's survival.

Epilogue

*J*ewish gangsterism declined after the Second World War. The urban ghettoes that spawned these men — New York's Lower East Side and those of Detroit, Philadelphia and Newark — no longer contained Jews. Jews moved to the suburbs, sent their children to universities and became part of America's economic, educational and occupational elite. Third and fourth generation American Jews no longer needed crime to "make it." Unlike the Italian Mafiosi, Jewish gangsters did not want members of their families to go into their "business." Hence, the activities of these men were one-generational. They had no successors. The Jewish gangster in America became history, something for their grandchildren to read about.

And what of the gangsters? Despite their depravity and violence, a part of these men remained a son of immigrants, still tied to his parents, his family, his people and to the American dream.

Author's Note and Acknowledgement

*M*y approach to the subject of Jewish gangsters in the United States has been selective. I did not attempt to be all-encompassing and include every important Jewish mobster.

The men I chose to include in my narrative lived in American cities which had large Jewish communities and whose rackets were, in large measure, influenced or dominated by Jews.

Chicago, whose organized crime was governed by Al Capone and his Italian successors, does not exactly fit my criteria. Nonetheless, Jack Guzik was such a character that I felt impelled to include him.

Another factor influencing my choices was the availability of written and oral sources on the various Jewish gangsters which suited my purposes.

Works on crime, whether recounted by the criminal, the lawman or the journalist, are filled with inaccuracies, errors, hearsay, misstatements and whitewashes. Using these sources frequently poses problems for the researcher seeking the truth. Since I used an anecdotal approach, I have avoided many of the dilemmas faced by historians who must make judgements on the reliability of the evidence.

Nonetheless, this is not a book of fiction. Wherever possible, I verified the accuracy of my sources and based my narrative on fact. The dialogue contained in the anecdotes is transcribed as related to me or as it appears in written accounts. In some instances, I edited the material and changed punctuation or capitalization to enhance readability. In all cases, I strove for accuracy without sacrificing the tone, flavor and spirit of the stories and the storyteller.

In this revised and expanded edition of the original, *But — He Was Good to His Mother*, I have added source notes as well as new material.

A number of persons were especially helpful to me and I want to acknowledge them. "Mervin," Irving "Itzik" Goldstein, Max "Puddy" Hinkes, Heshey Weiner, Faye Skuratofsky, Jerry Kugel, Myron Sugerman, Eli Golan, David Stern, Herb Brin, Lester Schaffer, Charles Jacobs, Carol K., Reuven Dafni, Jeremiah Unterman, David Avivi, A. Rubin, Murray Greenfield and Lori Levinski, gave generously of their time and reminiscences. Their input added spice and substance to the book. I also want to thank Dena Rubens, David Levitt, and Fay Newman Rubenstein, who took the time to write and share their memories with me. In addition, I wish to credit people who spoke to me but are no longer living, including Meyer Lansky, Harry Fleisch, Hershel Kessler, Sam Hessel, "Dutch," Philip Slomovitz, Leonard Simons and Elsie Proskie. Then, too, are those persons who spoke to me on condition of anonymity. In citing them in the text, I used an alias in place of their real names. I am also grateful to Professors Menachem Amir, Alan Block and Peter Lupsha for sharing their expertise and sources on organized crime with me.

For twenty years, I have used the good services of the people who administer the Freedom of Information Act at the Department of Justice. My thanks to all those who helped process my requests, including James K. Hall, Thomas H. Bresson, David G. Flanders, Emil P. Moschella, J. Kevin O'Brien, Linda Kloss, Marshall R. Williams and Helen Ann Near.

My thanks also to Danna Har-Gil whose editing skills proved most helpful in my revisions of the text. Lastly, I want to acknowledge, with thanks, Ilan, Dror and Murray Greenfield of Gefen Publishing House for their continuing interest and encouragement.

— Robert A. Rockaway
Arsuf, Israel

Source Notes

Chapter One: Crime Barons of the East

1. According to the FBI, Meyer Lansky made this comment to his wife in a wiretapped conversation; however, no written record of this comment survives. What does exist is the FBI agent's paraphrase of what Lansky supposedly said. Once this papraphrase became public it turned into a direct quotation. Lansky always denied having said it. Robert Lacey, *Little Man: Meyer Lansky and the Gangster Life* (Boston, 1991), pp. 284-285, offers a plausible analysis of how this phrase came to be attributed to Lansky.

2. Andrew Sinclair, *Era of Excess: A Social History of the Prohibition Movement* (New York, 1962), pp.166-170. At the time of repeal of Prohibition in 1933, the Roosevelt administration issued a report declaring that the total cost of Prohibition to the United States, in terms of lost revenue and enforcement, amounted to over 26 billion dollars, 10 billion dollars more than the cost of America's participation in the First World War (Ibid., pp. 396-399; William Helmer with Rick Mattix, *Public Enemies: America's Criminal Past* [New York, 1998], p. 65).

3. Larry Engelmann, *Intemperance: The Lost War Against Liquor* (New York, 1979), p. x.

4. Gangs and crime syndicates did not begin with Prohibition. They rose to power through the saloons, gambling houses and brothels of the nineteenth century, and through the murderous wars of labor and capital in the days of the robber barons. The simultaneous advent of automobiles, Thompson submachine guns and telephones allowed successful local gangsters to extend their control over entire cities and states (Sinclair, p. 221).

5. Sinclair, pp. 230-231.

6. Ibid., pp. 198; 438, note 62.
7. Robert Schoenberg, *Mr. Capone* (New York, 1992), p. 176; Laurence Bergreen, *Capone: The Man and the Era* (New York, 1994), pp. 356-357.
8. Hershel Kessler, interview by author, Los Angeles, Calif., 14 September 1989.
9. Mark Haller, "Bootleggers and American Gambling, 1920-1950," in Commission on the Review of National Policy Toward Gambling, *Gambling in America*, Appendix I (Washington, D.C., 1976); Stephen Fox, *Blood and Power: Organized Crime in Twentieth Century America* (New York, 1989), pp. 24-35; Albert Fried, *The Rise and Fall of the Jewish Gangster in America* (New York, 1980).
10. Leo Katcher, *The Big Bankroll: The Life and Times of Arnold Rothstein* (New York, 1959), p. 8.
11. Dennis Eisenberg, Uri Dan, Eli Landau, *Meyer Lansky: Mogul of the Mob* (New York, 1979), p. 108.
12. Katcher, p. 12.
13. Donald Henderson Clarke, *In the Reign of Rothstein* (New York, 1929), p. 13.
14. Jill Jonnes, "Founding Father: One Man Invented the Modern Narcotics Industry," *American Heritage*, February/March 1993, pp. 48-49; Katcher, pp. 287-299; David Courtwright, Herman Joseph, and Don Des Jarlais, *Addicts Who Survived: An Oral History of Narcotic Use in America, 1923-1965* (Knoxville, 1989), pp. 110-111, note 2; 199-200.
15. Alan Block, book review of *Addicts Who Survived*, in the *Journal of Social History* 24 (Winter 1990), pp. 396-399.
16. Courtwright et al., pp. 187, 193.
17. Ibid., p. 188.
18. Martin A. Gosch, Richard Hammer, *The Last Testament of Lucky Luciano* (Boston, 1974), p. 57.
19. Ibid., p. 41.
20. Katcher, pp. 138, 300.
21. *New York Times*, 5 November 1928; Katcher, p. 6.
22. *New York Times*, 8 November 1928; Arthur Goren, "Saints and Sinners: The Underside of American Jewish History," Brochure Series of the American Jewish Archives, Number VII, 1988, pp. 8-9.
23. *New York Times*, 2 December 1933.
24. Alan Block, *East Side-West Side: Organizing Crime in New York, 1930-1950* (New Brunswick, 1985), pp.133-134.
25. Jenna Weissman Joselit, *Our Gang: Jewish Crime and the New York Jewish Community, 1900-1940* (Bloomington, 1983), pp. 95-97.

26. Paul Sann, *Kill the Dutchman! The Story of Dutch Schultz* (New York, 1971), pp. 99-100.
27. *New York Times*, 25 October 1935.
28. Carl Sifakis, *The Encyclopedia of American Crime* (New York, 1982), p. 642.
29. Fox, p. 29.
30. Sann, p. 218.
31. Gosch, Hammer, p. 176.
32. Sifakis, p. 642.
33. Sann, p.106.
34. Sann, pp. 154, 166-167.
35. Sifakis, p. 642.
36. Max "Puddy" Hinkes, interview by author, Newark, N.J., 19 August 1990; Myron Sugerman, interview by author, Tel-Aviv, Israel, 19 April 1991.
37. Sifakis, p. 642.
38. *New York Times*, 22 June 1947; Lacey, p. 35. Eisenberg et al., p. 56.
39. Eisenberg et al., p. 56.
40. Ibid., p. 57.
41. Ibid., p.57.
42. Ibid., p. 122.
43. Stanley Feldstein, *The Land That I Show You: Three Centuries of Jewish Life in America* (New York, 1978), p. 323.
44. Eisenberg et al., p. 143.
45. In describing this incident, Peter Maas, *The Valachi Papers* (New York, 1968), p. 103, cites Case No. 133 of the 60th squad, New York Police Department.
46. *New York Sun*, 11 September 1931; Maas, *Valachi Papers*, pp. 112-116; Humbert Nelli, *The Business of Crime* (Lexington, 1976), p. 206.
47. Bureau of Prisons, Notorious Offenders File, "Louis 'Lepke' Buchalter," National Archives, Washington, D.C. (henceforth, Notorious Offenders File).
48. Ibid.
49. Gosch, Hammer, pp. 38-39.
50. Louis Buchalter, Admission Summary, 8 May 1940, Bureau of Prisons, Notorious Offenders File.
51. *New York Times*, 10 June 1947. FBI File 60-1501, "The Furdress Case," pp. 26-36. The FBI files cited are located at the Federal Bureau of Investigation Headquarters, Washington, D.C.
52. FBI File 60-1501; Burton B. Turkus and Sid Feder, *Murder, Inc.* (New York, 1992 [1951]), p. 332.
53. *New York Times*, 5 March 1944.

54. Turkus and Feder, p. 337.

55. FBI File 60-1501.

56. Ibid.

57. On Lepke's involvement in the narcotics traffic see, "Report on Convicted Prisoner by United States Attorney," U.S. Penitentiary Leavenworth, Kansas, 24 May 1940, in National Archives, Washington, D.C.; *New York Evening Journal-American*, 8 August 1939; *New York Times*, 6 April 1940; Turkus and Feder, p. 347.

58. U.S. Senate Special Committee to Investigate Organized Crime in Interstate Commerce (henceforth, IOC), 1951, Part 2, "Testimony of Harry J. Anslinger, Commissioner of Narcotics," pp. 89-91; see also Turkus and Feder, p. 348.

59. Turkus and Feder, pp. 332-333.

60. *New York Times*, 26 October 1935, 10 November 1935.

61. Nelli, pp. 211-218, maintains that no national crime organization was ever created, but various local syndicate leaders did meet periodically. On the other hand, Hank Messick, *Lansky*, pp. 72-79, maintains that a national syndicate was created.

62. Turkus and Feder, pp. 3-22; 350.

63. The information on Louis Amberg comes from the *New York Times*, 30 October 1932, 3 November 1932, 12 November 1932, 6 May 1934, 23 October 1935, 24 October 1935, 25 October 1935, 26 October 1935, 27 October 1935.

64. Carl Sifakis, *The Mafia Encyclopedia* (New York, 1987), p. 10.

65. Ibid.

66. IOC, Part 12, "Testimony of Abner Zwillman," p. 617. See FBI File 62-36085 for information about Zwillman's criminal activities.

67. Mark Stuart, *Gangster #2: Longy Zwillman, the Man Who Invented Organized Crime* (Secaucus, N.J, 1985), p. 22.

68. IOC, Report 725 (31 August 1951), pp. 65-66.

69. Ibid., pp. 66-67; Stuart, p. 32.

70. Hank Messick, *Secret File* (New York, 1969), p.278.

71. Ibid.

72. Fox, p. 31.

73. FBI File 62-3608.

74. FBI File 62-36085-10.

75. Ibid.

76. Irving "Itzik' Goldstein, interview by author, Newark, N.J.,16 August 1990.

77. Stuart, pp. 54-55.

78. Goldstein, interview.
79. Jerry Kugel, interview by author, Newark, N.J., 15 August 1990.
80. Stuart, pp. 80-89.
81. *New York Times*, 28 April 1941.
82. Philadelphia Grand Jury Report, 1928, Committee of Seventy Collection, Urban Archives Center, Temple University, Philadelphia, Pennsylvania; *New York Times*, 7 September 1928, 8 September 1928, 30 December 1928; *New Outlook*, November 1933, pp. 27-28.
83. Philadelphia Grand Jury Report, Ibid.
84. Ibid.
85. *New York Times*, 28 April 1941.
86. IOC, Part 11, pp. 72-98.
87. Fox, p. 72.
88. *New York Times*, 5 September 1957, 6 September 1957, 28 October 1957, 29 October 1957, 5 February 1958, 18 February 1958, 26 March 1958, 24 April 1958, 2 April 1958, 11 April 1958.
89. Lester Schaffer, interview by author, Philadelphia, Penn.,14 August 1991.
90. *Philadelphia Jewish Exponent*, 5 January 1979.
91. Information about Solomon is from the *New York Times*, 25 January 1933, 22 August 1933; National Archives, Record Group 60, File 12-1751; *Boston Globe*, 11 April 1933, 12 April 1933, 9 May 1933, 13 December 1933, 18 May 1934; and *Boston Evening Transcript*, 24 January-26 May, 1933.
92. The description of the murder is taken from the *Boston Globe*, 14 June 1933.

Chapter Two: Rogues of the Midwest

1. On Dalitz and the Cleveland Four, see Hank Messick, *The Silent Syndicate* (New York, 1967). On the gang during Prohibition, see the eleven part series of articles in the *Cleveland Plain Dealer* from 23 December 1933 to 5 January 1934.
2. IOC, Part 2, pp. 174-177 (testimony of Virgil Peterson).
3. Ibid.
4. *New York Times*, 10 September 1973; Ibid.
5. Ibid., 10 November, 1975, 22 November 1975.
6. IOC, Part 10, p. 923.
7. Sifakis, *Mafia Encyclopedia*, p. 96.
8. *Forbes*, 13 September 1982, p. 146.

9. FBI File 62-23190-178.

10. FBI File 32-15941.

11. Schoenberg, p. 102.

12. Ibid., pp. 102-103; George Murray, *The Legacy of Al Capone* (New York, 1975), pp. 120-122.

13. Murray, p. 341.

14. Bergreen, p.92.

15. Records of the Bureau of Prisons, National Archives, Notorious Offenders Files, HM FY91, Box 42.

16. Murray, p. 339.

17. Ibid., p. 337.

18. Ibid., p. 336.

19. FBI File 62-69850-1, 62-69850, 92-2720; Paul Maccabee, *John Dillinger Slept Here: The Crooks' Tour of Crime and Corruption in St. Paul, 1920-1936,* (St. Paul, 1995), p. xiii.

20. *New York Times,* 11 December 1935.

21. IOC, Part 2, pp. 170-171, testimony of Virgil Peterson.

22. Maccabee, p. 29.

23. Ibid., p. 35.

24. Ibid., pp. 39-41.

25. *Chicago Daily Jewish Courier* (Yiddish), 18 March 1924.

26. *Philadelphia Jewish Exponent,* 21 September 1928, p. 16.

27. Fried, pp. 112-113.

28. Leonard Simons, interview by author, Detroit, Mich., 20 August 1985.

29. Philip Slomovitz, interview by author, Detroit, Mich.,10 September 1989. While the Jewish English-language press printed almost nothing about Jewish crime, the New York Yiddish dailies, like the general press, were filled with stories about Jewish gangsters.

30. Leonard Dinnerstein, *Antisemitism in America* (New York, 1994), pp. 78-127.

31. Harry Fleisch, interview by author, Detroit, Mich., 20 July 1985.

32. Eisenberg et al., p. 34.

33. Schaffer, interview.

34. Herb Brin, interview by author, Los Angeles, Calif., 27 August 1991.

35. Mickey Cohen, *In My Own Words: The Underworld Autobiography of Michael Mickey Cohen* (Englewood Cliffs, N.J., 1975), p. 257.

Chapter Three: The Purple Gang

1. The following account of the "Collingwood Massacre" and its aftermath is based on C. H. Gervais, *The Rumrunners: A Prohibition Scrapbook* (Ontario, 1980), pp. 133-142; and the *Detroit News*, 11 November 1931, 12 December 1931, 28 November 1937.
2. Gervais, p. 133; *Detroit News*, 11 November 1931.
3. *Detroit News*, 22 August 1965; *Detroit Free Press*, 19 September 1965.
4. Gervais, p. 138.
5. *Detroit News*, 22 August 1965.
6. Robert A. Rockaway, *The Jews of Detroit: From the Beginning, 1762-1914* (Detroit, 1986), p. 59; Sidney Bolkosky, *Harmony and Dissonance: Voices of Jewish Identity in Detroit, 1914-1967* (Detroit, 1991), pp. 59-60.
7. Bolkosky, p. 59.
8. Rockaway, p.63.
9. Ibid., pp. 59, 61; Bolkosky, p. 59.
10. Rockaway, pp. 62-63.
11. Ibid., p. 63.
12. FBI File 62-26664. This profile is based on interviews with family members and former neighbors of the Purple gangsters. These sources wish to remain anonymous.
13. Haskel Adler, interview by author, Detroit, Mich.,3 July 1985.
14. *Detroit News*, 14 January 1945.
15. Engelmann, p. 125.
16. Ibid., p. 126.
17. Ibid.
18. Ibid., p. 127
19. The stories about Izzy and Moe are taken from Sifakis, *Encyclopedia of American Crime*, pp. 364-365; and Izzy Einstein, *Prohibition Agent No. 1* (New York, 1932).
20. Engelmann, p. 127.
21. Ibid., p. 139.
22. Ibid., p. 143.
23. Ibid.; FBI File 62-2664-1320, memo, SAC (Special Agent in Charge), New York, to Director, FBI, 1 June 1932.
24. FBI File 62-26664-13200.
25. Gervais, p. 133; Engelmann, p. 144.
26. Gervais, p. 131.
27. *Detroit News*, 28 November 1937, 13 March 1939, 14 March 1939.
28. Ibid.

29. David Levitt, letter to author, 20 July 1990.
30. *Detroit Times*, 27 November 1933; *Detroit News*, 14 January 1945.
31. Sifakis, *Mafia Encyclopedia*, p. 117.
32. *Detroit Times*, 27 November 1933; *Detroit News*, 14 January 1945.
33. *Detroit Times*, 27 November 1937.
34. Ibid.
35. Ibid.
36. Ibid.
37. Ibid.
38. Fox, p. 81.
39. *Detroit Free Press*, 20 August 1927.
40. Engelmann, p. 144.
41. Schoenberg, pp. 207-229.
42. Sifakis, *Mafia Encyclopedia*, p. 222.
43. Schoenberg, p. 209.
44. Ibid., pp. 207-229.
45. Ibid., pp. 228-229; FBI File 62-39128, serials 137-207, section 4; *Detroit News*, 16 February 1929, 18 February 1929.
46. FBI File 62-296321-11, Letter to J. Edgar Hoover, 25 June 1936.
47. Engelmann, p. 143.
48. *Detroit Free Press*, 25 June 1927.
49. Red Rudensky, *The Gonif* (Minnesota, 1970), p. 115.
50. *Detroit Times*, 27 November 1933.
51. Bolkosky, p. 143.
52. Ibid.
53. *Detroit News*, 14 January 1945.
54. Ibid.; *Detroit News*, 13 September 1928.
55. FBI File 62-29632-3, Letter to Mr. Hoover, 4 August 1934.
56. Engelmann, pp. 144-145.
57. *Detroit News*, 25 July 1929.
58. Levitt, letter to author.
59. *Detroit News*, 20 September 1930, 28 November 1937, 22 October 1965.
60. *Detroit News*, 14 January 1945.
61. *Detroit News*, 22 October 1965.
62. *Detroit Free Press*, 3 April 1964.
63. Ibid.
64. Ibid.
65. Richard Bak, "Dusting Off the Purple Gang," *Detroit Monthly*, December 1992, p. 68.
66. Ibid.; *Detroit News*, 28 November 1937.

67. *Detroit Times*, 27 November 1933.
68. *Detroit News*, 14 January 1945.
69. *Detroit News*, 25 November 1937, 28 November 1937.
70. *Detroit News*, 25 November 1937.
71. Ibid.
72. Ibid.; Turkus and Feder, p. 9.
73. Engelmann, pp. 145-147; Nelli, p. 170.
74. Engelmann, pp. 146-147.
75. Sifakis, *Mafia Encyclopedia*, pp. 351-352.
76. Gervais, pp. 143-144.
77. Elsie Proskie, interview by author, Tel-Aviv, Israel, 1 January 1991.
78. Melvin Holli, ed., *Detroit* (Detroit, 1976), p. 126; Bak, p. 109.
79. Ibid.
80. Ibid.; Robert Conot, *American Odessey* (New York, 1974), pp. 343-344.
81. Nelli, p. 170.
82. Meyer Lansky, telephone interview, 27 August 1980.
83. *Daily Variety* (Hollywood), 8 January 1960; *The Hollywood Reporter*, 8 January 1960.

Chapter Four: In the Beginning

1. Joselit, p. 1.
2. Thomas Byrnes, *1886 Professional Criminals of America* (New York, 1969 [1886]), pp. 224-225.
3. Ibid., pp. 261-262.
4. Ibid, pp. 268-269.
5. Ibid., pp. 152-154.
6. Benjamin P. Eldridge and William B. Watts, *Our Rival, The Rascal* (Boston, 1897), p. 88.
7. Ibid., p. 328.
8. For immigration statistics, see Simon Kuznets, "Immigration of Russian Jews to the United States: Background and Structure," *Perspectives in American History* IX (1975), pp. 35-124; and Abraham Karp, *Haven and Home: A History of the Jews in America* (New York, 1985), pp. 374-378.
9. See Arthur A. Goren, *New York Jews and the Quest for Community: The Kehilla Experiment, 1908-1922* (New York, 1970); and Joselit, *Our Gang* for descriptions of East Side vice and crime.
10. Herbert Ausbury, *The Gangs of New York* (New York, 1927), p. 359; Joselit, pp. 39-40.

11. For Fein's career, see Ausbury, pp. 362-368; and Joselit, pp. 107-112.
12. Ausbury, p.274. For Eastman's career, see Ausbury, pp. 273-287, 295-298.
13. Ibid., p. 276.
14. Ibid., p. 298.
15. Cornelius W. Willemse, *Behind the Green Lights* (Garden City, 1931), p. 288. See also Ausbury, pp. 287-290, 292-295.
16. Ausbury, p. 295.
17. Ibid., p. 329.
18. Sifakis, *Encyclopedia of American Crime*, p. 306.
19. Ausbury, p. 343. For Zelig's career, see Ausbury, pp. 331-336, 339-342.

Chapter Five: The Perils and Pitfalls of the Gangster Life

1. The story about Jake Skuratofsky was told to me by Myron Sugerman, Newark, N.J., 16 August 1990.
2. The following excerpt is from SAC, New York, to Director FBI, 21 June 1962, FBI File 92-2831.
3. Ibid.
4. For the life and gangbusting career of Thomas E. Dewey, see Thomas E. Dewey, *Twenty Against the Underworld* (Garden City, New York, 1974); and Richard Norton Smith, *Thomas E. Dewey and His Times* (New York, 1982).
5. Gosch, Hammer, pp. 140-141; Eisenberg et al., pp. 88-89.
6. The material on Gordon appeared in the *New York Times*, 28 April 1933, 2 December 1933, 7 December 1933, 9 December 1933, 9 October 1942; see also Fried, pp. 178-181.
7. Sifakis, *Encyclopedia of American Crime*, p. 291.
8. Ibid.
9. The material on Stacher is taken from, Eisenberg et al., and Lacey.
10. Material about Stacher's life in Israel comes from interviews with "Mervin," an alias for an individual who prefers to remain anonymous. Concerning Stacher's trial against Porush, see Eisenberg et al., pp. 297-298.
11. Lacey, p. 334.
12. The FBI files contain a great deal of hearsay and unsubstantiated accusations from anonymous correspondents.
13. David Stern, interview by author, Tel-Aviv, Israel, 3 September 1992.
14. *Yedioth Ahronoth* (Hebrew), 17 March 1972. The plot to kidnap Meyer

Lansky was disclosed to me by a source close to the murdered man, Ilan Asherov. This source prefers to remain anonymous.

15. Hinkes, interview.
16. Jack Guzik to Sanford Bates, 18 June 1934, Jack Guzik file, Records of the Bureau of Prisons, Notorious Offenders File.
17. Ibid.
18. Max Guzik to Parol Officer, 29 September 1933, Ibid.
19. Ibid.
20. Herman Lando, M.D. to Parol Officer, 9 October 1933, Ibid.
21. Rabbi M. Kohn to Parol Agent, 11 October 1933, Ibid.
22. Mike Lyman to Honorable Judge Woods, 18 September 1933, Ibid.
23. Fred Kohler to Board of Paroles, 23 October 1933, Ibid.
24. Hearing in the case of Jack Guzik, 12 December 1933, Ibid.
25. *New York Times*, 22 February 1956; Murray, p. 334.
26. FBI File 60-1501; *New York Times*, 10 June 1947.
27. Joselit, p. 123.
28. Turkus and Feder, pp. 336-337.
29. *New York Daily Mirror*, 10 June 1947; Sifakis, *Encyclopedia of American Crime*, p. 653.
30. Turkus and Feder, p. 349.
31. Ibid., p. 350.
32. *New York Times*, 5 March 1944.
33. Turkus and Feder, p. 350; *New York Mirror*, 22 August 1939.
34. *New York Times*, 29 September 1939.
35. Gosch, Hammer, pp. 239-245.
36. Turkus and Feder, p. 357.
37. *Time*, 4 September 1939, p. 12.
38. FBI File 65-1501.
39. *New York Times*, 2 January 1940.
40. Ibid., 6 April 1940.
41. *New York Times*, 19 April 1940.
42. Ibid.
43. Ibid., 20 April 1940.
44. Louis Buchalter to James V. Bennett, 21 June 1940, Bureau of Prisons, Notorious Offenders File, Louis Buchalter file.
45. Ibid.
46. Grand Jury report, 28 May 1940, Ibid.
47. The People of the State of New York vs. Louis Buchalter, alias "Lepke," 2 December 1941, Ibid.
48. Ibid.

49. *New York Daily News*, 5 March 1944.
50. Ibid.
51. *New York Journal American*, 5 March 1944.

Chapter Six: The Hit Parade

1. Ed Reid, Ovid Demaris, *The Green Felt Jungle* (New York, 1963), pp. 32-33.
2. Turkus and Feder, p. 134.
3. Gosch, Hammer, p. 186.
4. Sann, p. 257.
5. Turkus and Feder, p. 139.
6. Sann, p. 254.
7. This incident and the quotes are taken from Sann, pp. 21-32.
8. Ibid., p. 35.
9. Gosch, Hammer, pp. 183-184.
10. Sann, p. 89.
11. On the killing of Dropper, see the *New York Times*, 29, 30, 31 August 1923; and Asbury, *The Gangs of New York*, pp. 369-372. Detective captain Cornelius Willemse, who was in charge of transporting Dropper to his arraignment, offers a different version of his killing and says the killer's name was Louis Kintzler, or Louis Cohen. (Willemse, *Behind the Green Lights*, pp. 334-339.).
12. Asbury, p. 373. For Orgen's murder and funeral, see the *New York Times*, 16, 17, 18 October 1927.
13. Sifakis, *Encyclopedia of American Crime*, p. 169.
14. Charles Jacobs, interview with author, Boston, Mass., 20 August 1992.
15. Gosch, Hammer, pp. 87, 139.
16. On Harry Strauss, see the *New York Times*, 21, 23 March, 12 June, 2 August, 5 September, 27 September 1940; 25 April, 13 June 1941; and Turkus and Feder.
17. Turkus and Feder, pp. 307-312.
18. Ibid., pp. 217-218.
19. Ibid., pp. 206-215, 329.
20. On Reles, see Turkus and Feder; and the *New York Times*, 26, 29, 30 October 1935; 26 August 1937, 31 August 1940; 13, 14 November 1941; 5 March, 5 June 1942.
21. Turkus and Feder, p. 59.
22. Ibid., p. 65.
23. Goldstein, interview.

24. Gosch, Hammer, p. 248.
25. Ibid., p. 253.
26. Lacey, p. 407.
27. Fay Newman Rubinstein [Ben Newman's daughter], letter to author, 29 November 1998.
28. Goldstein, interview.
29. Ed Reid, Ovid Demaris, p. 19.
30. Quoted in, Sidney Zion, *Loyalty and Betrayal: The Story of the American Mob* (San Francisco, 1994), p. 46.
31. Lacey, p. 152.
32. FBI File 62-8158, Memo to Director, 31 January 1947.
33. FBI File 62-8158-433; Dean Jennings, *We Only Kill Each Other: The Life and Bad Times of Bugsy Siegel* (Englewood Cliffs, N.J., 1968), pp. 317-318.
34. *Los Angeles Times*, 21, 22, 23 June 1947; *Los Angeles Examiner*, 21, 22, 23 June 1947; *New York Times*, 22 June 1947; FBI File 62-81518. 34
35. Jennings, p. 205.
36. Lacey, p. 158; Eisenberg et al., p. 241.
37. Jennings, pp. 15-18.
38. SAC, Newark to Director, FBI, 30 March 1956, FBI File 62-36805-34.
39. Stuart, p. 216.
40. SAC Newark, to Director FBI, 22 January 1959, FBI File 58-4441-4.
41. Stuart, p. 217.
42. Ibid., p. 224.
43. Goldstein, interview.
44. Gosch, Hammer, p. 405.
45. Eisenberg et al., p. 247.
46. *New York Times*, 28 February 1959.
47. Stuart, p. 231.
48. *New York Times*, 25, 29 October 1974; 30 July 1976.
49. Ibid., 30 July 1976.
50. FBI File 62-89947-22.
51. Memo, Mr. Rosen to Mr. Ladd, 20 July 1949, FBI File 62-89947-16; *Los Angeles Mirror*, 20 July 1949.
52. Cohen, p. 78.
53. Ibid., p. 135.
54. IOC, Part 10, Testimony of Michael (Mickey) Cohen, p. 261.
55. *New York Times*, 30 July 1976.
56. Hearing in the Case of Jack Guzik, 12 December 1933, Records of Bureau of Prisons, Notorious Offenders File.
57. Goldstein, interview.

58. FBI File 29-HQ-5892.
59. IOC, Part 10, Testimony of Moe Sedway, pp. 87-88.

Chapter Seven: The Family Came First

1. Cohen, pp. 182-183.
2. The biographical material on Berman is from Susan Berman, *Easy Street* (New York, 1981), and FBI File 29-5892.
3. Berman, p. 127.
4. Ibid., p. 130.
5. *New York Times*, 24 November 1927.
6. FBI File 29-5892.
7. Berman, p. 47.
8. Ibid, p. 211.
9. Francis A.J. Ianni, "The Mafia and the Web of Kinship," in Francis A.J. Ianni and Elizabeth Reuss-Ianni, *The Crime Society: Organized Crime and Corruption in America* (New York, 1976), pp. 42-59.
10. See, James M. O'Kane, *The Crooked Ladder: Gangsters, Ethnicity, and the American Dream* (New Brunswick, N.J., 1992), for a discussion of the one-generational aspect of Jews in organized crime.
11. Goldstein, interview.
12. Stuart, p. 122.
13. *New York Times*, 7 December 1933.
14. Sann, p. 251-252.
15. Ibid., p. 253.
16. Ibid., pp. 253-254.
17. Turkus and Feder, pp. 153-154.
18. Sann, p. 293.
19. Ibid., p. 303.
20. Ibid.
21. Ibid., p. 304.
22. Ibid., p. 311.
23. Eisenberg et al., p.229.
24. During my conversation with Meyer Lansky in 1980, he spoke with pride of his son Paul's attending and graduating from West Point (telephone interview with Meyer Lansky, 27 August 1980).
25. Eisenberg et al., pp. 230-231.
26. Lacey, p. 434.
27. On Annenberg, see Messick, *The Silent Syndicate*, pp. 153-166.

28. Ibid., p. 152.
29. Moses L. Annenberg, Bureau of Prisons, Notorious Offenders File.
30. Fox, p. 105.
31. Ibid., p. 107.
32. *Washington Star*, 4 June 1942.
33. Fox, p. 173.
34. Louis Buchalter, Probation Department Investigation Report, 18 December 1939, Bureau of Prisons, Notorious Offenders File.
35. Turkus and Feder, p. 348.
36. Zena Smith Blau, "In Defense of the Jewish Mother," in Peter I. Rose, ed. *The Ghetto and Beyond* (New York, 1969), pp. 57-68.
37. Mark Slobin, *Tenement Songs* (Chicago, 1982), p. 204.
38. Fox, pp. 78-82.
39. Eisenberg et al., p. 34.
40. Lacey, pp. 75-76.
41. Stuart, p. 117.
42. Max Hassel, interview by author, Detroit, Mich., 23 July 1986.
43. "Mervin," interview by author, Newark, N.J., 19 April 1990. Mervin prefers to remain anonymous.
44. Ibid.
45. The correspondence between Guzik and the members of his family repose in the Guzik file, Records of the Bureau of Prisons, Notorious Offenders File, HM FY91 Box 42.
46. Grandpop [Jack Guzik] to Billy Jack, 22 November 1935, Notorious Offenders.
47. Joe and Lila to Jack, 28 September 1935, Ibid.
48. Guzik family to Jack, 28 September 1935, Ibid.
49. Jack Guzik to Jeanette, 3 September 1935, Ibid.
50. Jeanette to Jack, 14 February 1935, Ibid.
51. Jack to Jeanette, 15 January 1935, Ibid.
52. Charles and Mom to Jack Guzik, undated, Ibid.
53. Jack Guzik to wife, 4 December 1934, Ibid.
54. Stuart, pp. 122, 228.
55. The name of the family has been changed at their request.
56. The source of this story, a relative of the former mobster, prefers to remain anonymous.
57. *Jewish Daily Forward* (Yiddish), 23 March 1940.
58. Dorrie Shapiro Grizzard, quoted in Zion, p. 48.
59. Dena Rubens, letter to author, 22 April 1990.
60. Eisenberg et al., pp. 323-324.

Chapter Eight: Defenders of Their People

1. Kenneth Allsop, The Bootleggers: The Story of Chicago's Prohibition Era (London, 1961), p. 250; Walter Roth, "The Story of Samuel 'Nails' Morton: A Twentieth Century Golem?" Chicago Jewish History 13 (October 1989), pp. 1, 6-9; Chicago Daily News, 19 November 1925.
2. John Landesco, Organized Crime in Chicago (Chicago, 1968 [1929]), pp. 196-198.
3. Bill Reilly, "'Nails Morton: The White Knight Gangster," Inside Chicago (March\April 1990), pp. 30-31.
4. Landesco, pp. 196-198.
5. Ibid., p. 197.
6. Lori Levinski, interview by author, Tel-Aviv, Israel, 5 April 1990.
7. Landesco, p. 214.
8. Joel Slonim, "The Jewish Gangster," The Reflex 3 (July 1928), p. 38.
9. Abe Shoenfeld, Story 14, File 1780, Magnes Archives, Jerusalem. Subsequent quotes by Shoenfeld about Zelig are taken from this source and will not be cited.
10. Arthur A. Goren, "Saints and Sinners: The Underside of American Jewish History," p. 18.
11. Stuart, pp. 20-21.
12. Myron Sugerman, interview by author, Tel-Aviv, Israel, 19 April 1991.
13. Kugel, interview.
14. Howard Simons, Jewish Times: Voices of the American Jewish Experience (Boston, 1988), 133-134. The attitude displayed by the Jewish community toward the Jewish gangsters was not very different from that of the general community. Despite a certain fear and abhorrence for the gangster, Americans have viewed him as something of a folk hero. For a discussion of American attitudes toward the gangster, see David E. Ruth, Inventing the Public Enemy: The Gangster in American Culture, 1918-1934 (Chicago, 1996); and Robert Warshow, "The Gangster as Tragic Hero," The Immediate Experience, ed. Robert Warshow (New York, 1962), pp. 127-133.
15. Murray, p. 54.
16. Mark Haller, "Organizing Crime in Urban Society: Chicago in the Twentieth Century," Journal of Social History 5 (1971-1972), p. 227.
17. Lacey, p. 113.
18. Lansky, telephone interview; Eisenberg et al., pp. 184-186.
19. Eisenberg et al., p. 184.
20. Ibid., p. 185.

21. Judd L. Teller, *Strangers and Natives:The Evolution of the American Jew from 1921 to the Present* (New York, 1968), pp. 183-184.
22. Eisenberg et al., p. 185.
23. Teller, pp. 184-185; Ronald H. Bayor, *Neighbors in Conflict: The Irish, Germans, Jews and Italians of New York City, 1929-1941* (Baltimore, 1978), p. 136.
24. Lansky, telephone interview.
25. Hinkes, interview.
26. Ibid.
27. Heshey Weiner, interview by author, Newark, N.J., 15 August 1990.
28. Invitation, "A Tribute to Max 'Puddy' Hinkes," in possession of author.
29. Brin, interview.
30. Ibid.
31. David H. Bennett, *The Party of Fear: From Nativist Movements to the New Right in American History* (Chapel Hill, 1988), p. 245.
32. John Higham, "Social Discrimination Against Jews, 1830-1930," in *Send These to Me: Jews and Other Immigrants in Urban America*, ed. John Higham (New York, 1975), p. 163.
33. Berman, pp. 144-145.
34. Ibid.
35. Cohen, pp. 67-68.
36. Ibid., p. 68.
37. Jennings, pp. 76-77; Lacey, p. 112.
38. The following material is from FBI File 65-53615.
39. David Stern to German Ambassador, 23 March 1933, FBI File 65-53615-X.
40. FBI File 65-53615-X.
41. Ibid.
42. R.G. Harvey, SAC, to Director, 3 May 1933, FBI File 65-53615-X4.
43. SAC, Memo, 21 August 1933, FBI File 65-53615-X13.
44. J.M. Keith to Director, 19 August 1933, FBI File 65-5365-X13.
45. Dwight Brantley to Director, 2 September 1933, FBI File 65-53615-X14.
46. "Dutch," interview by author, Herzlia, Israel, 15 August 1988. This source prefers to remain anonymous.
47. Letter from Dr. S.S. Hollender, 9 June 1980.
48. Lacey, pp. 7, 163-164, 261; A. Rubin, interview by author, Tel-Aviv, Israel, 10 June 1980.
49. "Invitation" to the State of Israel Tribute Dinner for Moe Dalitz, 18 October 1970; *New York Times*, 1 September 1989.
50. IOC, Part 10, p. 91.

51. Ira Berkow, *Maxwell Street* (New York, 1977), p. 139.
52. Stuart, p. 107.
53. Ibid., p. 109.
54. Ibid.
55. Ibid., pp. 210-211.
56. Jeremiah Unterman, interview by author, Boston, Mass., 16 December 1986.
57. Donald R. Cressey, *Theft of a Nation: The Structure and Operations of Organized Crime in America* (New York, 1969), pp. 274-275; Joseph Bonanno, *A Man of Honor* (New York, 1983), p. 319.
58. M.S. (this source prefers to remain anonymous), interview by author, Newark, N.J. 16 April 1990.
59. The story of gunrunning on behalf of Israel is told in Leonard Slater, *The Pledge* (New York, 1970).
60. Ibid., p. 133.
61. Lacey, p. 163; Eisenberg et al., p. 296.
62. Daniel Avivi, interview by author, Herzlia, Israel, 26 June 1991.
63. Reuven Dafni, interview by author, Jerusalem, Israel, 7 June 1989.
64. Ibid.
65. Murray Greenfield, interview by author, Tel-Aviv, Israel, 15 May 1988.
66. Ibid.
67. Ovid Demaris, *The Last Mafioso: The Treacherous World of Jimmy Fratiano* (New York, 1981), pp. 28-29.
68. Ibid.
69. *Jewish Week Examiner*, 18 January 1981.
70. Howard Sachar, *A History of Israel* (New York, 1976), pp. 329-330.
71. Brin, interview.
72. Ibid.
73. Lacey, p. 338.
74. Dafni, interview.
75. Cohen, pp. 90, 234. The information about Cohen was provided by a Los Angeles Jewish businessman who was threatened and extorted by Cohen. This source prefers to remain anonymous.
76. *Cleveland Plain Dealer*, 8 April 1953.
77. Ibid., 19 December 1951.

Bibliography

Government and Archival Sources

Department of Justice. Bureau of Prisons. Notorious Offenders File. National Archives, Washington, D.C.
Files of Moses L. Annenberg, Louis "Lepke" Buchalter, Jack Guzik, and Charles Solomon.

Department of Justice. Federal Bureau of Investigation. Washington, D.C.
Files on:
Isadore Blumenfeld, Files 62-69850, 92-2720
Lepke Buchalter, Files 60-1501, 62-99379
Mickey Cohen, File 62-89947
Arthur Flegenheimer, File 23-2130
Louis Fleisher, Files 7-142, 62-29632, 15-1089, 62-1383
Max Hoff, Files 62-22444-1-86, 62-31642, 62-91933
Meyer Lansky, File 92-2831
Purple Gang, Files 60-1501, 62-29632, 62-25345, 62-81093, 62-26664
Arnold Rothstein, Files 62-57444, 62-32855
Moe Sidwertz [Sedway], File 29-HQ-5892
Benjamin "Bugsy" Siegel, Files 62-81518, 62-2837
Mert Wertheimer, Files 62-44462, 62-34294
Abner Zwillman, File 62-36085

Organized Crime in Interstate Commerce. Hearings Before the Special Committee to Investigate Organized Crime in Interstate Commerce. 81st Congress, 2nd Session, and 82nd Congress, 1st Session. Interim Reports, Final Report, Hearings in twelve parts and index. Washington, United States Government Printing Office, 1950-1951.

Magnes Papers, Central Archives for the History of the Jewish People,

Jerusalem. Abe Shoenfeld's reports on Jewish Criminality on the Lower East Side of New York, and on Jack Zelig.

Committee of Seventy Collection, Urban Archives Center, Temple University, Philadelphia, Pennsylvania. Philadelphia grand jury report (1928), on Max Hoff's syndicate.

Newspapers

Boston Globe, 1933-1934
Boston Evening Transcript, 24 January-26 May 1933.
Chicago Daily Courier (Yiddish), 1924.
Chicago Daily News, 1925.
Cleveland Plain Dealer, 1951, 1953.
Daily Variety, 8 January 1960.
Detroit News, 1920-1945, 1965.
Detroit Free Press, 1927, 1945, 1964.
Detroit Times, 1933-1937.
Forbes, 13 September 1982.
Hollywood Reporter, 8 January 1960.
Jewish Daily Forward (Yiddish), 1944.
Jewish Week Examiner, 1981.
Los Angeles Examiner, 1947.
Los Angeles Times, 1947.
New York Daily News, 1944.
New York Mirror, 1939, 1947.
New York Journal American, 1939,1944.
New York Sun, 1931.
New York Times, 1920-1947, 1956, 1959, 1973-1976, 1989.
Philadelphia Jewish Exponent, 1928.
Time, 4 September 1939.
Washington Star, 1942.
Yedioth Ahronoth (Heb.), March 1972

Interviews

Adler, Haskel. Detroit, Mich., 18 August 1989.
Avivi, Daniel. Herzlia, Israel, 3 April 1991.
Brin, Herb. Los Angeles, Calif., 27 August 1991.
Dafni, Reuven. Jerusalem, Israel, 7 June 1989.

"Dutch." Herzlia, Israel, 24 November 1989

Fleisch, Harry. Detroit, Mich., 20 July 1985.

Golan, Eli. Herzlia, Israel. 26 November 1992.

Goldstein, Irving "Itzik." Newark, N.J., 16 August 1990.

Greenfield, Murray. Tel-Aviv, Israel, 15 May 1988.

Hessel, Sam. Detroit, Mich., 23 July 1986.

Hinkes, Max "Puddy." Newark, N.J., 16 August 1990.

Jacobs, Charles. Boston, Mass., 20 August 1992.

Kessler, Hershel, Los Angeles, Calif., 14 September 1989.

Kugel, Jerry. Newark, N.J., 15 August 1990.

Lansky, Meyer. telephone conversation, 27 August 1980.

Levinsky, Lorri. Tel-Aviv, Israel, 5 April 1990.

"Mervin." Tel-Aviv, 19 April 1991.

M.S. Tel-Aviv, Israel, 16 April 1991.

Prosky, Elsie. Tel-Aviv, Israel, 1 January 1991.

Rubin, A. Tel-Aviv, Israel, 10 June 1980.

Schaffer, Lester. Philadelphia, Penn., 14 August 1991.

Simons, Leonard. Detroit, Mich., 20 August 1985.

Skuratofsky, Fay. Newark, N.J., 16 August 1990.

Slomovitz, Philip. Detroit, Mich., 10 September 1989.

Stern, David. Tel-Aviv, Israel, 3 September 1992.

Sugerman, Myron. Tel-Aviv, Israel, 19 April 1991.

Unterman, Jeremiah. Boston, Mass., 16 December 1986.

Weiner, Heshy. Newark, N.J., 16 August 1990.

Books

Allsop, Kenneth. *The Bootleggers: The Story of Chicago's Prohibition Era.* London, England: Hutchinson, 1961.

Asbury, Herbert. *The Gangs of New York: An Informal History of the New York Underworld.* New York: Knopf, 1927.

Bayor, Ronald H. *Neighbors in Conflict: the Irish, Germans, Jews and Italians of New York City, 1929-1941.* Baltimore: Johns Hopkins University Press, 1978.

Bennett, David H. *The Party of Fear: From Nativist Movements to the New Right in American History.* Chapel Hill: Duke University Press, 1988.

Bergreen, Laurence. *Capone: The Man and the Era.* New York: Simon & Schuster, 1994.

Berkow, Ira. *Maxwell Street.* Garden City, N.Y.: Doubleday, 1977.

Berman, Susan. *Easy Street*. New York: Dial Press, 1981.

Block, Alan. *East Side-West Side: Organizing Crime in New York, 1930-1950.* New Brunswick: Transaction Books, 1983.

Bolkosky, Sidney. *Harmony and Dissonance: Voices of Jewish Detroit, 1914-1967.* Detroit: Wayne State University Press, 1991.

Bonanno, Joseph, with Sergio Lalli. *A Man of Honor: The Autobiography of the Boss of Bosses.* New York: Simon & Schuster, 1983.

Byrnes, Thomas. *1886 Professional Criminals of America.* New York: Chelsea House, 1969 [1886].

Cohen, Mickey, with John Peer Nugent. *In My Own Words: The Underworld Autobiography of Michael Mickey Cohen.* Englewood Cliffs, N.J.: Prentice-Hall, 1975.

Clarke, Donald Henderson. *In the Reign of Rothstein.* New York: Vanguard Press, 1929.

Conot, Robert. *American Odyssey.* Detroit: Wayne State University Press, 1986 [1974].

Courtwright, David, Herman Joseph, and Don Des Jarlais. *Addicts Who Survived: An Oral History of Narcotics Use in America.* Knoxville: University of Tennessee Press, 1989.

Cressy, Donald R. *Theft of a Nation: The Structure and Operations of Organized Crime in America.* New York: Harper & Row, 1969.

Demaris, Ovid. *The Last Mafioso: The Treacherous World of Jimmy Fratiano.* New York: Times Books, 1981.

Dewey, Thomas E. *Twenty Against the Underworld.* Garden City, N.Y.: Doubleday, 1974.

Dinnerstein, Leonard. *Antisemitism in America.* New York: Oxford University Press, 1994.

Einstein, Izzey. *Prohibition Agent Number 1.* New York: Frederick A. Stokes, 1932.

Eldridge, Benjamin P. and William B. Watts. *Our Rival, the Rascal.* Boston: Pemberton Publishing Company, 1896.

Engelmann, Larry. *Intemperance: The Lost War Against Liquor.* New York: The Free Press, 1979.

Eisenberg, Dennis, Uri Dann, Eli Landau. *Meyer Lansky: Mogul of the Mob.* New York: Paddington Press, 1979.

Feldstein, Stanley. *The Land That I Show You: Three Centuries of Jewish Life in America.* Garden City: Anchor Press, 1978.

Fox, Stephen. *Blood and Power: Organized Crime in Twentieth Century America.* New York: William Morrow and Company, 1989.

Fried, Albert. *The Rise and Fall of the Jewish Gangster in America*. New York: Holt, Rinehart and Winston, 1980.

Gervais, C.H. *The Rumrunners: A Prohibition Scrapbook*. Ontario, Canada: Firefly Books, 1980.

Goren, Arthur. *New York Jews and the Quest for Community: The Kehilla Experiment, 1908-1922*. New York: Columbia University Press, 1970.

Gosch, Martin and Richard Hammer. *The Last Testament of Lucky Luciano*. Boston: Little, Brown and Company, 1974.

Helmer, William, and Rick Mattix. *Public Enemies: America's Criminal Past, 1919-1940*. New York: Facts On File, 1998.

Holli, Melvin G., ed. *Detroit*. New York: New Viewpoints, 1976.

Jennings, Dean. *We Only Kill Each Other: The Life and Bad Times of Bugsy Siegel*. Englewood Cliff, N.J.: Prentice-Hall, 1968.

Joselit, Jenna Weissman. *Our Gang: Jewish Crime and the New York Jewish Community, 1900-1940*. Bloomington: Indiana University Press, 1983.

Karp, Abraham. *Haven and Home: A History of the Jews in America*. New York: Schocken Books, 1985.

Katcher, Leo. *The Big Bankroll: The Life and Times of Arnold Rothstein*. New Rochelle, N.Y.: Arlington House, 1959.

Lacey, Robert. *Little Man: Meyer Lansky and the Gangster Life*. Boston: Little, Brown and Company, 1991.

Landesco, John. *Organized Crime in Chicago*. Chicago: University of Chicago Press, 1968 [1929].

Maas, Peter. *The Valachi Papers*. New York: Putnam, 1968.

Maccabee, Paul. *John Dillenger Slept Here: The Crooks' Tour of Crime and Corruption in St. Paul, 1920-1936*. St. Paul: Minnesota Historical Press, 1995.

Messick, Hank. *Lansky*. New York: Putnam, 1971.

Messick, Hank. *Secret File*. New York: Putnam, 1969.

Messick, Hank. *The Silent Syndicate*. New York: Macmillan, 1967.

Murray, George. *The Legacy of Al Capone*. New York: Putnam's, 1975.

Nelli, Humbert, *The Business of Crime: Italians and Syndicated Crime in the United States*. New York: Oxford University Press, 1976.

O'Kane, James M. *The Crooked Ladder: Gangsters, Ethnicity, and the American Dream*. New Brunswick: Transaction Publishers, 1992.

Reid, Ed, and Ovid Demaris. *The Green Felt Jungle*. New York: Trident, 1963.

Rockaway, Robert. *The Jews of Detroit: From the Beginning, 1762-1914*. Detroit: Wayne State University Press, 1986.

Rudensky, Red. *The Gonif*. Blue Earth, Minnesota: The Piper Company, 1970.

Ruth, David E. *Inventing the Public Enemy: The Gangster in American Culture, 1918-1934*. Chicago: University of Chicago Press, 1996.

Sachar, Howard. *A History of Israel*. New York: Knopf, 1976.

Sann, Paul. *Kill the Dutchman! The Story of Dutch Schultz*. New York: New Rochelle, N.Y.: Arlington House, 1971.

Schoenberg, Robert J. *Mr. Capone*. New York: William Morrow and Company, 1992.

Sifakis, Carl. *The Encyclopedia of American Crime*. New York: Facts On File, 1984.

Sifakis, Carl. *The Mafia Encyclopedia*. New York: Facts On File, 1987.

Simons, Howard. *Jewish Times: Voices of the American Jewish Experience*. Boston: Little, Brown and Company, 1988.

Sinclair, Andrew. *Era of Excess: A Social History of the Prohibition Movement*. New York: Harper & Row Publishers, 1962.

Slater, Leonard. *The Pledge*. New York: Simon and Schuster, 1970.

Slobin, Mark. *Tenement Songs: The Popular Music of the Jewish Immigrants*. Chicago: University of Illinois Press, 1982.

Smith, Richard Norton. *Thomas E. Dewey and His Times*. New York: Simon & Schuster, 1982.

Stuart, Mark. *Gangster #2: Longy Zwillman, the Man Who Invented Organized Crime*. Secaucus, N.J.: Lyle Stuart, 1985.

Teller, Judd. *Strangers and Natives: The Evolution of the American Jew from 1921 to the Present*. New York: Delacorte Press, 1968.

Turkus, Burton B. and Sid Feder. *Murder, Inc*. New York: Da Capo Press, 1979 [1951].

Willemse, Cornelius. *Behind the Green Lights*. Garden City, New York: Garden City Publishing Company, 1931.

Zion, Sidney. *Loyalty and Betrayal: The Story of the American Mob*. San Francisco: Collins Publishers, 1994.

Articles

Bak, Richard. "Dusting Off the Purple Gang." *Detroit Monthly* (December 1992): 67-70, 109.

Goren, Arthur. "Saint and Sinners: The Underside of American Jewish History." Cincinnati: Brochure Series of the American Jewish Archives, Number VII (1988).

Haller, Mark. "Bootleggers and Gambling, 1920-1950." Commission on the Review of National Policy Toward Gambling. Appendix I. *Gambling in America*. Washington, D.C.,1976.

Haller, Mark. "Organizing Crime in Urban Society: Chicago in the Twentieth Century." *Journal of Social History* 5 (1971-1972): 210-234.

Higham, John. "Social discrimination Against Jews, 1830-1930." In *Send These to Me: Jews and Other Immigrants in Urban America*, edited by John Higham, 138-173. New York: Atheneum, 1975.

Ianni, Francis A.J. "The Mafia and the Web of kinship." In *The Crime Society: Organized Crime and Corruption in America*, edited by Francis A.J. Ianni and Elizabeth Reuss-Ianni, 42-59. New York: New American Library, 1976.

Jonnes, Jill. "Founding Father: One Man Invented the Modern Narcotics Industry." *American Heritage* (February/March 1993): 48-49.

Kuznets, Simon. "Immigration of Russian Jews to the United States: Background and Structure." *Perspectives in American History* IX (1975): 35-124.

Reilly, Bill. "'Nails' Morton: the White Knight Gangster." *Inside Chicago* (March\April 1990): 30-31.

Roth, Walter. "The Story of Samuel 'Nails' Morton: A Twentieth Century Golem?" *Chicago Jewish History* 13 (October 1989): 1, 6-9.

Slonim, Joel. "The Jewish Gangster." *The Reflex* 3 (July 1928): 36-41.

Warshow, Robert. "The Gangster as Tragic Hero." In *The Immediate Experience*, edited by Robert Warshow, 127-133. Garden City, N.Y.: Doubleday, 1962.

Index of Gangsters

A

Abbandando, Frank "the Dasher," 28, 159
Accardo, Tony, 52, 165
Adonis, Joe, 22, 23, 28, 165
Alberts, William (see Zelig, Jack)
Alderman, Willie "Ice Pick," 153, 189
Alpert, Alexander "Red," 158
Alterie, Louis "Two Gun," 219
Altman, Hymie, 49, 76
Amberg, Louis "Pretty," 29-31
Anastasia, Albert, 23, 46, 138, 161, 246
Annenberg, Moses "Moe," 203-206
Axler, Abe, 79-81, 84-86, 89

B

Berman, Davie, 182-191, 233, 234
Berman, Otto "Abbadabba," 145
Bernstein, Ray, 48, 63-69, 87, 92
Bloom, Harry, 54
Bloom, Yiddy, 54
Blumenfeld, Isidore "Kid Cann," 54-56, 188, 233

Bonnano, Joe, 46, 244
Bruno, Angelo, 41
Brotki, Samuel, 99, 101
Buchalter, Louis "Lepke," 7, 24-29, 35, 43, 132, 134-143, 144, 145, 150, 151, 161, 165, 206, 238

C

Capone, Al, 8, 50, 51, 81, 83, 109, 165
Caspar, Samuel, 95
Catalanotte, Samuel, 91
Catena, Gerry, 35, 170
Cohen Mickey, 61, 62, 175-178, 182, 234-236, 249-252, 253
Colbeck, Dinty, 78
Costello, Frank, 13, 22, 28, 35, 40, 46, 161, 165, 188, 244
Cowan, Louis "Diamond Louie," 50

D

Dalitz, Morris "Moe," 44, 46, 47, 48, 241
Davis, Sam "the Gorilla," 48
De Carlo, Angelo "Gyp," 35

Diamond, Jack "Legs," 13, 20, 31, 150, 151

Dragna, Jack, 166, 176, 177

E

Eastman, Monk, 104-108

Egan, Jellyroll, 78

Eisen, Maxie, 50

F

Fein, Benjamin "Dopey Benny," 15, 102, 103

Feinstein, Puggy, 155

Flegenheimer, Arthur "Dutch Schultz," 7, 13, 15, 16-20, 23, 28, 31, 43, 144-150, 197, 208

Fleisch, Harry, 61

Fleisher, Harry, 48, 63, 65, 69, 76, 87, 90

Fleisher, Louis, 88, 89

Fletcher, Eddie, 79, 80, 83, 85, 86, 89

Fratianno, Jimmy "the Weasel," 250-252

G

Gaetz, Bendick "the Cockroach," 96

Gambino, Carlo, 46, 174, 192

Genovese, Vito, 23, 148, 174, 192

Giancana, Sam, 52

Gleckman, Leon, 56, 57

Goldstein, Martin "Buggsy," 28, 135, 160, 161, 162

Gordon, Waxey, 13, 15, 16, 119-122, 132, 144, 195, 196

Greenbaum, Gus, 169

Greenthal, Abe "the General," 95, 96

Guzik, Jack "Greasy Thumb," 51-54, 128-132, 165, 178, 212, 213, 241, 242

H

Hassel, Maxie, 210

Hinkes, Max "Puddy," 18-20, 126, 224, 225, 231, 232

Hoff, Max "Boo Boo," 7, 39, 40, 57, 208, 238

Horowitz, Harry "Gyp the Blood," 110, 111

J

Jacobson, Sam "Sammy the Greener," 50

K

Kaplan, Nathan "Kid Dropper," 150, 151

Katz, Sam "Big Sue," 170, 171

Kay, Sam, 247

Kelly, Paul, 109

Kessler, Hershel, 9

Keywell, Harry, 63, 65, 66, 68, 69, 76, 83, 85, 92

Keywell, Phillip, 49, 83, 86, 87, 92

Klein, Julius "Sheeny," 97

Klein, Sidney "Big Red," 114

Kleinman, Morris, 44, 47

Kurtz, Michael "Sheeny Mike," 97, 98, 99

Kushner, Harry, 214

Kushner, Irving, 214

L

LaMarre, Chester, 91

Landau, Abe, 145

Lansky, Meyer, 7, 9, 15, 20-24, 28, 35, 40, 43, 46, 59, 61, 93, 115-117, 119, 120, 122, 124, 125, 137, 144, 153, 154, 163, 165, 167-169, 174, 188, 189, 201-203, 205, 208, 209, 217, 218, 228-231, 238, 241, 246, 252

Lebovitz, Joseph "Nigger Joe," 63-65, 67

Leebove, Arthur, 253

Levine, Abraham "Pretty," 28, 215

Levine, Hymie "the Loudmouth," 50

Levine, Solomon, 63, 65, 69

Levine, Samuel "Red," 23, 154

Licavoli, Peter, 92, 192

Licavoli, Yonnie, 92

Lowenthal, Frank "Sheeny Irving," 96

Lucchese, Thomas "Three Finger Brown," 137, 192

Luciano, Charles "Lucky," 13, 14, 17, 22-24, 28, 35, 46, 109, 119, 120, 137, 144, 145, 148, 154, 161, 162, 165, 169, 174, 188

M

Maione, Harry "Happy," 28, 91, 159

Maranzano, Salvatore, 23, 149, 154

Marcus, Joe, 187

Masseria, Joe, 22, 23, 119, 149

Milberg, Irving, 63-66, 68, 69, 76, 80, 81, 85-87, 92

Miller, Davey, 227-228

Millman, Harry, 49, 90, 91

Moran, George "Bugs," 81, 83

Moretti, Willie, 35

Morton, Samuel "Nails," 219-221

N

Nitti, Frank, 52

O

O'Banion, Dion, 219

Orgen, Jacob "Little Augie," 150-152

Osterman, Edward (see Monk Eastman)

P

Paul, Herman "Hymie," 63-65, 67

Pioggi, Louis "Louie the Lump," 108-109

Polizzi, Al, 46

Porter, Billy, 98-99

Profaci, Joseph, 192

R

Raider, Morris, 76, 87, 92

Raider, Phil, 76

Reinfeld, Joseph, 33

Reles, Abe "Kid Twist," 28, 135, 137, 158-162

Ricca, Paul, 52

Rosen, Nig (see Harry Stromberg)

Rosenkrantz, Bernard "Lulu," 145-146

Rosenthal, Herman "Beansie," 111
Rosenzweig, Louis "Lefty Louie," 222
Rothkopf, Louis, 44, 47
Rothstein, Arnold, 9-15, 29, 133, 203
Rudensky, Morris "Red," 84
Rudnick, George, 155

S

Schultz, Dutch (see Arthur Flegenheimer)
Sedway, Moe, 153, 166, 169, 179-181, 189, 242
Seidenshner, Jacob "Whitey Lewis," 222
Selbin, Ziggy, 89
Shapiro, Jake "Gurrah," 132-134, 151, 198, 215
Shaw, Edward, 49
Shorr, Henry, 76, 90
Siegel, Benjamin "Bugsy," 7, 15, 20-24, 28, 35, 43, 46, 119, 122, 135, 144, 153, 162-170, 176, 188-190, 236, 247-248
Smiley, Allen, 247-248
Solomon, Charles "King," 7, 42, 43, 208
Stacher, Joseph "Doc," 21, 22, 33, 38, 122-124, 178, 202
Stein, Sam, 253
Strauss, Harry "Pittsburgh Phil," 28, 91, 135, 154-157, 159, 162
Stromberg, Harry, 40-41
Sutker, Joseph, 63-65, 67
Sutton, Willie "the Actor," 17

T

Tane, George, 216, 217
Tannenbaum, Albert, 145, 198
Toblinsky, Joseph "Yoski Nigger," 102, 103
Tocco, William, 192
Torrio, John, 52, 109, 165
Tucker, Sam, 44, 47

V

Valachi, Joe, 23
Vaccarelli, Paolo (see Paul Kelly)

W

Weinberg, Abe "Bo," 23
Weiss, Mendy, 145, 161
Weisberg, Willie, 41, 42, 61
Wexler, Irving (see Waxey Gordon)
Wolensky, Moe "Dimples," 137
Workman, Charley "Bugs," 145, 196-201

Z

Zelig, Jack, 104, 109-112, 222-223
Zerilli, Joseph, 44, 91-93, 192
Zweibach, Max "Kid Twist," 108, 109, 222
Zwillman, Abner "Longy," 7, 18-20, 28, 31-39, 43, 46, 59, 122, 126, 135, 144, 165, 17—175, 191, 193, 194, 205, 208-210, 214, 224, 231, 238, 242, 243

Index of Photos

Arnold Rothstein *(PHOTO: UPI/BETTMANN)* 11

Louis (Pretty) Amberg *(PHOTO: AP/WIDE WORLD)*. 19

Benny (Bugsy) Siegel *(PHOTO: AP/WIDE WORLD)* 28

Arthur (Dutch Schultz) Flegenheimer *(PHOTO: AP/WIDE WORLD)* 38

Abner (Longey) Zwillman *(PHOTO: UPI/BETTMANN)* 43

Jack Guzik *(PHOTO: AP/WIDE WORLD)* 50

Morris Dalitz 55

Louis (Lepke) Buchalter *(PHOTO: UPI/BETTMANN)* 60

Police Dept. picture of the "Purple Gang" *(BURTON ARCHIVES)* 70

Bugsy Siegel 82

Jack Zelig *(PHOTO: UPI/BETTMANN)* 100

Harry Horowitz *(PHOTO: UPI/BETTMANN)* 107

Waxey Gordon *(PHOTO: UPI/BETTMANN)* 118

Jack Guzik *(PHOTO: UPI/BETTMANN)* 127

Jacob Shapiro 136

Marty Goldstein and Harry Strauss *(PHOTO: UPI/BETTMANN)* 147

Longy Zwillman *(PHOTO: AP/WIDE WORLD)* 156

Abe Reles *(PHOTO: AP/BETTMANN)*. 164

Mickey Cohen 172

Meyer Lansky *(PHOTO: AP/WIDE WORLD)*. 187

Max (Boo-Boo) Hoff *(PHOTO: AP/WIDE WORLD)* 200

Isidore (Kid Cann) Blumenfeld *(PHOTO: UPI/BETTMANN)* 245